THE COLLECTED WORKS OF

ERIC VOEGELIN

VOLUME 5

MODERNITY WITHOUT RESTRAINT

PROJECTED VOLUMES IN THE COLLECTED WORKS

The Editorial Board offers grateful acknowledgment to the Earhart Foundation, Liberty Fund, Inc., Robert J. Cihak, M.D., and John C. Jacobs, Jr., for support provided at various stages in the preparation of this book for publication. A special thanks for support goes to the Charlotte and Walter Kohler Charitable Trust.

The University of Missouri Press offers its grateful acknowledgment for a generous contribution from the Eric Voegelin Institute.

THE COLLECTED WORKS OF

ERIC VOEGELIN

VOLUME 5

MODERNITY WITHOUT RESTRAINT

THE POLITICAL RELIGIONS,
THE NEW SCIENCE OF POLITICS, AND
SCIENCE, POLITICS, AND
GNOSTICISM

EDITED WITH AN INTRODUCTION BY
MANFRED HENNINGSEN

UNIVERSITY OF MISSOURI PRESS

COLUMBIA AND LONDON

Copyright © 2000 by
The Curators of the University of Missouri
University of Missouri Press, Columbia, Missouri 65201
Printed and bound in the United States of America
All rights reserved

5 4 3   18 17 16 15

Library of Congress Cataloging-in-Publication Data

Voegelin, Eric, 1901–
  Modernity without restraint / Eric Voegelin ; edited with an introduction by
Manfred Henningsen.
      p.   cm.—(The collected works of Eric Voegelin ; v. 5)
  Includes bibliographical references and index.
  ISBN 978-0-8262-1245-0 (alk. paper)
      1. Political science.   2. Church and state.   3. Gnosticism.   4. Religion and
politics.   I. Henningsen, Manfred.   II. Title.
JC251.V58   1999
320'.01—dc21   99-044762

⊗™ The paper meets the requirements of the American National Standard
  for Permanence of Paper for Printed Library Materials, Z39.48, 1984.

Designer: Albert Crochet
Typesetter: BookComp, Inc.
Printer and binder: Thomson-Shore, Inc.
Typeface: Trump Mediaeval

The New Science of Politics © 1952 by the University of Chicago. All rights
reserved. Published by arrangement with the University of Chicago Press.

Science, Politics, and Gnosticism Copyright © by Regnery
Publishing. All rights reserved. Reprinted by special
permission of Regnery Publishing Inc., Washington, D.C.

Contents

Acknowledgments

I would like to thank my colleague Jon Goldberg-Hiller for retrieving a lost part of the manuscript from my hard drive; Julie Schorfheide for doing remarkable editorial work, especially on my introduction and on the new translation of *The Political Religions*; Liza Cawana for her computer assistance; and Thomas Maretzki from the Department of Anthropology for some basic linguistic advice.

MODERNITY WITHOUT RESTRAINT

Editor's Introduction

I

The three books by Eric Voegelin that are published in this volume were written in remarkably different phases of his life, reflecting the circumstances of his respective Austrian, American, and German biographies. When the study *Die politischen Religionen* was first published in Vienna in April 1938, Austria had been annexed a month earlier by Nazi Germany. Voegelin was informed at the end of March that he should not expect any successful employment at an Austrian university in the future and should therefore look for a job at an American university.[1] When he received the letter with the friendly suggestion he was still a *Privatdozent* and adjunct professor at the university, officially employed as an assistant at the law school. On April 22, 1938, he lost the right to teach; the so-called *venia legendi* was withdrawn by the ministry. On May 17 he was fired from the position of an assistant, effective at the end of the month. When the Gestapo tried to get hold of his passport he fled to Switzerland. He and his wife, Lissy, ended up in Cambridge, Massachusetts, where, on Christmas 1938, he wrote the preface for a new edition of *Die politischen Religionen*, which his publisher, Bermann-Fischer, issued in Stockholm in 1939. This preface was also meant as an answer to Thomas Mann, who—after having read the book—had written Voegelin a highly critical letter about the lack of passionate denouncement of the Nazis.[2]

The second book, *The New Science of Politics*, is a series of lectures he gave at the University of Chicago in the winter quarter

1. The letter from the Austrian Ministry of Culture was dated April 1, 1938. Eric Voegelin Papers, Hoover Institution Archives, Increment Box.
2. Thomas Mann letter, ibid., box 24, file 11.

of 1951. These lectures, which were published in 1952 and are still in print, marked the beginning of his American career as a political philosopher. More than any of his earlier German publications or even the five volumes of *Order and History* (1956–1987), the Chicago lectures on truth and representation shaped his professional and intellectual reputation in the United States. The strategic assault on the positivist foundations of the American social sciences at the onset of the behavioral revolution in political science was almost suicidal. One of Voegelin's Austrian teachers, the world renowned legal scholar Hans Kelsen, then teaching at Berkeley, wrote the longest (125 manuscript pages) and most scathing critique—still unpublished—which was a defense of positivism against the "pseudo science" of the "New Science," as he called it.[3] Robert A. Dahl, who wrote a review for *World Politics*, was especially dismayed by Voegelin's statement that the "future is really 'unknown' " because "by definition it cannot be predicted."[4] In addition to the concerns of the professional policy advisers whose political influence depended on predicting the future, Voegelin's *New Science* gained instant political and cultural recognition when *Time* featured it in a cover story on the intellectual crisis of the West. *Time* called it an "intellectual detective story, a quest through the history of Western thought for the culprits responsible for contemporary confusion."[5] The notion that Gnosticism was at the core of modernity, thereby lending a kind of sectarian image to the Western Enlightenment, went against the self-understanding of all liberal intellectuals. They labeled Voegelin from then on "conservative" and dismissed him as irrelevant for their cultural agenda. This label survived Voegelin's death in 1985 and can be found regularly in the growing literature on Hannah Arendt because, almost without exception, the authors have only read one piece by Voegelin, namely, his review of her book *The Origins of Totalitarianism*.[6] Ironically it was just that book and his review of it that established the friendly relationship between the two until her death in 1975,[7] although Arendt already had praised his *Rasse und*

3. Hans Kelsen, "A New Science of Politics," MS ibid., box 63, file 13.
4. Robert A. Dahl, "The Science of Politics: New and Old," *World Politics* 7 (1955): 489.
5. "Journalism and Joachim's Children," *Time*, March 9, 1953, 57.
6. Eric Voegelin's critique and the exchange between him and Arendt appeared in *Review of Politics* 15 (1953): 68–85.
7. This information I received from Lissy Voegelin.

Staat (1933) in her book on totalitarianism as the "best historical account of race-thinking in the pattern of a 'history of ideas.' "[8] In a letter to Karl Jaspers in November 1952, she recommended to him Voegelin's *New Science:* "I think the book is on the wrong track, but important nonetheless."[9] Albert Camus was so much intrigued by Voegelin's ideas on gnostic politics that he asked a visitor to give him an issue of the German cultural journal *Merkur* (which she carried with her) in which Voegelin had published in 1952 an essay under the title "Gnostische Politik." When Jacob Taubes, the Swiss scholar of comparative religion, wanted to establish contact with Voegelin, he wrote a letter to Voegelin on November 24, 1952, and introduced himself with this information about his wife's encounter with Camus in Paris.[10]

Voegelin introduced himself formally to his new academic audience at the University of Munich on November 26, 1958, with a lecture under the enigmatic title "Wissenschaft, Politik, und Gnosis." This lecture split not only his audience in the lecture hall but also the intellectual public. The leading liberal German newspaper, the *Süddeutsche Zeitung* of Munich, summarized the shocked reaction by suggesting in a front-page editorial (November 29/30, 1958) that the new professor who had characterized Hegel, Marx, Nietzsche, and Heidegger as Gnostics was indulging in "irrationalism." The editorial reminded its readers that Voegelin was the first professor since the death of Max Weber in 1920 to teach political science at the university. The editorial writer did not know that Voegelin, in his Chicago lectures, had criticized Weber for his intentionally "value free" teaching of politics after World War I, at the same university in the same lecture hall where Voegelin was giving his inaugural lecture. He blamed Weber for effectively surrendering to the irrationality of the ideologues among his students. Voegelin refused to make the same mistake and, with the inaugural lecture, set the tone for his teaching during the eleven years of his tenure in Munich. His students, the writer of this introduction among them, were never in doubt about his perspective and mostly enjoyed the often merciless and sarcastic answers he gave to their questions. Yet

8. Hannah Arendt, *The Origins of Totalitarianism* (Orlando: Harvest Book, 1979), 158.

9. *Hannah Arendt–Karl Jaspers Correspondence, 1926–1969,* ed. Lotte Köhler and Hans Saner (New York: Harcourt Brace Jovanovich, 1992), 203, letter no. 137.

10. Jacob Taubes, November 24, 1952, in Voegelin Papers, box 37, file 10.

the German students appreciated especially Voegelin's willingness to be questioned during lectures, since that was a breach of German university customs.

II

The different historical circumstances under which Voegelin wrote the three studies in this volume should not distract from the experiential background that motivated his theoretical analyses. The crisis of Western civilization he frequently refers to has distinctly German characteristics. This German ambience is quite obvious in *The Political Religions* when the Nazi movement is analyzed as a political religion. Yet even in the *New Science* and *Science, Politics, and Gnosticism* the German emphasis is striking. In all three studies he pursues questions of the German version of modernity. At the end of the *New Science* he identified the German area as the "most progressively modern stratum" of Western civilization.[11] Comparing the English, American, French, and German revolutions, Voegelin concluded his analysis with this statement: "The German Revolution, finally, in an environment without strong institutional traditions, brought for the first time into full play economic materialism, racist biology, corrupt psychology, scientism, and technological ruthlessness—in brief, modernity without restraint."[12] In a nutshell he repeated the indictment of modernity that the master thinkers of the Frankfurt School, Max Horkheimer and Theodor Adorno, had presented in their seminal book, *Dialectics of Enlightenment* (1947). Yet the Frankfurt thinkers who had written their radical critique during their World War II exile in Los Angeles did not distinguish among the various provinces of the West. Their critique was directed against Western Enlightenment as a whole. For them the Enlightenment transformation of the world was total and without any cultural and political exceptions. Voegelin's focus on the German historical formation underlined a progressive direction of development yet indicated the civilizing impact of cultural, political, and social traditions in other societies. Unlike the two Frankfurt thinkers, Voegelin left space for human agency. The prominent type of human agent that Voegelin

11. Eric Voegelin, *The New Science of Politics: An Introduction* (Chicago: University of Chicago Press, 1987), 189 (241 below).
12. Ibid., 188 f (241 below).

recognized in Italy, Austria, and Germany, however, was the representative of fascist politics. Alternative agents of political transformation were not visible for him on the European horizon of the 1930s.

In *The Political Religions* Voegelin continues his search for the body politic in Germany that he had begun in his two race books of 1933[13] and—with a primarily Austrian focus—in *The Authoritarian State* of 1936. In the Austrian case he noted the "nonexistence of a political people, a *demos*, that could have founded the state as democracy" beginning in 1918 after the collapse of the Austrian-Hungarian empire.[14] This collective human agent was more visible in the German context, although it presented itself as *Volk* without contours, and the Nazi movement tried to shape it into historical form under the leadership of the Führer. Voegelin's tone in skillfully analyzing the situations in Italy, Austria, and Germany in the middle of the 1930s is clinical as he describes the genesis and symptoms of a syndrome for which he apparently can prescribe no cure. He justifies his detached procedure in the preface to the Austrian book when he insists on the privileged knowledge interest for the theorist. The theoretically curious reader for whom he was writing as an "ideal reader" wanted to know "whether the struggle over the transformation of reality into truth has ended with victory or defeat."[15] But social reality mostly follows its own steering mechanisms without paying attention to the "truth" of the theorist, a fact Voegelin learned from the collapse of the authoritarian constitutional model he had so brilliantly explained and legitimated in his Austrian book. He began to study the tension between the truth claims of theory and the self-interpretation of society. *The Political Religions*, which appeared when Austria was swallowed by Nazi Germany, was a first attempt to understand the truth claims of a society that were obviously in conflict with truth in a more universal sense. Voegelin achieved full clarity of the tension in his Chicago lectures on truth and representation. He

13. Eric Voegelin, *Race and State*, ed. Klaus Vondung, trans. Ruth Hein, vol. 2 of *The Collected Works of Eric Voegelin* (1997; available Columbia: University of Missouri Press, 1999), and *The History of the Race Idea: From Ray to Carus*, ed. Klaus Vondung, trans. Ruth Hein, vol. 3 of *The Collected Works of Eric Voegelin* (1998; available Columbia: University of Missouri Press, 1999).

14. Eric Voegelin, *Der autoritäre Staat: Ein Versuch über das österreichische Staatsproblem* (Vienna: Julius Springer, 1936), 93.

15. Ibid., iv.

wrote in *The New Science,* "For man does not wait for science to have his life explained to him, and when the theorist approaches social reality he finds the field pre-empted by what may be called the self-interpretation of society."[16]

Voegelin's focus on the self-interpretation of the Nazi movement demonstrates his sense of urgency at that time. But the way in which he approached the subject indicates how unmoved he was by the available literature on the Nazis. He was interested in the religious aura that surrounded the rise of the Nazi movement in Germany and that also affected its Austrian version. In Voegelin's encoded response to Thomas Mann's complaint about his lack of decisiveness in making a moral judgment and condemnation, he confessed that "my store of educated and less-educated expressions of condemnation is impressive."[17] To him condemnation was not sufficient because it "diverts attention from the fact that a deeper and much more dangerous evil is hidden behind the ethically condemnable actions." He saw the root of evil in "religiousness" and recognized it as "a real substance and force that is effective in the world." He called it, without any conceptual qualifications, "satanical." For Voegelin, the response to the "satanic" challenge of the time was "religious renewal" within or outside "the framework of the historical churches" and primarily "initiated by great religious personalities." Voegelin did not see National Socialism as a "return to barbarism, to the Dark Ages, to times before any new progress toward humanitarianism was made" and realized that critics might consider this attitude itself "barbarism and a relapse into the Dark Ages." Anticipating the provocative moves he would make in later stages of his intellectual life, he actually welcomed being misunderstood by critics. After all, the "satanic" temptation is not "merely a morally inferior, dumb, barbaric, contemptible matter," it is "a force, and a very attractive force at that."[18] He wanted to understand the attraction of evil.

Much of what Voegelin said in 1938 about the religious foundation of political order in general and the Nazi movement in particular he would later find unclear, inadequate, too vague, and undifferentiated. He even questioned the concept of religion for the

16. Voegelin, *New Science,* 27 (109 below).
17. Voegelin, *Die politischen Religionen* (Stockholm: Bermann-Fischer, 1939), 7 (23 below).
18. Ibid., 8 f (24 below).

class of political phenomena he was writing about in the 1930s.[19] Yet the main charge against modernity as the juggernaut of spiritual disenchantment remained intact until the end of his life. In *The Political Religions* he rejects the conceptual nominalism that equates religion with the institutional churches and politics with the modern secular state. For Voegelin this neat compartmentalization makes it impossible to recognize that all political order is justified and legitimated through symbolic narratives that connect the respective society or movement with a larger order of things. The secularization of the world, this major achievement of modernity,[20] has not silenced the quest for meaning but has produced the urge to find alternative ways of satisfying this existential human need. The "satanic" seducers Voegelin tried to understand in 1938 forced him to search for other historical constellations in which the connection between social order and narratives of transcendent meaning manifests itself. All of these constellations, i.e., ancient Egypt, Greece, Rome, the Catholic and sectarian Christian Middle Ages, English Puritanism, and modern apocalyptic speculation, he revisits at length in other stages of his intellectual journey. Yet he returns only occasionally to the central and formative experience of his search, the rise of Nazi Germany. He never prepared his most extensive treatment of the Third Reich, his 1964 lectures on Hitler and the Germans, for the contractually promised publication. Voegelin's view of the "satanic" aspect of the Nazis had obviously changed. One can almost say that by 1964 he completely agreed with Hannah Arendt's political analysis that he had found spiritually wanting in 1953. His personal comments on Arendt's book *Eichmann in Jerusalem*, published in 1963, were full of praise.[21] In June 1961, when she was working in Munich on the manuscript for the essays in the *New Yorker*, Arendt gave a talk on the Eichmann trial in Voegelin's graduate seminar at the university and engaged his students in a spirited discussion. She told her husband in a letter (June 4, 1961) that an encounter with Voegelin at his home had been *"sehr nett"* (very nice).[22]

19. See Voegelin, *Autobiographical Reflections*, ed. Ellis Sandoz (1989; available Columbia: University of Missouri Press, 1999), 50 f.

20. See Giacomo Marramao, *Die Säkularisierung der westlichen Welt* (Frankfurt: Insel, 1996).

21. These comments were made to me in Munich in 1963.

22. Hannah Arendt to Heinrich Blücher, *Briefe, 1936–1968*, ed. Lotte Köhler (Munich: Piper Verlag, 1996), 549 f.

Voegelin's understanding of the Nazi temptation in 1938 is dominated by the secularization thesis, or rather by his opposition to it. Not unlike Carl Schmitt and Leo Strauss, whose respective Catholic and Jewish critiques of a secular modernity made them unusual bedfellows in 1932 and 1933,[23] Voegelin, the Protestant, saw the disintegration of meaning as the major cause of the legitimation crisis of politics on the continent. It would not be misleading to call his answer in 1938 "political theology," as Michael Henkel recently suggested with direct reference to Carl Schmitt.[24] However, since Voegelin abandons this approach in his writings in the United States, use of the term would create a wrong impression about the general thrust of his thinking. In *The Political Religions* he is quite clear about the consequences of secularization. He writes: "When God is invisible behind the world, the contents of the world will become new gods; when the symbols of transcendent religiosity are banned, new symbols develop from the inner-worldly language of science to take their place. Like the Christian *ecclesia*, the inner-worldly community has its apocalypse too."[25] The most radical trans-valuation of meaning would be the inversion of the mystic union, replacing a transcendent God with a social collective. Voegelin explained the inversion:

> They build the *corpus mysticum* of the collectivity and bind the members to form the oneness of the body. They are not rejected as crimes against the dignity of the person, and as a matter of fact, they are not merely tolerated by reason of being the dictates of the moment. They are rather promoted and desired as a means of achieving religious-ecstatic ties between man and his God. The formation of the myth and its propaganda by means of newspapers and radio, the speeches and celebrations, the assemblies and parades, the planning and the death in battle, make up the inner-worldly forms of the *unio mystica*.[26]

According to Voegelin, this mystical construction of social meaning is at the core of all totalitarian politics in the twentieth century, although he presents a detailed analysis only of German National Socialism. In order for totalitarian politics to be complete, the "death of God," i.e., the overcoming of all traditional religion, has

23. See Heinrich Meier, *Carl Schmitt and Leo Strauss: The Hidden Dialogue, Including Strauss' Notes on Schmitt's* Concept of the Political *and Three Letters from Strauss to Schmitt* (Chicago: University of Chicago Press, 1995), 41.
24. Michael Henkel, *Eric Voegelin zur Einführung* (Hamburg: Junius Verlag, 1998).
25. Voegelin, *Die politischen Religionen*, 51 (60 below).
26. Ibid., 56 (64 below).

to precede. After the divine "decapitation" has taken place, Führer-figures like Mussolini and Hitler become the representatives, mediators, and sovereigns of the new inner-worldly meaning. In the German case the inner-worldly circuit was additionally strengthened through the ties of blood and race. For Voegelin "the Führer becomes the speaker of the spirit of the people and the representative of people because of his racial unity with the people."[27] The imagined totalitarian reality was thus symbolically sealed against all trans-human leakage. For Voegelin this sealing-off was "abandonment of God," yet it remained "religiosity experienced by the collective body—be it humanity, the people, the class, the race, or the state—as the *realissimum*." He had nothing against the indictments of Christian thinkers who called these totalitarian inner-worldly beliefs "anti-Christian" because they concealed "the most essential parts of reality" within the "wealth of the stages extending from nature to God." Still, neither human knowledge nor Christian belief could explain why "God's creation contains evil, . . . [or why] the order of the community is built upon hate and blood, with misery and the apostasy of God." Voegelin's final question in *The Political Religions* was that of the theodicy, and it remained unanswered for him: "Why is it the way it is?"[28]

Voegelin's struggle with the theodicy in 1938 did not turn him into a theologian. Toward the end of the essay he intimated a design for a universal project of meaning, which he actually carried out in the volumes of his posthumously published *History of Political Ideas* and in the volumes of *Order and History*. He wrote:

> Humans live in political society with all traits of their being, from the physical to the spiritual and religious traits. We have only presented examples from the Mediterranean and Western European culture areas, but the thesis is universal and also applies to the political forms in the East. The political community is always integrated in the overall context of man's experience of the world and God, irrespective of whether the political sphere occupies a subordinate level in the divine order of the hierarchy of being or whether it is deified itself. The language of politics is always interspersed with the ecstacies of religiosity and, thus, becomes a symbol in the concise sense by letting experiences concerned with the contents of the world be permeated with transcendental-divine experiences.[29]

27. Ibid., 58 (66 below).
28. Ibid., 65 (71 below).
29. Ibid., 64 (70 below).

Voegelin began to work on this universal hermeneutics after he had settled at a U.S. university. Yet *The New Science of Politics*, the first book he published in the United States, remained solely focused on the Western context.

The Chicago lectures were not an ad hoc event. Word had gotten out that Voegelin was working on a major history of political ideas. The eight volumes of this history, now published in the *Collected Works*, finally confirm the substance of those expectations that surrounded Voegelin in the early 1950s. The lectures were a declaration of war against positivism, the dominant epistemology in the social sciences at that time. Although he spent only his first lecture on the false hope of using natural science methods in the social sciences, he made it quite clear that "if . . . the use of a method is made the criterion of science, then the meaning of science as a truthful account of the structure of reality, as the theoretical orientation of man in his world, and as the great instrument for man's understanding of his own position in the universe is lost,"[30] and that "the subordination of theoretical relevance to method perverts the meaning of science on principle. Perversion will result whatever method should happen to be chosen as the model method."[31] Despite these fighting comments he was disinterested in joining a "*Methodenstreit*" in the social sciences. Having been preoccupied for many years with the "History of Political Ideas" project, he was interested in substantive arguments or, as he would always say in an often misleading way, in "scientific questions." He obviously meant, not the American usage of *scientific*, but the German one, which alludes much more to the Greek notion of *episteme* and is equally applicable to the natural sciences (*Naturwissenschaften*) and the humanities (*Geisteswissenschaften*). Voegelin rarely bothered to explain to his American audience the more inclusive meaning of the German concept *Wissenschaft* (science), which was not limited to the natural sciences. Voegelin made it also clear in the introductory lecture that he was against an understanding of political science as the "handmaid of the powers that be." He was disinclined to reduce political science to policy analysis. He wanted to restore it to "its full grandeur as the science of human existence in society and history." Contrary to his conservative reputation, he

30. Voegelin, *New Science*, 5 (91 below).
31. Ibid., 6 (92 below).

did not intend to simply restore the grand narratives of Western political thinking. He told the Chicago audience:

> One cannot restore political science today through Platonism, Augustinianism, or Hegelianism. Much can be learned, to be sure, from the earlier philosophers concerning the range of problems, as well as concerning their theoretical treatment; but the very historicity of human existence, that is, the unfolding of the typical in the meaningful concreteness, precludes a valid reformulation of principles through return to a former concreteness. Hence, political science cannot be restored . . . by means of a literary renaissance of philosophical achievements of the past; the principles must be regained by a work of theoretization that starts from the concrete, historical situation of the age, taking into account the full amplitude of our empirical knowledge.[32]

The empirical knowledge Voegelin is invoking includes the full civilizational range from ancient Greece to the regimes of terror in the twentieth century. Strangely missing from his discussion of the history of political society in the West, however, are the *polis* of Athens and the United States. Michael Oakeshott was not totally off the mark when he entitled his positive review in the *Times Literary Supplement* "The Character of European Politics" and concluded it with the statement: "And if the reader puts it down with the conviction that he has been given a new understanding of European politics rather than a glimpse of a New Science of Politics, perhaps that is what was intended."[33] Certainly, the *History of Political Ideas*, which is the intellectual backdrop to the *New Science*, was not intended to privilege European politics as the culmination and civilizational peak experience of human history. Voegelin's critique of the Enlightenment was explicitly directed against this type of occidental self-aggrandizement. He basically agreed with Arnold J. Toynbee's understanding of history as a field of plural processes of civilizations, although critically distancing himself, in *Order and History*, from Toynbee's own constructions of meaning. He justified his focus on Western history in the Chicago lectures by mentioning "certain historical conditions that . . . are given only in the Occident. In the Orient . . . this type of articulation does not occur at all—and the Orient is the larger part of mankind."[34]

32. Ibid., 2 f (89 below).
33. *Times Literary Supplement*, August 7, 1953. The identification of Michael Oakeshott as the unsigned reviewer of the book is found in Voegelin's handwriting on the copy in the Voegelin Papers, box 63, file 12.
34. Voegelin, *New Science*, 41 (120 below).

Voegelin's exclusion of a broader exploration of Athenian and American politics from his new departure deserves special mentioning. After all, both cases are paradigmatic illustrations of the process of articulation through which, according to his theoretical understanding of politics, societies erupt into historical being and distinguish themselves from others through narratives of meaning. Voegelin presents the critical arguments of the Athenian philosophers against the *polis* and obviously sympathizes with their views. The self-interpretation of the *polis* and its remarkable career from the reforms of Cleisthenes in 507 B.C. to the conquest by Alexander in 336 B.C. remain absent in the *New Science*. The absence of the American story is even more remarkable, since Voegelin's first book, *On the Form of the American Mind* (1928), testified to the favorable impact the United States had left on the imagination of the European visitor in the 1920s. It could have been a confirmation of this early encounter with the United States if Voegelin, as an American citizen since 1944, had theoretically contrasted his adopted society with his native society on this particular occasion. But Voegelin was a political philosopher who, despite his insistence on experience, rarely made personal experiential references. The American story simply did not fit into his theoretical framework; therefore, it was left out. He never revisited American political themes in a major way after the first book.

Voegelin's disinterest in a new *Methodenstreit* in the social sciences was also caused by his realization that it would have been a lonely battle. Most political scientists would have been ill-prepared to enter into a discussion with him over substantive questions. Greek philosophy, the Roman Republic and Empire, medieval Christianity from the early to the late Middle Ages, Christian sectarian and other millenarian movements, English Puritanism, ancient and modern Gnosticism, to name only some of the major historical formations that are discussed in the *New Science*, were not knowledge domains in political science in the early 1950s. The wide range of historical knowledge itself, however, was not the greatest challenge for potential participants in such a debate. The claims of existential truth Voegelin connected with the various historical formations questioned the value-free assumptions that underlined the positivist epistemology of the social sciences. Political scientists who were in doubt about the truth status of their own professional work had difficulties making sense of the symbolic truth claims Voegelin recognized at the core of all the narratives of social self-interpretation.

The challenge of *The New Science* came from Voegelin's thesis that societies are not organized only to manage the basic affairs of the respective people that live within their boundaries. They represent types of truth that are articulated in narratives of symbolic meaning. He distinguished among cosmological, anthropological, and soteriological truths and connected them in his lectures with the early cosmological empires, the *polis,* and Christianity. In 1952 he insisted that

> Theory is bound by history in the sense of the differentiating experiences. Since the maximum of differentiation was achieved through Greek philosophy and Christianity, this means concretely that theory is bound to move within the historical horizon of classic and Christian experiences. To recede from the maximum of differentiation is theoretical retrogression.[35]

This affirmation of truth within specific civilizational boundaries was hard enough to accept for the average relativists, who refused to grant the status of privileged meaning to any symbolic formation. Yet it became unbearable for many when connected with the indictment of the Enlightenment and its assortment of narratives of human empowerment as modern Gnosticism. Voegelin's insistence on the truth claims of Greek philosophy and Christianity could have been written off as a particular form of spiritual nostalgia. The charges he raised in *The New Science of Politics* and in his inaugural lecture in Munich, namely, that the left and right regimes of terror in the twentieth century were the ideological offspring of the Enlightenment, aimed at the core of the liberal self-understanding of the post–World War II West on both sides of the Atlantic.

Voegelin's indictment of modern Enlightenment as Gnosticism was not simply a broadening of his earlier arguments. The texts from the intellectual fringe of political mass movements he had used in *The Political Religions* vanished. In *Science, Politics, and Gnosticism* he introduced major philosophical texts by Hegel, Marx, Nietzsche, and Heidegger. The confessional statement from the *Kommandant* of Auschwitz, Höß, was added in order to infuriate the detached intellectual reader. Voegelin wanted to make sure that nobody missed the conclusions of his analysis. He introduced

35. Ibid., 79 (152 below).

the German master thinkers in order to demonstrate how intimately connected their visions were with the labor camps of the
gulag system, the Nazi camps, and the other killing fields of this
century. Calling Marx an "intellectual swindler" resulted in the
attention Voegelin was hoping for to make people listen. His knack
for provocative formulations enabled him to express his intellectual
anger in a strategically successful fashion. *The New Science of
Politics* (1952) and *Science, Politics, and Gnosticism* (1959) are
not just responses to the collaboration of intellectuals with power.
Voegelin's critique goes further than moralism. His thesis on the
Gnosticism of the master thinkers supposes that they not only
"knew" how to change the world, they wanted to be present at
or in charge of the transformation of reality. This activist will
to power connected the master thinkers as much with Jewish-
Christian apocalyptic as with gnostic thinking. Voegelin became
aware of the frequent overlap of the apocalypse and Gnosticism in
his studies. This growing recognition may explain why the Gnosticism thesis lost importance for him. Ironically, Klaus Vondung's
critical observation in 1997 summarizes Voegelin's own views on
the subject at the time he was publishing *The Ecumenic Age* (1974)
and in the remaining decade of his life. Vondung writes:

> Although the Gnosticism thesis could be maintained with respect to
> its essential core, it seemed to be necessary, with respect to the histori-
> cal phenomena, to distinguish, for instance, Hermeticism from Gnos-
> ticism, and, above all, Apocalypticism, as expressed in Jewish and
> Christian visions and Millenarian, Chiliastic, and Messianic move-
> ments. Quite a few phenomena that Voegelin dealt with under the
> heading of Gnosticism . . . are usually attributed . . . to the apocalyp-
> tic tradition.[36]

If Voegelin recognized the complexity of the situation, why did
he not retract some of his statements and offer a new reading of the
field of spiritual deformations?

Voegelin's habits of scholarly work rarely motivated him to re-
visit completed projects. He never returned, for example, to the subject matter of his first four books. In addition, he was not interested
in publishing the volumes of his history of political ideas in later

---

36. Klaus Vondung, "Eric Voegelin, the Crisis of Western Civilization, and the
Apocalypse," in *International Interdisciplinary Perspectives on Eric Voegelin*, ed.
Stephen A. McKnight and G. L. Price (Columbia: University of Missouri Press, 1997),
119.

years, since it demanded the integration of new scholarship in the various periods of Western history. Once he had given his "Hitler and the Germans" lectures, he lost interest and did not want to prepare the lectures for publication. Voegelin's intellectual interests changed over time. He could not bring himself to the tedious task of editing or revising his earlier writings. With regard to the thesis on Gnosticism he had said in *The New Science* and the Munich lecture what he wanted to say. He therefore moved on without being bothered by the contradictions critics had pointed out to him. His initial thesis on Gnosticism was triggered during his work on the history of ideas, when the speculative similarities between German philosophy, medieval millenarian visionaries, and ancient gnostic systems became overwhelming to him. The question of speculative continuity from ancient through medieval to modern Gnosticism preoccupied him in the late 1940s, since it was directly connected for him with the regimes of terror. These regimes were defined at their core by a will to power of a select group of ideologues whose claims to a privileged knowledge about the structure and conditions of reality had turned the world for the "vast majority of all human beings alive on earth" into hell. The language he used in 1953 in his famous review of Hannah Arendt's *Origins of Totalitarianism* expresses the state of mind that drove his research in ancient Gnosis and modern Gnosticism:

> The putrefaction of Western civilization, as it were, has released a cadaveric poison spreading its infection through the body of humanity. What no religious founder, no philosopher, no imperial conqueror of the past has achieved—to create a community of mankind by creating a common concern for all men—has now been realized through the community of suffering under the earthwide expansion of Western foulness.[37]

This uncompromising language from 1953 illustrates the radical discursive shift from the more moderate tone of detached academic analysis in the preface to the Stockholm edition of *The Political Religions* in 1939. Voegelin had overcome the mode of detachment when he was writing about the gnostic origins of "Western foulness" and the collaboration by the philosophers. Once he had said about this spiritual syndrome what he wanted to say his intellectual interest in Gnosticism as the speculative signature of the modern

---

37. Voegelin, "The Origins of Totalitarianism," *Review of Politics* 15 (1953): 68.

West began to fade. He turned his attention to the civilizational formations of consciousness and their respective experiential specificity. In *Anamnesis* (1966) one finds only two entries for Gnosis; in *The Ecumenic Age* from 1974 Voegelin provides a searching analysis of Gnosticism in terms of his theory of consciousness in the introduction but few other direct references to the subject. Voegelin continued to follow the literature on the subject and stayed in contact with scholars on Gnosticism such as Gilles Quispel and Hans Jonas. Yet his interest in the ancient and modern gnostic mentality was not that of a historian of religion. He did not respect disciplinary boundaries in this area or any other. He constantly crossed them in order to get answers from specialists to questions he had encountered in his work. The specialists provided him with the historical answers, even though they did not always appreciate the way Voegelin made use of their knowledge. Both Quispel and Jonas considered Voegelin's symbolic transfer of meaning from ancient gnostic religion to modern ideological movements with some reservation. Their response, however, did not cause Voegelin to change his mind with regard to recognizing a fundamental equivalence in the ancient and modern gnostic experiences and, therefore, to drop the Gnosis thesis altogether.[38] He had simply lost interest in the genealogy of the deformation of modern consciousness.

III

In a surprising coincidence, all three texts of this volume became independently available in English and German editions in the late 1990s. This coincidence is difficult to explain, since Voegelin never succeeded in gaining major recognition in Germany. While he was teaching in Munich from 1958 to 1969 the cultural hegemony of the Frankfurt School in West German intellectual life overshadowed the reception of his work. Although his solid anti-Nazi credentials and the fact of his emigration from Nazi Germany to the United States saved him from being labeled and dismissed by the German left as conservative, this background prevented him from ever seeking close contact with West German conservatives themselves. Voegelin regarded the past of many conservatives with suspicion, and they reciprocated by distancing themselves from him and his

38. See for the comparison Giovanni Filoramo's introduction to his book *A History of Gnosticism* (Cambridge: Blackwell, 1992), xi–xix.

work. This complicated relationship between Voegelin and the Germans did not alter after his retirement and return to the United States in 1969. Change came in the 1990s with the publication of a series of texts, most of them edited by Peter J. Opitz, one of his former Munich students and now professor of political science at the same university. These texts included books that were out of print, had never been translated into German, or presented selected correspondence with people like Alfred Schütz and Leo Strauss.

The sudden availability in Germany of a whole number of books by Voegelin might not have made much of a difference if the unexpected collapse of state socialism in East Germany, Eastern Europe, and the Soviet Union from 1989 to 1992 had not seriously undermined the intellectual self-understanding of the left cultural élites in Germany. With the end of state socialism all certainties of cultural interpretation were gone. Suddenly Voegelin's *Die politischen Religionen*, *The New Science of Politics*, and *Wissenschaft, Politik, und Gnosis* enjoyed a new reading. The text that received much attention was the essay on mass movements as political religions, since it provided a different understanding of totalitarian regimes in general. Compared with approaches centered on events and institutions, personalities and economic factors, Voegelin's attempt to explain the religious fascination that totalitarian movements instilled in their followers was surprising. The way he made readers recognize the attraction of evil contradicted the liberal consensus about the Holocaust regime. In addition, this essay offered a conceptual vocabulary for understanding all the fundamentalist religious regimes at the end of the twentieth century that were responding to the global reach of Western modernity. Voegelin's ability to recognize the existential anxiety that accompanied the original delegitimation of traditional spiritual meaning in the West helps to comprehend similar responses in other societies whose patterns of traditional meaning have become undermined by Western modernity. Toward the end of the twentieth century, Voegelin's reading of the Western configuration has gained ecumenic importance.

MANFRED HENNINGSEN

The
Political
Religions

TRANSLATED BY

Virginia Ann Schildhauer

Per me si va ne la citta dolente.

CONTENTS

Preface

The treatise on "Political Religions" was published for the first time in Vienna in April of 1938. Since the national-socialist provisional management of the publishing house did not promote its circulation, the treatise remained almost unknown. However, it did become well enough known to find as critical a response among knowledgeable readers as my earlier writings. These criticisms reproach me for presenting my case in such an overly objective manner that it actually seemed to support those conceptions of the world and movements, in particular National Socialism, which it was intended to oppose. It lacked the decisiveness of making a judgment and condemnation, which would put beyond all doubt my own outlook.

These critics touch on the basic questions surrounding the present world situation and the individual's attitude toward it. Today there is one type of politicizing intellectual—and the critics meant here usually belong to this circle—who proclaims his deep aversion to National Socialism through strong ethical judgments. He considers it his duty to battle it with any literary means. I can do the same: Anyone able to read will recognize my deep aversion against any kind of political collectivism on the basis of the verse by Dante that precedes the treatise, and my store of educated and less-educated expressions of condemnation is impressive. There are reasons for my not spreading this aversion before a large audience in the form of politicizing outbursts. In fact, although there are many reasons supporting this attitude, I can only touch upon one essential reason here.

Political collectivism is not only a political and moral phenomenon. To me its religious elements seem much more significant.

23

Choosing to take up the struggle with literary means in the form of ethical counter-propaganda is important, but such a struggle will become questionable when it hides the essential. Doubly questionable, as a matter of fact, since it diverts attention from the fact that a deeper and much more dangerous evil is hidden behind the ethically condemnable actions. And its own means will become ineffective and questionable when it finds no deeper reason than a moral code. Thus, although I do not mean to imply that the struggle against National Socialism should not also be an ethical one, it is, in my opinion, not conducted radically enough, because the *radix*, the root in religiousness, is missing.

When considering National Socialism from a religious standpoint, one should be able to proceed on the assumption that there is evil in the world and, moreover, that evil is not only a deficient mode of being, a negative element, but also a real substance and force that is effective in the world. Resistance against a satanical substance that is not only morally but also religiously evil can only be derived from an equally strong, religiously good force. One cannot fight a satanical force with morality and humanity alone.

Nonetheless, this difficulty cannot be remedied by resolve alone. There is no distinguished philosopher or thinker in the Western world today who, firstly, is not aware—and has not also expressed this sentiment—that the world is experiencing a serious crisis, is undergoing a process of withering, which has its origins in the secularization of the soul and in the ensuing severance of a consequently purely secular soul from its roots in religiousness, and, secondly, does not know that recovery can only be achieved through religious renewal, be it within the framework of the historical churches, be it outside this framework. Such renewal, to a large extent, can only be initiated by great religious personalities, but everyone can be ready and willing to do his share in paving the way for resistance to rise up against the evil.

It is precisely in this respect that the politicizing intellectuals fail completely. It is dreadful to hear time and again that National Socialism is a return to barbarism, to the Dark Ages, to times before any new progress toward humanitarianism was made, without these speakers even suspecting that precisely the secularization of life that accompanied the doctrine of humanitarianism is the soil in which such an anti-Christian religious movement as National Socialism was able to prosper. For these secularized minds the religious question is a taboo, and they are suspicious of bringing it up seriously and radically—perhaps they would also consider this barbarism and a relapse into the Dark Ages.

Thus, I believe that discussing the basic religious issues of our times as well as describing the phenomenon of evil that is to be combated is more important than participating in that ethical defensive struggle. If my representation gives rise to the impression that it is too "objective" and "advertises" for National Socialism, then that to me seems to be a sign that my representation is good—for the Luciferian aspects are not simply morally negative or atrocious, but are a force and a very attractive force at that. Moreover, my representation would not be good if it gave rise to the impression that we are concerned with merely a morally inferior, dumb, barbaric, contemptible matter. That I don't consider the force of evil to be a force of good will be clearly evident to all readers of this treatise who are open to religious questions.

Cambridge, Mass.
Christmas 1938

1

The Problem

Speaking about political religions and construing the movements of our times not only as political but also, and primarily, as religious movements is not accepted as a matter of course yet, even though the factual situation would force the attentive observer to take this stand. The reason for the prevailing resistance can be found in the linguistic symbolism that has become established in the past few centuries since the dissolution of Western imperial unity and the growth of modern states. When one speaks of religion, one thinks of the institution of the Church, and when one speaks of politics, one thinks of the state. These organizations confront one another as clear-cut, firm entities, and the spirit with which these two bodies are imbued is not one and the same. The state and secular spirit conquered their spheres of power in the fierce battle against the Holy Empire of the Middle Ages, and in the course of this struggle linguistic symbols developed, which do not reflect reality as such but seek to capture and defend the opposite positions of the struggle.

The concepts of religion and politics followed the institutions and their symbols: They entered onto the battlefield and placed themselves under the authority of the linguistic symbols used in the struggle. For this reason, cognition today still involves the contrasts formed under the pressure of their conceptual instruments, although a critical look might reveal merely different examples of the effectiveness of closely related fundamental human forces. The currently prevalent concepts of religion and state in general European usage as well as in more limited scientific usage are oriented along certain models whose significance can be traced back to the intellectual struggles waged in Europe. By *religion* one understands such phenomena as Christianity and the other great redemptive religions; by *state* one means the political organizations of the type of the modern nation-state. For an adequate understanding of political religions, the concept of the religious must, therefore, be extended to include not only the redemptive religions but also all other phenomena accompanying the development of states, which we believe to be of a religious nature. Moreover, we must inquire whether the concept of the state really is limited to secular-human organizational relationships that do not have any relation to the sphere of the religious.

State

A standard definition, which no one up to now ever suspected of having religious pretensions, describes the state as an organizational unit of a sedentary body of people that is endowed with original power to rule. Some parts of this definition evidently refer to facts gained in past experience: people organized into a unit who have settled down in one area. However, another part, namely, that concerning the original power to rule, gives rise to doubts. *Original* can only mean that the power has no other source than the state itself, that it is not derived from anywhere else, that it is absolute. A close look at reality will quickly show that this claim is false. An absolute, an original power would be a power above all powers. It would have no power equal to it or superior to it, and any subordinate powers would be so only by its grace. The power of the ruler, however, is limited by internal barriers, because there are certain things that no ruler can do without being overthrown, and it is restricted by external barriers with respect to other powers.

A pluralism of powers forces one to look at their origins. The primacy of their power, their supremacy, contains a superlative, i.e., the assertion that the power concerned is the highest power. For Dante it was self-evident that a pluralism of powers would give rise to an inquiry into their legitimation and order. The objective of such an inquiry would be to find the formula for uniting the myriad powers and to attribute supremacy to the divine principle of unity that is part of the power structure. We do not notice such an obligation in the standard definition mentioned above. Supremacy is simply asserted to be part of a judgment based on experience that claims to be correct. The order of creation, which is excluded completely, is, as it were, decapitated by it, i.e., the divine head is cut off, and the state takes the place of the world-transcendent

God as the ultimate condition and the origin of its own existence. The multitude of powers that mutually hinder one another give rise to the notion of an all-encompassing unity—unless, of course, we refuse to take this intellectual step, decide to remain fixed at this point, and believe that the world is inhabited by demonic powers of equal primacy and that the question regarding unity is pointless. The assertion of primacy swerves from the path of ordered thought: It disregards the rules for examining experiences reasonably, it refuses rational discourse; and the spirit that adopts this assertion will change from being a discussion partner to an adherent of another order, the origins of which we need to study.

The standard definition, however, lets us down, and we can only grope our way forward by looking at the historical sources from which the assertion sprang forth. It was Hegel who advanced the thesis that the people in their role as the state were the spirit in its immediate reality and, consequently, the absolute power on earth. Its powerful mind does not stumble over trifles, and it draws the consequences firmly. If the state is absolute power, then it cannot have any internal barriers. For this reason, it would incorporate the mechanical aspects of order and service, complete obedience and dismissal of individual opinions and reasoning, absence of one's own spirit and, at the same time, an intensive presence of the spirit that blossoms within the state. The courage of the individual is not of a personal nature in the state, but a mechanical phenomenon. It is not the courage of a special person, but that of a link in the whole. Therefore the spirit that has become the state, and not any coincidence, invented the mechanical means of killing in order to transform the personal form of courage into the impersonal form: The intention to kill is directed against an abstract enemy, not against an actual person.

Now we feel more distinctly what is at stake: The issue is not the correctness of a definition; the issue is a matter of life and death. And even more so, the issue is the question as to whether man may exist personally or has to blend into a suprapersonal *realissimum*. Intrapersonal relationships are severed, nonhuman spiritual structures confront one another, and man is transformed into a machine component that runs along mechanically in the gearbox, abstractly fighting and killing toward the outside. Anyone who recognizes the state will no longer hold that the state's power is original or absolute; rather, this is the dogma of a believer. In the believer's realm of experience, the existence of man loses its reality. Instead the state takes over the reality and makes itself into the only true reality, from which a stream of reality is allowed to flow back to the people, providing them with new stimulus in their role as parts of the suprahuman reality. We are caught in the innermost heart of a religious experience, and our words describe a mystical process.

Toward the outside, the national spirits manifested in states bear a certain relationship with one another and with the prevailing world spirit (*Weltgeist*). Their relationship to the world spirit as steps toward its realization in history is similar to that between man and the state, where man is but a component part of the whole machine. The rise and fall of states in history reflect the "Day of Judgment" of the spirit, when all types of national spirit are condemned to death after they have served their time. The power struggle between states is not guided by blind destiny; rather, it lays bare the reason of the world. The destinies of peoples, as they experience themselves as actors in the course of world history, are as insignificant before the decree of reason as the destinies of people are before the absolute power of the state. Faced with the reality of the state, people sink down into the impersonal nothingness of their instrumentality; and faced with the reality of the world spirit, people and states do the same. It cannot be said with certainty what is more surprising at this point in the Hegelian speculation: the imperatorial, world-ordering reason that forces history into the revelation of the spirit, or the lack of feeling for the deep problem of theodicy, i.e., that the world spirit has no other means at its disposal besides blood and the misery of mankind. The gigantic structure of the system and its strict order is woven over an abyss of human nihilism and torn by the desire for fulfillment in reality through a collective body.

Religion

Man experiences his existence as being natural (*kreatürlich*) and, therefore, questionable. Somewhere in his innermost self, at the navel of his soul, at the place where his soul is linked to the cosmos, this question keeps tugging at him. This is where those states of excitation arise that are often inadequately referred to as emotions and, consequently, easily mistaken for the superficial state of agitation of the soul that goes by the same name. It is not easy to comprehend the nature of these innermost emotions. Religious people describe them with images that correspond only to those features that they recognize in their own states of excitement. They speak of primal emotions when they want to describe the level at the bottom of our soul that is deeper than other feelings and that reverberates through our existence from this depth. They speak of the infinitude of this feeling when they mean that it is not oriented toward specific objects but is a directionless, agitated surge deep within us at the bottom of our soul. They call it a feeling of simple dependency when they want to describe the experience of being bound to a suprapersonal, all-powerful something. They speak of dereliction and desolation when the agitations of existence are overwhelmed by the recognition that they were previously held in the womb and are now released from it. They pick themselves up from *distentio*, the dispersion of their existence, to return to the point of their origin so as to rediscover themselves and God in the act of *intentio*, focus (*Rückspannung*) on God. And the feeling of reunion can intensify to such a degree that optical phenomena of the Divine are experienced. All the states of agitation arising from the condition of creatureliness can be variously colored by anxiety, hope, despair, bliss, peacefulness, searching restlessness, indignation, rebellion, humbleness, and so on.

The range of nuances that we have tried to point out unfolds on one single dimension of the religious experience, namely, in connection with the agitations of naturalness. They are multiplied by the many different types of Being in which this agitation finds fulfillment and provides deliverance. The Beyond surrounding us can be searched for and found in all the directions in which human existence is open toward the world: in the body and in the spirit, in man and in community, in nature (*Natur*) and in God. The large number of fundamental possibilities and the infinitude of historically concrete instances that become apparent are linked with attempts at self-interpretation, including all the misunderstandings and misrepresentations arising in the course of this struggle to form an inexhaustible supply of experiences as well as rationalizations and systemizations of such experiences. For one the gates of existence stand wide open, granting a view of the levels of being that range from inanimate nature to God; the world unfolds itself to him, the rational relations between its contents become apparent, and they form an order of being in which the levels of being are classified in a hierarchy, and in response to the question as to the reason of being they form an order of creation. A maximum of absorption of reality is combined with the maximum of rationality in the order and interrelationship, and it is crowned by the perfect dogmatic development of the spiritual-religious experience in terms of an idea of God, such as that developed in the Occident in the *analogia entis.* For others, only scanty glimpses of reality are granted, perhaps only one single view: of nature, a great person, one's people, mankind—what such a person sees becomes the *realissimum,* the paramount reality; in fact, it takes the place of God and, thus, hides all else also, and above all, God.

We have sharpened the question concerning the complications that arise for religious experiences due to the types of reality identified as fundamental, in order to illustrate the difficulties of cognition we pointed out in the beginning. Wherever a reality discloses itself in the religious experience as sacred, it becomes the most real, a *realissimum.* This basic transformation from the natural to the divine results in a sacral and value-oriented recrystallization of reality around that aspect that has been recognized as being divine. Worlds of symbols, linguistic signs and concepts arrange themselves around the sacred center; they firm up as systems, become filled with the spirit of religious agitation and fanatically defended as the "right" order of being. Our time is overcrowded with religious orders of this kind, and the result is a Babylonian confusion of tongues, since the signs or symbols of a language have immensely different holy, magic, and value-related qualities, depending on the speaker using them. Today language no longer can be considered universally binding within one people. Instead, it is torn into special languages according to the lines of political-religious splintering. We do not have self-evident words that could be used to name the spiritual facts of this sphere. Followers of movements that want to be anti-religious and atheistic refuse to concede that religious experiences can be found at the root of their fanatical attitude, only venerating as sacred something else than the religion they fight. For this reason, we need to draw a linguistic distinction: The spiritual religions, which find the *realissimum* in the Ground of the world (*Weltgrund*), should be called trans-worldly religions (*überweltliche Religionen*); and all others, i.e., those that find the divine in subcontents of the world, should be called inner-worldly religions (*innerweltliche Religionen*).

Let us turn away from the realities (*Realia*), from the facts of being, in which the divine is recognized, and from the recrystallization of reality surrounding the *realissimum*, and back to the humans who seek and find. New manifestations of keen perception and broadness of vision, of emphasis of volition and emotion, of spirituality and instinctiveness, will become apparent. When the heart is sensitive and the mind is perceptive, one look at the world will suffice to see the misery of the human creature and to guess at ways of salvation; when they are insensitive and dull, massive impressions will be needed to trigger even some weak feeling. The sheltered son of a prince saw a beggar, a sick person, and a corpse for the first time—and he became Buddha; a contemporary writer sees the piles of corpses and witnesses the gruesome destruction of thousands of people in Russia after the war—and he realizes that something is awfully wrong in the world and writes a number of mediocre novels. One person sees in suffering the essence of the human creature and searches for deliverance in the ground of the world; another sees it as a grievance that can and must be actively remedied. Some souls react more strongly to the inadequacies of the world, some to the magnificence of the creation. Some only experience a Beyond as real if it appears as a powerful person and organization accompanied by glamour and noise, by force and terror. For others the face and gestures of every person are transparent, letting his solitude with God shine through. And wide is the space for places of the soul from which ecstasies arise, the experiences in which humans transcend their existence: from the *unio mystica* in spirit to the exaltation in the celebration of community; to the dedication to the fraternity of companions; to the loving extension of oneself into the landscape, the plants and the animals; up to carnal convulsions in the sexual act and in bloodlust.

2

Akhenaton

The oldest political religion of a highly civilized people was the Egyptians' worship of the sun. Its beginnings merge with the dawning of history, but its development—which we can trace up to its climax in the sun cult of Akhenaton and the subsequent catastrophe—illustrates the contours of the problem almost more clearly than the later and better known cases of the Mediterranean and European culture groups.

The factors that defined the development of the myth can be found at the beginning of historical time. The kings of the first dynasties already considered themselves to be successors to the sun god Horus, one of the rulers of the dynasty of gods who reigned over the country during its mythical beginnings. The pre-dynastic kings of the two distinct kingdoms of Upper and Lower Egypt were summarily called "servants of Horus." They attained the status of semi-gods, and later they were venerated as gods in the cities over which they ruled. The first kings known in history carried the title of Horus, since they were considered to be his successors, as well as the title of a "good God"; and after their death they were also worshipped as gods in their temples. Moreover, the "state form of religion" can already be found at the beginning of historical time. The king is the mediator between humans and the gods. Theoretically, he alone has the right to worship the gods, but in practice he has high priests and colleges of priests carry out his mediatorship in the different temples.

Thus, the main figures of the inner-political religious power struggle have been introduced. There were numerous local deities whose powers were not always clearly delineated, and in the large cities there was not only one Sun God but several. Each god had its priesthood, and the colleges of priests struggled with each other to increase the standing of its god so that he would be considered the highest God. The decisive point in this struggle was the recognition by the God mediator, the king. For this reason each of the colleges of priests had to try to gain such influence over the king that its god would be acclaimed as the god closest to the pharaoh, as the "state God."

At the time of transition from the Fourth to the Fifth Dynasty (ca. 2750 B.C.) the struggle of the priesthoods had been decided in favor of the sun god of Heliopolis, Ra (Re). The names of several kings of the Fourth Dynasty had already contained a reference to Ra; in the course of the transition to the Fifth Dynasty the priesthood proved its power to topple kings and to make kings. Most likely the first king of the Fifth Dynasty was a high priest of Ra, whereas the office of the vizier was held by a priest of Ptah. The structure of the state theology was further elaborated: The king became Ra's own son, and Ra appeared on earth every time to become the father of the king. The king's official name always included the name of Ra, and as of the end of the Fifth Dynasty, the title "Son of Ra" was added to the old Horus title. The Horus of Edfu was repressed, and the cult of Ra became the state cult. The political transformation, which was also a religious change, was reflected in the revisions made in the myths of the gods. Old myths were transformed and new ones were added. Ra, who had once ruled the kingdom as a mortal king together with Toth as his vizier, became the king of Upper and Lower Egypt. From now on the state theology very closely follows the political development.

Another phase of the sequence was completed after the period of the internal upheavals that resulted in the separation of the Old Kingdom from the Middle Kingdom during the reign of the Twelfth Dynasty (ca. 2000 to 1788 B.C.). The cult of Ra had survived the centuries, and Ra's renown had increased so much that many priesthoods interpreted their respective god as being a special form of the Ra in order to take advantage of his fame. The focus of political life shifted from Memphis in the north to Thebes in the south, and consequently, the god of the new capital of the empire, Amon of Thebes, who had been an unimportant local deity up until then, became the AmonRa in order to underscore the city's new political significance. Together with the restoration of political unity, the local deities were unified into forms of the one sun god. Another step toward monotheistic myth formation was accomplished.

After the Hyksos period the state religion in the New Kingdom followed the newly created stringent military organization. "The hitherto distinct priesthoods of the different temples were united into one large upper college which comprised the whole country. The head of the state temple in Thebes, the high priest of Amon, headed this priesthood, and hence his power far surpassed that of his old rivals in Heliopolis and Memphis." Following the victory of the Theban dynasty, the Amon of Thebes had risen to the status of the highest god of the state. The queen became the wife of God; the wife of the priest of Amon became God's first concubine.

The new military state expanded beyond the borders of the Old Kingdom of Upper and Lower Egypt. Egypt entered the period of world empire; and against the background of the territorial expansion, the knowledge of new lands and people, the influx of gold and slaves, the newly attained luxuries and blossoming arts, and the new overall political situation as a world power involved in lively traffic with Asian and Mediterranean kingdoms, the state religion also changed. "Just as the gods were considered kings who reigned over the Nile Valley at the time that the myths were created because the tellers of the legends lived under such kings, so the priests of the New Kingdom, seeing as they were living under kings who ruled over a world empire, saw before them a tangible form of world supremacy and a world plan—the prerequisites for the creation of a world god." The priesthoods of all major deities began to intersperse into the myth of their god cosmological and demiurgical speculations. Yet, these speculations generally made sure that the boundaries of the effectiveness of the god overlapped with the land of the Nile. Only in connection with the sun god did the speculations go farther. Already during the reign of Amenhotep III (1405–1370 B.C.), an old name for the sun—"Aton"—had frequently been used instead of the name of the sun god. The new usage is significant and completes the work that had been started by unifying the sun gods as forms of one Ra during the Middle Kingdom. Amenhotep IV inaugurated the worship of Aton as the highest god. Although he did not dispute its identity with Ra, his intentions exceeded beyond the cult of the sun as that of a visible god. He stated that Aton was, not the sun's disk, but "the glow that is in the sun." Aton is "the lord of the sun"; the new god is the life-giving principle as such, as it is revealed in the effect of the sun. Amenhotep builds a new temple for his god, and now the political struggle between the new god and the old priesthood begins, which ends by abolishing not only the old priesthoods but the old gods as well. The old gods were no longer venerated, and their names were obliterated on public monuments wherever they were found. As a matter of fact, even the name of the king's father, Amenhotep III, was eliminated from all temples in Thebes because it contained the name of the god Amon. Finally, the king changed his own name to Akhenaton ("It pleases Aton"). The king completed this work by building three new cities in the three parts of the kingdom—Egypt, Nubia, and Asia—for Aton, the new god of the empire, which took the place of Thebes, the old city of Amon. The Egyptian city Akhetaton (the modern Tel el Amarna) became the residence of the king.

Aton takes over the functions of an imperial god that, during the time of expansion, had incipiently been performed by the old gods. The gods who had originally reigned solely over the Nile Valley led, during the wars of conquest, the king's troops beyond the borders of the old country. By moving the kingdom's border stones forward into new territories in Nubia and Egypt, the sphere of power of the gods was also enlarged. According to the state theology, the king conquered the world for God, and God was asked to help in enlarging the conquered territories and, thereby, his supremacy. Since the king himself is God, the divine and human spheres are merged. The territory conquered by humans and the world created by God—human and divine rule, human and divine creation—cannot be distinguished clearly. Based on these ideas, Akhenaton developed his conception of God, which we know from his hymns to Aton. Because of his brightness he is the source of all life; he is the creator of humans and animals, of the earth and the Nile, the seasons and their changes. And he crowns creation by revealing himself in the heart of Akhenaton. The hymns still speak of the origins of Aton as being the deities of the Nile Valley, for instance in the following verses:

> Thou drivest away the darkness.
> When thou sendest forth thy rays,
> The Two Lands are in daily festivity.[1]

1. Translator's note: The passages from the "Hymns of Akhenaton" are from James Henry Breasted, *The Dawn of Conscience* (New York: Scribner's Sons, 1968), 281–86, quoted in Eric Voegelin, *Order and History*, vol. 1, *Israel and Revelation* (1956; available Columbia: University of Missouri Press, 1999), 107 f.

The "Two Lands" are Upper and Lower Egypt. Yet, in another passage, the creation is enlarged:

> Thou didst create the world according to thy desire,
> While thou wert alone,
> The countries Syria and Nubia,
> And the land of Egypt.

The earth thus created extended over three parts, with Egypt actually being named last. Aton is a world-god, the God of the whole universe; his creative love and care extend to all forms of life on the whole earth and all people without distinguishing between race and language:

> Thou settest every man into his place,
> Thou suppliest their necessities:
> Everyone has his food and the time of his life is reckoned.
> Their tongues are divers in speech,
> And their forms as well;
> Their skins are distinguished,
> As thou distinguishest the foreign peoples.

The break with orthodox Egyptian tradition is very sharp: The king shows an extraordinary ability to liberate himself from the bonds to a world that is identical with the land of the Nile and to comprehend the vastness of the world in its variety as structured creation. He was the first great religious individuality in world history.

Yet, no matter how admirable the wisdom and greatness of soul of this unique character may be in historical context, he does not break with the Egyptian state religion. Aton is the one and only god, but he is not a savior of all people. He is the god of the Egyptian Empire. Although he cares for the well-being of all, he only descends to one, to the king, who says:

> Thou art in my heart,
> And there is no other that knows thee,
> Save thy son [Akhenaton].

The old hierarchy of sacred substance remains intact. Creation is traced back to its creator only through the son of God. Only one single individual in the world lives with an immediate relationship to God, and that is the mediator, the king. Only he is cognizant of the will of God, and he is the force who carries out these plans:

For thou hast made him arise in thy designs and in thy might.

A clear distinction is made between world periods and flows of energy. Aton created the world out of loneliness:

> O sole god, beside whom there is no other!
> Thou didst create the world according to thy heart,
> While thou wert alone.

The act of creation extends beyond the first act. It continues as the permanent re-creation of the world with each rising sun:

> The world subsists in thy hand,
> Even as thou hast made them.
> When thou hast risen they live,
> When thou settest they die;
> For thou art length of life of thyself.
> And men live through thee.
> All eyes see thy beauty
> Until thou settest.

And now the circle closes. The flow of life that pours throughout the world does not produce meaningless life, but meaningful action as service to Aton and his son:

> All work is laid aside when thou settest in the west.
> When thou risest again,
> Everything is made to flourish for the king
> . . . .
> Since thou didst found the earth
> And raise it up for thy son,
> Who came forth from thy body.[2]

The world and the empire are one, the son of God is the king, the flow of divine energy created the world and keeps it alive through the radiance of the sun and the commands of the king, who knows the divine will. And from below, creation rises up again to God through service.

In the reforms of Akhenaton, the sun cult reached the limits of its development. Following the king's death, conservative reaction

2. Editor's note: Translation by John A. Wilson, in *Ancient Near Eastern Texts Relating to the Old Testament*, ed. James B. Pritchard (Princeton: Princeton University Press, 1950), 371.

sets in and returns in a few generations to the old veneration of gods. The powerful proponents of such the conservative reaction were the repressed priesthoods and the military who had watched in anger as the empire and its grand armies declined under the dominion of the reformer. However, the reinstatement of former traditions found a broad base of support among the people, who had been strongly agitated by the religious reform. This brings us to a final and most significant aspect of the creation of Akhenaton, namely, the point at which the conditions and limits of political religion become evident. We said before that the old gods and their worship had been abolished by the establishment of the cult of Aton. That measure, at least with respect to the former state god, concerned primarily the priesthood and the social classes close to the state god. However, besides the state religion and its gods, nonpolitical gods and their cults also existed in the polytheistic culture of Egypt, such as the Osiris cult and its mystery plays. The Osiris cult and cult of the dead had united to form a comprehensive faith that covered the morality of earthly existence, the judgment of the dead, life after death, and the punishment and rewards for the individual soul in the other world. It was the main religion of the lower classes, who had been too distant from the hierarchy of the sacred substance of the sun god to have gained any significant meaning from the state religion for their personal lives. Ontologically, the sun cult touched on the problems of the world and the state; the cult of Osiris touched the fate of the individual soul. In terms of a systematic understanding of religion, polytheism permitted the coexistence of religious realms without their getting into conflict or without any rational construction forcing them into a system. In social terms, the sun cult found its followers in the ruling classes; the Osiris cult had its adherents in the dominated people. In the course of Akhenaton's reform, Osiris and his priesthoods were abolished just like the other gods, and Egypt's religious life, which had been finely balanced by polytheism, experienced a serious setback. Within the scope of political religion, there had only been a change of personnel within the ruling class. The monotheistic rationalization may have proven successful if the king had been capable of maintaining the expansionary force of the country. Yet, the religion of the people had been eliminated without the Aton cult providing any substitute. The overall system of religious life connected to the Osiris cult was not satisfied by the monotheistic cult of the empire. The creative religious work of Akhenaton did not go beyond developing the sun myth; moreover, it contained no elements of personal ethics or answers to questions about life and death. The pure state cult with its hierarchy of ecclesiastical substance and the distance of the subjects to God had only been able to exist in a polytheistic system, in which the other characteristics of man were allowed to develop their own religion next to the political religion.

3

Hierarchy

We now shall characterize some of the most important sacred symbols used to link the political aspects of human life with the divine.

A basic form of legitimization for the rule of people over people is found in the radiation of power along a hierarchy of rulers and offices that ranges from God at the top down to the subject at the bottom. This symbol has a manifold history, and we will hint only at some significant manifestations. We can already find it in the sun cult of Akhenaton, at a very high degree of spiritualization, and the development in Egypt could have had consequences for later European developments. It is obviously no coincidence that the sun-images called forth in connection with the doctrine of the emanation of divine substance occupy such a significant position, in particular for the Egyptian Plotinus. Moreover, Philo of Alexandria's work on monarchy tells us to what extent the natural star myth pushed aside the spiritual myth during the Ptolemian Age, because he decidedly opposes any belief in the sun or moon as sovereign gods and insists that the rulers, in exercising their power, are subject to the invisible logos. The image of sacral effusion was perfected by Maimonides, who absorbed the entire eastern Mediterranean culture and conveyed its streams to Western Europe through complex and many-branched channels. A century after Maimonides, we find the symbol of outpouring from the source— which the Jewish thinker, together with that of the radiation of light, had minutely established at the Egyptian court—in Dante's *De Monarchia*: "It is now clear that the authority for temporal world-government must come directly, without intermediary, from the universal fount of authority, which, though it flows pure from a single spring, spills over into many channels out of the abundance of its goodness." And the emperor "in the light of paternal grace . . .

will better enlighten our globe, over which it [the government] rules through Him alone who is the ruler of all things spiritual and temporal."[3] Louis XIV makes the sun the symbol of a monarch again. In his memoirs, he explicates the reasons for choosing this symbol in verses reminiscent of the "Hymns of Akhenaton":

> Due to its unique characteristics, due to the luster that surrounds it, due to the light it shines onto the other stars that form a court around it, due to the equal and just distribution of light to all realms on earth, due to the good, which it creates everywhere by spreading, without interruption, life, joy and activity all round, due to its untiring movement which always seems peaceful, due to its constant and unchanging course from which it never deviates, the sun surely is the most lively and most beautiful image of a great monarch.

Toward the end of the sixteenth century, Bodin, the great theo-retician of the French monarchy, brought the symbol of the sacral hierarchy into a rational order that covered in detail all the stages of state and law. The highest power in the world is God; he is the seigneur of all princes, who serve him as vassals. The ruler is not sovereign in the absolute sense but only with respect to his subjects. He himself is subject to the laws of God, just as his subjects are bound by those of their ruler. From the ruler, the right of issuing commands radiates along the pyramid of state organs down to the subjects. And the train of connections operates in the opposite direction, too: "For just as contracts and deeds of gift of private individuals must not derogate from the ordinances of the magistrate, nor his ordinances from the law of the land, nor the law of the land from the enactments of a sovereign prince, so the laws of a sovereign prince cannot override or modify the laws of God and of nature."[4] The strict order in this system of emanation of divine will through the various ranks is loosened only by the Christian belief of man's immediacy to God: The king is bound only to God, but the magistrates are bound to God and the king, and the subjects are bound to God ("for He must always be placed above all else"), the king, and the magistrates. It is in this respect, the recognition of the human person in its immediacy to God, that the sacral-political hierarchy deviates from the symbolism of Akhenaton, where the

3. Translator's note: Quotations taken from Dante, *De Monarchia* (*On World Government*), trans. H. W. Schneider (New York: Liberal Arts Press, 1957), 79–80.
4. Translator's note: Quotation taken from Jean Bodin, *Six Books of the Commonwealth*, trans. M. J. Tooley (Oxford: Blackwell, 1955).

ruler was considered the exclusive intermediary between God and man. As for the rest, the hierarchical order established by Bodin remained the structure of Europe's inner state order up until the propagation of the new secularized theories of legal gradations. The hierarchy of offices and standards immanent in the state did not follow any rules, and following the decapitation of God, it was able to ally itself with any symbolism to attain legitimation.

Ecclesia

In the symbolism of hierarchy, the state is not an entity closed in itself; rather, it is composed of the various ranks of authority that range from the ruler on earth up to God. Although the person of the subject seems to be cut off from God through the mediatorship of the hierarchy, there is, even though their immediacy to God is not exclusively ensured as declared by Bodin, still a single divine stream of power that flows from the source down the ranks of the pyramid to its base. The order of domination is sacral in character, but it is not the Most Holy Sacrament. The divinization of the worldly order of domination, its inner-worldly closure and the simultaneous decapitation of the trans-worldly God, is linked to manifold prerequisites.

The closure of a community based on organized domination demands, above all, that the community is experienced as an entity with a center of existence that rests in itself. The natural starting point for the growth of a special, inner-worldly, sacral-political community in the primitive period—irrespective of whether it was matriarchal or patriarchal—is always a community based on genealogical descent. Numerous fragments of its symbolic world can be found in the high civilizations and up to our time. The Greek polis was firmly based on tribal clans, and the acceptance by the political entity could only be gained through entry into the tribal clan. Apart from that, probably under oriental influence, the Greek world—like the Egyptian world—had the personal, apolitical religiosity of the mystery cults. In the full light of history stands the political-religious tragedy of Socrates, the man who was called by the divine voice of his daimon and the charge by the oracle at Delphi to conduct a political-religious reform in his polis and was destroyed by its resistance. He refused to flee because any form of existence outside the sacral community was senseless to him. A recent historian determined that, like Plato and Aristotle, Socrates had reached a less-developed stage of spirituality as compared to that of the Christian Age, because these philosophers were not yet able to go beyond the boundaries of the sacral-political inner-worldly community and recognize the possibility of a religious existence immediately under God.

Modern inner-worldly political entities are much more thoroughly and clearly defined by the transformation of the substance of ecclesia than by the remnants of the symbolism of tribal communities. The Christian concept, as elucidated in the epistles of Paul and the closely related Epistle to the Hebrews, considers the ecclesia, the community, to be the mystical Body of Christ. The organic analogy is developed in several variations. Sometimes the offices of the ecclesia are arranged as the "limbs" of the body and supplement each other to form the worldly body, whose *pneuma* is Christ; at other times the allegory to the body is extended beyond the earthly visible "limbs" of the body up to Christ himself, who becomes the head of the body; vice versa, the spiritual contents can dominate, and the spirit (*pneuma*) of Christ pours forth by virtue of its *pleroma*, its fullness, into the worldly "limbs," so that the personality of the spirit of the Savior is almost nullified. The analogy is supported by remnants of the symbolism of descent insofar as Christ is viewed as the second Adam, the second progenitor of mankind, and by the version of the Lord's Supper propounded by the mystery cults.

The Paulinian fluctuations trace possible further developments. The charismata that radiate from the *pneuma* of Christ and determine the functions of the "limbs" of the body can be expanded beyond Paul's scheme of ranks of the early Christian community and supplemented by the political-sovereign functions. Thus the function of reigning attains its status in the *corpus mysticum* and, with respect to this characteristic, can no longer be distinguished from the functions of priests and teachers. There is no boundary between the political and the religious spheres; the *corpus mysticum* is an entity structured in itself, in which a sacrament of royal unction exists next to a sacrament of ordination. Performing the duties of a king is one sacral function among many. In terms of history, for example, this concept became reality in the *sacrum imperium* of the ninth century. Other forms take up the possibility of developing a hierarchy among the offices of the *corpus mysticum* in such a way that one of the offices becomes the highest, with the others remaining part of the *corpus* and its charismata, only through the mediatorship of such highest authority. This is reflected by the concept of papal supremacy over the ruler. Yet, the functions' immediacy to God may also be made a principle, as in Dante's idea of the emperor; and in principle, the symbol of a community constituted through the *pneuma* of Christ can be transformed to inner-worldly bodies when the spiritual unity that once became reality is replenished again with natural contents. The possibility of replenishment already can be found in the early Christian centuries when the ecclesia of the Christians became a people among peoples as the *populus Christianus*. The subsequent transformation can be traced back to such historical sources as the ancient empire of the God-man and the *acclamatio des populus Romanus*, which bound the ruler to the people, and the Germanic tribal and royal conceptions.

The ecclesia constituted by Christ has changed in many ways. Nonetheless, despite all the transformations, the basic structure—which is what matters—is still evident. The Christian churches stem from it in a direct line, yet certain parts of the idea have remained alive in political communities. We stand everywhere in the continuum of the ecclesia where particular communities, which have become inner-worldly, acknowledge the equality and fraternity of all parts of the community, even when these communities and movements proclaim strongly anti-Church and anti-Christian attitudes until a new state religion is introduced, as was the case in the French Revolution. The continuation of the Christian community based on love in the French solidarism was acknowledged by the laical thinkers of the Third Republic, and the idea of solidarity was interpreted as a secularized Christian charity. The Pauline idea of separating the *corpus mysticum* from the complementary functions of the community plays a part in the theories of the division of labor propounded by English and French economists and sociologists. The ecclesiastical interspersion of the American national community is common knowledge. Because of the tradition of Puritanism the ideas have not undergone significant changes, and we can find such Pauline categories as the "like-mindedness" of the members of the body as basic sociological principles in science.

Furthermore, because of the special social-historical position of the United States, the idea of equality was developed more clearly into the idea that only those men who are really equal in spirit can be full members of the community. The inner-worldly ecclesia reacts particularly irritably to any threat to the spirit constituting the community of equals, and it has found the means to incorporate the heterogeneous elements that built up the natural *corpus* during the period of immigration in pedagogical psychology and its efforts of assimilation. And even where the religious contents of the inner-worldly ecclesia conflict severely with those of the Christian ecclesia, as is the case in German National Socialism, the basic form of the mystic—bound into a *corpus* through the *pneuma*—lives on through the demand for spiritual conformity, just as the Christian "caritas" lives on in the secularized forms of charitable organizations for poor national comrades.

Spiritual and Temporal

One of the most important factors contributing to the formation of inner-worldly communities was the schism within the ecclesia along spiritual and temporal lines. In historical terms, the contrast is more than one pair, yet we can only discuss two or three main types.

The first significant historical-philosophical interpretation of the issue was presented by Saint Augustine. World history is the enormous struggle between the heavenly and the earthly *civitas*, the kingdom of Christ and the kingdom of evil. Neither kingdom should be conceived as an institution, for example as the church and the state (although Augustine occasionally tended to view the state as the *magnum latrocinium*), but as communities made up of followers of Christ and his enemies. The *civitas terrena* split off from the *civitas Dei* by the defection of the evil angels. The *civitas Dei* begins as a city of angels and ends as the kingdom of God, and its citizens all lead righteous lives according to God. The church is the representative of God's state on earth, but its sacramentally bound limbs also include citizens of the *civitas terrena*, and citizens of the *civitas Dei* can also be found outside the church. The symbols developed during a time of struggle of Christianity, on occasion of the conquest of Rome by the Visigoths (410). They were directed against an idea that threatened the Church, namely, that Christianity, the young state religion of the Roman Empire, had not protected the state from disaster. In order to make clear to this threatening public opinion that Christianity was not a form of life or accident insurance, Augustine develops the image of genuine Christian attitude and the meaning of allegiance to Christ. The great conceptual framework is confusingly complex and not completely of one piece; everywhere the problems to be encountered in the future are evident. The *civitas Dei* is identical neither with the Church, nor with the age initiated by Christ's act of redemption, nor with the eternal sabbath of the divine end realm. It comprises all of these in whole or in part as well as the pre-Christian following of God. It reflects to the extreme the tensions that resulted when the institutional elements of the Church were forced together into a unity with the apocalyptic elements of the new secular age and the eschatological elements of the end realm. The result was the myriad of dualisms ranging from the sacramental communities of the Church and its surrounding milieu, the terrestrial-worldly and spiritual-transcendent affiliation with the *civitas Dei*, from God's realm to Satan's realm. And, finally, the institutional reality of the state and the concept that in order to achieve happiness on earth the kingdoms best be small and numerous, just as a city is composed of numerous families, did not occupy a completely clear place in the system. The tension in the system reflects the tension of the struggle being fought by Christianity. There were yet no reduced schemes of the contradiction between spiritual and worldly power in the institutions of Church and state, or of human life in this or in the next world. Instead Augustine responded to the lamentation about the Roman massacre with harsh, contemptuous formulas: "Many perished in different terrible ways. If one has to lament this, then one should remember that it is the destiny of all who were born to this life. As far as I know, not one man died who wouldn't have had to die sometime anyway." These kinds of statements can be found in political-religious communities today, as, for instance, when Ernst Jünger, in response to the horror of death in war, says that death was always bitter, whenever it came—a hardship that is legitimized in faith: "The fallen went, by falling, from an imperfect to a perfect reality, from the Germany in its current form to the eternal Germany."

The problem is narrower and more sharply outlined at the height of Scholasticism, when the fissures in the *sacrum imperium* were already visible in the political theory of Thomas Aquinas. The offices within the great ecclesia have become firmly established and independent of one another. The dissolution of the empire through the formation of large feudal organizations had set in. The feudal church was established as the first "state in the realm"; it was followed by the princes, the first and most radical being Frederick II in the Sicilian state. The reception of Aristotelian political philosophy enabled Thomas to determine the relation between the functions of the Church and the prince. Following the contents of the *Politics,* Thomas attributed to the prince the task of exercising worldly rule over his subjects in such a way that their material and spiritual existence allowed them to pursue the salvation of their souls; the spiritual care is the task of the Church. In accordance with the higher rank assigned to the spiritual purpose, as compared to the temporal, the function of the prince is of subordinate rank to that of the Church. The significance and limits of this idea become evident when Aquinas's teaching is compared to Aristotle's. The Greek philosopher still moves in the political-religious system of the *polis.* The meaning of personal and political life is understood analogously, and the analogy becomes expanded from man and the state to the world and God. The most valuable life is a life of activity of the mind, because when man is intellectually active, he is the most sufficient unto himself and requires no outside means. Thus, he becomes most like God, who rests in and is by himself. And in the same way, an autarchic, self-sufficient state that is not extremely involved in relations with other states is the optimal kind of state because it is an analogy of divine-cosmic being. This final stage of an intellectualized religion of the *polis* is complete in itself. Although wide areas of Aristotle's *Politics* remain intact when transferred to the Thomistic system, their central meaning is destroyed. The cosmos of the divinely analogous state is broken up, the personal and communal existence is divided into two realms, and the political-temporal sphere is subordinated to the spiritual sphere. The problem of the political institution, which Augustine had not considered important, now takes center stage; and consequently it is only a question of what the historical situation will be when the political institution will break away from its subordination under the feudal church and usurp the sacral contents itself. Frederick II had already taken this step. Following the conquest of Jerusalem and his self-elevation as the Messiah-king, the emperor speaks as an autocrator, a heathen God-man. The ancient Justitia becomes the declared state virtue;

her cult the state religion; the people are forced into service; and the triumphal arch at Capua is erected as an altar. The pope declares the emperor an antichrist. The first inner-worldly political religion had been established on the soil of the Christian ecclesia.

Apocalypse

So far we have singled out individual characteristic phases from the organization of the ecclesia and its history in order to illustrate how the political-religious world of images is arranged and remains the basic structure of European development up until today. History was viewed from outside as a sequence of variations of a religious world of symbols. Now we will turn to a new dimension of symbolism, namely, to the interpretation of the development from inside, from the standpoint of the people and powers involved.

The basic pattern of a religious interpretation of history already was provided by the Pauline classification of world history into three areas: the heathen *lex naturalis,* the *lex mosaica* of the Old Testament, and the third, the Christian empire. The interpretation develops further from these beginnings by taking up the historical material that is significant for the time up to the climax in the German symbolism in the twelfth century and the proclamation of the Third Age in that century by Joachim of Fiore and Dante. The interpretation of history is symbolic insofar as the material is ordered and interpreted as an expression of divine will in history. The rational scheme of order is the sacred numbers: the "three" of the Trinity, the "seven" of the gifts of the Holy Spirit, the hexameron, God's six-day works, the numbers of lineage in the Old Testament of the forty-two generations from Abraham to Christ, and the half of this number in the twenty-one generations before Abraham. We have already touched upon the first great Christian philosophy of history that uses symbolism, namely, the Augustinian: The era of Christ is the sixth and, at the same time, the last earthly era; the following seventh is the blessed, transcendent end realm. At the height of German symbolism in the twelfth century, the method is completed in order to undergo with Joachim of Fiore the transformation that significantly influenced the ecclesiastical dynamics of the ecclesia and its inner-worldly splinter groups. Joachim found the formula for a spiritual and intellectual movement that had aspired to gain public attention and acknowledgment for a long time and according to which the empire of Christ, in contrast to the old classification, was not the last worldly empire but would be followed by a third. In this counting, the first was the divine empire of the Old Covenant; the second, the Christian; the third was that of the third divine person, Holy Spirit, which coincided with the seventh world era and would be followed by the eternal sabbath of the end realm. Each of the empires is divided into seven eras, and the eras of the pre-Christian as well as Christian empire, for which historical material is available, are symbolically determined by their leaders. Following the forerunners Zacharias and John, Christ stood at the beginning of the second kingdom. At the beginning of the third kingdom, which is rapidly approaching, stands an appearance that is simply called DUX, the leader (*Führer*). Joachim of Fiore calculates that the third empire would begin in 1200; the Joachitic Franciscan spiritualists calculate the beginning to be in 1260. The historical models that formed the basis for the apocalypse of the third kingdom were the foundings of monastic orders, the new *religiones*, in which the growing development of perfect life within the Holy Spirit became visible. The first generations of the Franciscans condensed the revelation into the belief that Francis of Assisi was the prophesied Dux, with Joachim of Fiore and Dominic being the forerunners. The work of Joachim was acknowledged as the *evangelium aeternum* of the Apocalypse (Rev. 14:6). The third empire of Joachim is not a new institution that was to take the place of the Church but a process of spiritualization of the ecclesia and transformation of the universal Church toward a new contemplative and spiritual monastic order. Contrary Paul's imperial apocalypse, the revelation of Joachim of Fiore, therefore, contains no references to the social order of the third empire. In the empire of the *spiritualis intelligentia*, the people would lead contemplative lives, i.e., no longer active-contemplative like the clergy of the universal Church; they would live spiritually, in poverty and fraternally, all would have equal rank, and there would be no coercive order.

The Christian apocalypse of the empire and the symbolism of the late Middle Ages form the historical basis for the apocalyptic dynamics in modern political religions. As a result of the Christian monastic movements since Benedict and, above all, the development of mendicant orders as well as the formation of new *religiones* within Christianity, the spiritual view of the renewal of the soul and the partaking in the perfection of the Christian ideal of existence are considered part of this world. The rising line of perfection of spiritual being has become one of the strongest elements of inner-worldly dynamics since the Renaissance: in the belief in the *perfectibilitas* of human reason; in the infinite further development of humankind to an ideal, final condition during the Enlightenment; in the deistic formations of orders of Freemasonry to perfect the world structure; and in the belief in progress as the religion of the people in the nineteenth century. The symbolism of the apocalypse of the empires lives on in the symbolism of the nineteenth and twentieth centuries: in the three empires of Marx and Engels's philosophy of history, in the Third Reich of National Socialism, and in the fascist third Rome, following the Rome of antiquity and the Christian Rome. Also the content-related definitions of the third empire have remained intact: the belief that the institution of the universal Church will be dissolved through spiritualization into orders of perfect life through the descent of the Holy Spirit; in the belief in the "withering away of the state" and the fraternal and free association of people in the communist third realm; in the belief in the deliverers of the empire, Dante's five hundred, five, and ten (DVX); in the figures and myths of leaders in our time; and in the orders of the new empires in the communist, fascist, and national-socialist associations and élite groupings as the core of the new imperial organizations.

4

The Leviathan

The process by which the Western ecclesia dissolves into political subentities continues throughout the Middle Ages and reaches a decisive stage during the period of Absolutism, when territorial states were increasingly sealing themselves off against each other. Not all regions of Europe reached this stage at the same time: The western nation states were carriers of the development and have remained the great prototypes up until today. They were also the first to think through the theology of the new ecclesia and to reform it as particular communities existing among others, in such intimate worldly political and sacral interpenetration, with state and Church in such close unity that the contradiction between temporal and spiritual become meaningless.

The great theologian of the particular ecclesia with immediacy to God was Thomas Hobbes. He is frequently considered to be the theorist of absolute monarchy, which he is; but he is more than that, because he created the symbol of the Leviathan, the omnipotent state immediately under God and acting upon divine orders.[5] The construction of the symbol is based on two steps: first, a natural construction of the personality of the state (*Staatsperson*), which is to be binding for all times, and then the construction of the natural unity as one Christian ecclesia based on the historical circumstances of the seventeenth century. In order to construct the

5. Hobbes took the image of the Leviathan from the Bible. The monster is described in Job 40 and 41: "His heart is firm as a rock, firm as the nether millstone. When he raises himself, strong men take fright, bewildered at the lashings of his tail. Sword or spear, dagger or javelin, if they touch him, they have no effect" [41: 24–27]. "He has no equal on earth; for he is made quite without fear. He looks down on all creatures, even the highest; he is king over all proud beasts" [41: 33–34]. [Translator's note: Quote taken from *The New English Bible* (New York: Oxford University Press, 1970).]

new natural unity of the political nation, Hobbes uses, because of the biblical tradition of the Old Covenant, contract theory. Men in the state of nature have committed themselves through a contract to place by majority vote a sovereign above themselves and to surrender to him. Because of this construction, Hobbes has been called a contract theorist. That is not entirely incorrect, but it only applies to an instrument of his theory, one that is bound to tradition and time and not to its essence. The essential can be extracted from the formulae that determine the results of the covenant: The previously unformed multitude do not elect a ruler but combine their multiplicity into the unity of one person; the multitude becomes the unity of the commonwealth in which the bearer of their personality is procured; the commonwealth—not the elected sovereign—is the person who now appears as the actor in history. We already mentioned that the most important prerequisite for forming an inner-worldly communal religion is that the community understands itself as a unit centered in itself. The symbol of the Leviathan chosen by Hobbes takes an important step in this direction, and although it does not achieve the spherical and cosmos-related conciseness of Aristotle's polis, it does eliminate to a great extent the open structure of the Christian ecclesia. Even though the hierarchy still extends up to God and the commonwealth is created according to God's commission, the hierarchy no longer flows down to persons who occupy the ranks of the ecclesia but to the community as a collective person; it goes to the sovereign, not considered as the ruler of subjects, but as the personality carrier of the commonwealth. If one wanted to make historical comparisons, then one would have to grant Hobbes a similar position for the particular inner-worldly ecclesia as was previously ascribed to Paul for the creation of the symbolism of the Christian community. The new community attains its unity through the sovereign in the same symbolic-mystical way as the Pauline ecclesia attained its unity through the *pneuma* and *kephale* of Christ [Eph. 4:15]. The worldly substrate of the commonwealth is the particular nations, but their unity is a *corpus mysticum*, just like that of the Christian one. The only parallel to this process within the more narrow context of European history can be found in the Germanic world during the period of migration of peoples. There, we find as in Hobbes, the creation of the personhood of a tribe through the appointment of a king, and the loss of that personhood through his death. The relationship between *rex* and *gens* is so close that the investiture or loss of the king means gaining or losing the historically immediate existence of the national being. In the same way, Hobbes's covenant of sovereignty declared the state to be a historical person, the "Mortal God," the worldly God, to whom mankind owes next to the "Immortal God," the eternal God, their peace and security.

The commonwealth is a closed cosmos not only with respect to political power, it is also closed intellectually (*geistig*), because the sovereign, irrespective of whether he be a monarch or an assembly, has the right to judge which opinions and teachings are suitable to maintain and promote the unity of the commonwealth; he decides which people be allowed to speak in assemblies, and he has the right to censor any printed material. The justification for this power could have been written by a modern minister of propaganda: The actions of people are determined by their opinions, and whoever directs the opinions in the right direction will also direct the actions to support peace and harmony. Although the teachings have to be true, a conflict could not arise in any case, because any teachings disrupting the peace of the community cannot be true.

Thus, the Leviathan is a sacred, pagan symbol, and if we want to transform it into a Christian symbol, we would have to compare and contrast it to the previous symbol of the Christian ecclesia. The high scholastic construction put forth by Thomas, in which the temporal was of lower rank than the spiritual order and organizationally distinguished, was crumbling. And the worldly order— as it began to be filled with national elements—developed into a unit with its own personality. Thus the polemic of Hobbes is directed against the fragment of the *sacrum imperium,* which still laid claim to being the personal representation of Christianity and to having spiritual priority, against the Catholic Church. He uses his theory of the commonwealth to prove that the Church was not a commonwealth and did not have any personality. The new ecclesia, therefore, could not be part of a comprehensive empire of God but would only be immediate to God as an individual person. The Pauline concept of the empire that, supplemented by the charisma of the king, dominated the ninth century—and according to which the pope, emperor, king, clergy, and laymen were the parts ("limbs") of the ecclesia—is vehemently rejected, because it would lead to the absurd consequence that undoubtedly historical communal figures as France, Spain, or Venice would no longer be recognized as such but would instead be parts of the ecclesia without any status of personality immediate to God. Each commonwealth would be a Christian ecclesia on its own, if its sovereign made the Bible and Christendom binding by national law. Then the state and the Church would be one; the sovereign would be the head of the Church, immediately under God, and would not require the mediatorship of the *Vicarius Christi.* A spiritual commonwealth in the form of a church that is not the state would be absurd; the distinction between spiritual and temporal was introduced to the world only to confuse the people, to alienate subjects from their sovereign, and to disrupt the peace of the commonwealth-church.

Hobbes supports his arguments by referring to the history of the Old and New Covenants. The religious potency of the Jewish theocracy strikes the world of the English Reformation with full force and unites with the national consciousness in the symbol of the sacral communal person. The stages of Jewish history are traced in great detail from the covenant with Abraham and the subjection of Israel to God, to the leadership of Moses and his successors, to the crisis of apostasy when Israel gives up God as its Lord in order to have a king like the other peoples. Abraham is taken as an example to develop the image of a spiritual head of state. God has spoken directly to Abraham, since he was the representative of his people, and therefore each subject in the commonwealth (since he experienced no divine revelation) had to subject himself to the laws of the sovereign with regard to all external religious acts and declarations. Subjects were free and subjected only to God as far as their innermost feelings and thoughts were concerned, which were not shown on the outside and could not be known by the human ruler.

The sovereign of the Christian commonwealth had the same position as Abraham had toward his family. God speaks only to him; only he knows God's will, and he alone is entitled to interpret the word and will of God. Taking the Jewish theocratic concept as the pattern, the symbol of the Leviathan gains characteristics related to those of Akhenaton's imperial religion. Once more the ruler becomes the mediator of God; God reveals himself only to the ruler; he alone conveys the will of God to the people—with the single reservation that a spark of God's personal revelation remains in the private, innermost life of a person.

The appearance of Christ did not change the situation. Its purpose was to renew the covenant with God, which had been broken in the rebellion that resulted in the selection of Saul as king. Christ had been sent to save mankind from the sin of rebellion and to lead it back to the kingdom of God; yet this kingdom was a kingdom of mercy and not of this world; Christ will rule as king only after the general Resurrection of the dead. The ecclesiastical power in this world was transferred from Christ to the Apostles, from the Apostles to successors by laying on of hands until sovereign persons adopted Christendom by subjecting themselves to the immediate revelation of God—and not to the Apostles. The Christian sovereigns hold the ecclesiastical power; and through their mediatorship, God's rule in this world over the ecclesia subjected to their rule will be restored again.

The new ecclesia struggles with the old Christian ecclesia, and from its position as the ecclesia willed by God it has to prevail over claims that can only be described as the work of Satan. Hobbes, therefore, has to confront the symbol of the Leviathan with the symbol of Satan's empire. As far as Christian mankind is concerned, it disintegrates in the ecclesiae of the Christian political communities; the attempt to maintain a universal Christian ecclesia as an institution with a personality is considered the work of Satan. The Catholic Church and its claim to spiritual supremacy over all Christians is understood as the kingdom of darkness, which wanted to disturb the unilinear continuation of the people of God from the Jewish time before the kings until the time of the Christian commonwealth. The state was the church, and whoever came forth as an opponent to this new ecclesia, the Leviathan, is Satan—just as, in Jewish history, Palestine was the kingdom of God and the neighboring, hostile nations were the kingdom of the archfiend, Satan.

The contradiction stayed alive in England for a very long time. Defoe wrote an extensive political history of Satan, and in 1851 Cardinal Newman thought it necessary to illustrate the absurdity of the Catholic Church's interpretation of Satan by using Blackstone's commentary to the English constitution to depict the English state as the kingdom of Satan corresponding to the images of Satan put forth by anti-Catholic literature. He did this to prove that the method could be applied to anything. The cardinal's satire has been outdone by reality: Like the symbol of the commonwealth, Hobbes's symbol of Satan has shown its propensity to be permeated with any historical contents. In the course of the political-religious history of Europe, the particular ecclesia developed further into a closed, inner-worldly ecclesia and also gave rise to the corresponding empires of Satan.

5

The Inner-Worldly Community

Nothing essential has changed in the basic characteristics of the European political-religious symbolism since the seventeenth century. Hierarchy and orders, universal and particular ecclesia, the empires of God and of Satan, *Führertum* and apocalypse, remain the expressive forms of the communal religion up until today. Yet, the contents are gradually changing toward those traced out in *Leviathan*. The ecclesia is increasingly breaking away from the association of the universal empire that has its hierarchical peak in God until, in some instances, it becomes independent and closes itself off in an inner-worldly way. There is no longer any sacral permeation from the highest source; rather, it itself has become an original sacral substance. Remnants of the old structure can still be found in formulae without significance: for example, the statement that the sacral, closed community "acted at the order of God" when it spread out. But "at the order of God" is synonymous with such inner-worldly formulae as "order of history," "historical mission," "order of blood," etc. We must, therefore, complete lines drawn even earlier and point out the symptoms of the new meanings, which are widely known as facts but rarely interpreted as expressions of political religiosity.

The tremendous foundation of the new inner-worldliness, which has been built in the centuries since the late Middle Ages, is the knowledge of the world as an inventory of existential facts about all stages and as knowledge of its essential and causal contexts. The knowledge of space and nature, of the earth and the peoples who live on it, of their history and intellectual differentiation, of plants and animals, of man as an embodied being and as a mind, of his historical existence and his ability to gain knowledge, of the life of his soul and his desires, fills up the new understanding of the world and pushes all knowledge about divine order to the edges and beyond. The radical metaphysical question posed by Schelling—"Why is there something; why is there not nothing?"—reflects the worries of a few; it means nothing to the religious attitude of the masses. The world as contents has suppressed the world as existence. The methods of science as the sole forms to study the contents of the world are declared to be the generally obligatory basis of man's attitude toward the world. Since the nineteenth century and for long periods up until today, the word *metaphysical* has been considered to be an abusive word (*Schimpfwort*), religion to be "opium for the people" and, in a more recent turn, an "illusion" with a doubtful future. Counter-formulas against the spiritual religions and their worldviews are coined and legitimated by the claims of secular science as the valid form of cognition, contrary to revelation and mystical thought. The "scientific *Weltanschauungen*," "scientific socialism," and "scientific race theory" emerge; inventories are taken of the "mysteries of the world," and they are solved. At the same time, the general knowledge of fundamental questions of being and of the expressive forms used to study them shrinks into small groups. Indifference, laicization, and atheism become the characteristics of the publicly binding worldview.

Men can let the contents of the world grow to such an extent that the world and God disappear behind them, but they cannot annul the human condition itself. This remains alive in each individual soul; and when God is invisible behind the world, the contents of the world will become new gods; when the symbols of transcendent religiosity are banned, new symbols develop from the inner-worldly language of science to take their place. Like the Christian ecclesia, the inner-worldly community has its apocalypse, too; yet, the new apocalyptics insist that the symbols they create are scientific judgments. We have already drawn several lines from the Joachitic symbols to modern times in order to illustrate the continuum of the expressive forms. The inner-worldly apocalypse needs only to remove from Joachim's thinking the transcendent end realm, the eternal Sabbath, the Beyond, to have at its disposal a language of symbols suitable for the secular world. The end realm is no longer a transcendent community of the spirit but an earthly condition of perfected humanity. In his essay "Ideen zu einer Geschichte in weltbürgerlicher Absicht," Kant propounds a view of history in which the rational and enlightened person climbs to ever-higher stages of perfection as inner-worldly being until, finally, he moves forward to the repression-free, cosmopolitan community with suitable leaders. Mankind is that great collective body, to whose progress each man has to contribute. It is terrestrially closed; it progresses only as a whole, and the meaning of individual existence is to participate instrumentally in the collective progress. This conception is radically collectivistic; it is so radical that, with respect to his own construction, Kant expressed his "astonishment" at the circumstance that a man would not gain from his activities for the collective body because only the last generations would enter into the perfection of the earthly paradise. Christian resistance is roused, and Kant finds a way out through personal immortality, even if this reader has the impression that he does not seem to consider this an adequate substitute for the earthly life of perfect, rational persons.

Whereas Kant's revelation encompasses all mankind, other apocalyptics narrow their symbolism to the mission of one particular community. Fichte develops his revelation in connection with the symbolism of the Gospel of John. The end realm, as a terrestrial realm, is the kingdom of God, and no other people than the ancient Germans are qualified to regenerate mankind and bring about the kingdom of God. Comte transformed the theories of Vico and Saint-Simon into the law of the three stages of world history—the "theological age," the "metaphysical age," and the upcoming "positivistic-scientific age"—and finds that the French are the carriers-proponents of the positivist spirit. Marx divides history into the original communist period, the class-based period, and the final communist society and recognizes the proletariat as carrier of the development toward the end realm. Since Gobineau, race theorists understand world history as movement of and struggle between the races, and they see as carrier a chosen Nordic or Germanic race. Within the course of European history, each of the revelations also created its own group of symbols for Satan. We already mentioned the conception of the Catholic Church as Satan who belongs to the Leviathan. Kant's devil is human desires; Fichte drew up the figure of Satan Napoleon; for the positivist apocalypse, religion and metaphysics are Evil; the bourgeoisie belongs as evil to the proletariat; the chosen race is tied to an inferior race, above all the Jews as "counter race."

The common trend of the new symbolism is its "scientific"

character. This introduces a peculiar dynamic that has significantly changed the spiritual structure of the inner-worldly community in less than one century. The apocalyptic revelations enumerated above are "naïve," i.e., they credulously claim that their theses are of scientific character. Since the middle of the nineteenth century, proceeding from Marxism, there has been an increasingly radical tendency to criticize the apocalypse by disclosing inherent ideologies. The proponents of these disclosures want to prove that the symbolic systems do not meet the requirements of scientific methods and that they are formed to promulgate certain interests. By putting forth the claim of being scientific, the revelations opened themselves up to scientific discussion and are being corroded by their own prerequisites. Now, one could believe that the consequence of mutual ideology-critical corrosion is a return to criticism-proof images of the world; but instead, something remarkable occurs: The adherence to inner-worldly religiosity is so strong that its revelations do not break apart under the attack of scientific criticism; the concept of truth is transformed instead. In the first phase of this development the nonscientific character of the symbols is acknowledged. Yet it is not dropped by political-religious man; rather, the symbol maintained its capacity to bind the masses, even if it does not meet scientific standards. The naïve apocalypse is replaced by a conscious apocalypse; the system claiming to be rational-theoretical, national-economic, or sociological is replaced by "myth." The "myth" is created purposely to bind the masses emotionally and to arouse in them the politically effective expectation of salvation. Since the myth cannot legitimize itself through transcendent revelation or stand up to scientific criticism, a new concept of truth is developed in the second phase—a concept, as Rosenberg put it, of the so-called organic truth. We can find first signs of this in Hobbes's thesis that any teaching that disrupts the unity and peace of the commonwealth cannot be true. The theory is now developed further into the opinion that only that is true which promotes the existence of the organically closed, inner-worldly national community. Knowledge and art, myth and customs are true if they serve the purpose of the racially bound nationhood (*Volkstums*). "From there they come, and there they go again. And their decisive criterion is whether they increase, add to, or strengthen the inner values of these racial national characteristics." Thus the formation of myths is withdrawn from rational discussion and becomes more similar to the actual symbolism of a kingdom of spiritual forms, in which inner-worldly and transcendent experiences are combined into a tangible unit.

As a consequence of the pragmatic elements of the inner-worldly faith, people following this type of religion will not allow their faith to be disrupted even though they know of the psychological techniques used for creating myths, the propaganda of the myths, and the social dissemination. If whatever promotes society is true, then the means for interspersing the myths that strengthen the community are not only correct in a technical sense but also permissible and necessary in a communal-religious sense. It is, therefore, possible to develop the techniques of myth propaganda to its current high status without the facts of the propaganda destroying its own purpose. It is possible to utilize the insights that depth psychology has gained into the instinctual life of individuals and of the masses without the appeal to the desires arousing any resistance. Just as the criticism of ideology did not result in the destruction of the inner-worldly belief in revelations, the insight into the depths of the life of desires has not led to a rationalization of the personality; on the contrary, it has given rise to the recognition that hate is stronger than love, and that, therefore, the appropriate means for realizing common objectives are to disinhibit man's aggressiveness and to build up hate.

The significance of this phenomenon as a characteristic of inner-worldly religiosity becomes more evident when it is compared to a transcendent consideration of the necessary means to an end, such as the one put forth by Ignatius of Loyola. The reflections of Ignatius concern the selection of the right means for man's one goal: to live for the worship of God and the salvation of the soul. The most appropriate means must be selected to achieve this objective, "so that I do not subordinate and forcefully submit the objective to the means, but the means to the objective." Bearing in mind human desires, it is recommended that one take great care to determine whether a form of the conduct of life does not correspond to "unordered inclinations" and is chosen in the hope that God would show himself accommodating toward the soul anyway, instead of completely subordinating the conduct of life to the salvation of the soul and the worship of God. Thus the conduct of life is an earthly means that gains its significance from the transcendent objective and must not contain anything that is not compatible with the holy purpose. When the inner-worldly collective existence takes the place of God, the person becomes the link serving the sacral contents of the world, i.e., an instrument, as Kant already—and still—noted with "astonishment." The problem of the person's conduct of life, its physical and spiritual existence, is only important in connection with the existence of the overall community as its *realissimum*. When an individual has assumed the attitude of inner-worldly religiosity, he accepts this position; he views himself as a tool, as a "Hegelian" machine-part working in the overall whole, and voluntarily submits himself to the technical means with which he is integrated into the collective organization. The knowledge of the contents of the world and the techniques based on such knowledge are not the temporally subordinated means for attaining the eternal goal of life in the other-worldly God; they are rather the life-blood of the inner-worldly God himself. They build the *corpus mysticum* of the collectivity and bind the members to form the oneness of the body. They are not rejected as crimes against the dignity of the person, and as a matter of fact, they are not merely tolerated by reason of being the dictates of the moment. They are rather promoted and desired as a means of achieving religious-ecstatic ties between man and his God. The formation of the myth and its propaganda by means of newspapers and radio, the speeches and celebrations, the assemblies and parades, the planning and the death in battle, make up the inner-worldly forms of the *unio mystica*.

Symbolism

The symbolism of the completely closed inner-worldly ecclesia did not have to move far beyond the symbol of the Leviathan—the decisive step was the decapitation of God. In Hobbes's symbolism, the multitude was joined in the body of the commonwealth according to the laws of God; the Christian commonwealth in its form as a collective person was subordinate to God, and the sovereign was the mediator with God. We already pointed out the similarities to the imperial religion of Akhenaton and the orientation of the symbols along the lines of Abraham's chosen people. Now the link to God in the perfectly inner-worldly symbolism is severed and replaced by the community itself as the source of legitimation of the collective person. The symbolism's language is rational, fairly well developed, and uniform, because the theorists of the two radically inner-worldly ecclesia, the fascist Italian and the national-socialist German, draw from the common vocabulary of German Romanticism. For both, the sacral substance is the national spirit or the objective spirit, i.e., *realissimum* that lasts throughout the period, which becomes historical reality in individuals as members of their nation and in the works of such individuals. Mussolini describes Fascism as a religious idea and the politics of the regime as religious politics, because Fascism proceeded from the assumption that man was in touch with a *volonta obiettiva* and, therefore, gained personality in a spiritual empire, in the empire of his people.

Taking this assumption as its basis, the structure of the symbolism rises in the forms that Hobbes has created in detail. The people (*Volk*) is the "people in its plurality," as a community of language, customs, culture, economic activity, and it becomes the "people in its unity," the historical person, through the political organization. The Hobbesian hypothesis of the covenant and the election of the sovereign are replaced by a different inner-worldly sacral principle for selecting the personality carriers of the community: In the Italian and the German theories, the person of the comrade of the people is admittedly related to the spirit of the people, because the comrade of the people can gain the status in the people as of a spiritual body only through this relationship; but the status is not the same for all. In some people, the few, the spirit of the people lives stronger; in others, the many, it is weaker, and it finds total expression in one person only, namely, in the Führer. "The 'Führer' is permeated with the idea; it acts through him. But he is also the one who can give this idea a living form. The spirit of the people becomes reality in him and the will of the people is formed in him; in him is won the manifest form of the race—encompassing a people which is therefore never concretely assembled in its entirety. He is the representative of the people," writes a German theorist. The Führer is the point where the spirit of the people breaks into historical reality; the inner-worldly god speaks to the Führer in the same way the transcendent God speaks to Abraham, and the Führer transforms god's words into commands for his immediate followers and for the people. The connection with the symbolism of the Leviathan is so close that even the same words are used to describe the mystical personification of the ecclesia: In the German theory, the Führer is the "representative" in the same sense as Hobbes's sovereign is the representative, the carrier of the personality of the commonwealth. There is a certain difference in this respect between the Italian and the German symbolism; whereas the Italian spirit of the people is considered more spiritual, the German spirit of the people is blood-based, and the Führer becomes the speaker of the spirit of the people and the representative of people because of his racial unity with the people.

Another part of the theory is not as carefully rationalized as the previous parts: The difficult point is the personality status of the comrades of the people. On the one hand they are members of the people, because the spirit of the people is alive in them; on the other hand they are linked to the spirit of the people in political-organizational terms through the mediatorship of the Führer. The imperial religion of Akhenaton solved this problem in a radical manner by awarding the function of mediator to the pharaoh and letting the will of the god descend from him to the people. In the inner-worldly symbolism, the Führer and the people are bound to each other through the sacral substance, which lives in one and the other; the god does not stand on the outside, but lives in the humans themselves. The spirit of the people, therefore, could also express itself in the will of the people, and the voice of the people could become the voice of god. The theorists master this problem on the one hand by acknowledging the historical existence of the people as an expression of the spirit of the people in customs and morals, language and culture, and—in particular in the German theory— by viewing the political organization as a structure, within the protective walls of which the people's characteristics can develop appropriately. On the other hand, they reject the political deter-mination of will by the people—again especially in the German theory, where the Führer is the only carrier of the people's will. In the teaching on plebiscite, the idea that the act of voting is an act of national will is decisively rejected. The plebiscite is to express and enforce the concordance between the objective will of the people embodied in the Führer and the subjective convic-tions of the people. The plebiscite is a declaration of loyalty to the Führer not an announcement of an individual's will. If, therefore, the plebiscite does not confirm the will of the Führer, the Führer need not step back before the will of the people, because the denial is not the objective will of the people but only the expression of a subjective arbitrariness. As far as this construction is concerned, the symbolism resembles closely that of Egypt. The god speaks only to the Führer, and the people are informed of his will through the mediation of the Führer.

Belief (*Glaube*)

The world of symbols is a complete, an ultimate, world—we want to descend to the original sources, to the forces that created the symbolic forms. Gerhard Schumann's "Lieder vom Reich" are one of the strongest expressions of political-religious agitation. They allow us to trace the movements of the soul that form the basis for the symbols and historical reality of the inner-worldly community. The roots of such religious excitation can be found in the experience of creatureliness, but the *realissimum* in which they find redemption is not God, as in Christian religious experience, but the people and the sworn fraternity of comrades. Moreover, the ecstasies are not spiritual but anchored in desire, and they end in the bloodlust of the deed. We would like to quote the verses, in which the poet describes his experience.

The basic emotion of natural abandonment (*kreatürlichen Verlassenheit*) is described as a state of dreamlike unreality, of coldness, of sealed-off loneliness. The soul breaks out of this state with a burning fervor to be united with the sacred whole. A hot flood of excitement tears it from its solitude into the fraternity of "earth, light and thing." The transition from rigid pride to merging into and flowing with the fraternity is both active and passive; the soul wants to experience itself and does experience itself as an active element in breaking down resistance; and at the same time, it is driven and swept along by a flood, to which it only has to abandon itself.

The soul is united with the fraternal flow of the world: "And I was one. And the whole flowed." The stream carries the soul along, breaks through any walls, and lets the soul flow into the whole of the people. The soul becomes depersonalized in the course of finding and unification, it frees itself completely of the cold ring of its own self, and it grows beyond its own chilling smallness to become "good and great." By losing its own self it ascends to the grander reality of the people: "I lost myself and found the people, the empire [*Reich*]." In another vision, German soil is rejuvenated, a new sky arches over it, and out of the chaos rises the Grail, the image of the new order, which the soul and its comrades serve in a sworn confraternity. Yet, reality is still depressing, time weighs heavily on the Reich, and the "strict followers" turn away, magically bound by their oath, "awaiting the hour of the flames, which they spoke of." Dire need weighs down oppressively, life stops short until—from the embers of the last moment before the collapse—thousands cry out: "The Führer! Make us slaves! Lord, free us!" In a vision of the Mount of Olives—"Then night fell. One stood and struggled"—the longed-for Führer accepts the command of god to save his people:

> And descending He carried the torch into the night.
> The millions submitted to him in silence.
> Saved. The sky was ablaze in the pale light of morning.
> The sun grew. And with it grew the "Reich."

The last vision also does not go beyond the religious excitation of an individual soul. The need of the people and salvation through the Führer are not outside historical events that the poet forms into a picture; the need is the need of the soul that has lost itself ecstatically within the overall nation, whose suffering is the suffering of the nation. And the Führer, who, after his struggle with god, descends from the mountain as the savior to save the people, saves the individual soul that has devoted itself to serve the Grail, to construct the dome of the Reich.

The religious agitation is not calmed through unification with the whole. It needs the tension of the struggle and the ecstasy of the deed. The deed of salvation of the Führer and the victory of the league of the sworn "strict followers" culminate in the empirical establishment of the Reich. This unambiguously expresses what had been heard before, namely, that the personal religious drama and the drama of the whole people could break apart. During the period of tension and waiting, the servants of the Grail are the upholders and champions of the coming Reich. After the political and organizational establishment of the Reich, a schism opens up between the fervor of the strict followers and the daily routine of battle-relieved business and commercial activities. In the poem this is described as follows: "And after the victories come those who celebrate. Then they are great and the soldier falls silent." The poet turns against the shallow and ignorant, industrious people who strive to interpret the events while the soldiers shudder at the new commands of Fate as they continue to be driven to new battles: "There is no time to drowse at celebrations. We are hammering out the 'New Reich.' " And while the others do not grasp that "Fate [*das Schicksal*] is getting ready to perfect itself," a prayer is sent forth:

> Do not permit me to settle down.
> Do not permit me to have my fill and to call for peace.
> Thrust me into every despair and restlessness of the heart.

Another verse admonishes further: "Throw yourself also over your will! Over the stars! Up!" The will to lose oneself and to break away ecstatically is driven by a deeply agitating existential fear, as is described in the "Münstergedicht" below:

> And all fear, the terrible horror
> Breaks open: from tower to tower upwards, upwards!

The poem "Die Tat" illustrates the stages of agitation starting from the excitement of acting to the point of relaxation. The sense of the deed is not the victory but the deed itself; the pain inflicted upon the enemy is to be resumed to the soul of the perpetrator: "And when you strike, hit your own heart." Friends have to be destroyed up to the point of total desolation. By committing the deed, the evil, destructive deed, the actor strikes himself until his own desires and his own will are extinguished. The naked, purposeless deed as well as the act of becoming absorbed and tormenting oneself are acts of mythical self-dissolution and communion with the world up to the point of relaxation in bloodlust: "The deed was good if red blood flows."

For these actors, marked by the struggle, the new world after victory is hollow and dull. They are strangers to everyday life and the celebrations: "In hard and unmoved expressions, / They bear only scaffolds, and no mercy." Dazed, gloomy, sometimes writhing, they "wait for orders." They come together from out of the general crowd as "a group of resolute men" united among themselves, "because life pulls the hearts of men to it"; the core, the soul of the Reich devoted only to "the Führer who is alone," the Führer, whom they dream of at night.

> The blood court echoes in their steps.
> In their soul they carry the Grail.
> Slaves of the "Führer," protectors and avengers at the same time.
> The Reich burns in them, the Reich grows with them.

6

Epilogue

We have tried to study the political religions as knowledgeable persons, so let us, first of all, sum up the conclusion: The life of people in political community cannot be defined as a profane realm, in which we are concerned only with legal questions and the organization of power. A community is also a realm of religious order, and the knowledge of a political condition will be incomplete with respect to a decisive point, firstly, if it does not take into account the religious forces inherent in a society and the symbols through which these are expressed or, secondly, if it does include the religious forces but does not recognize them as such and translates them into areligious categories. Humans live in political society with all traits of their being, from the physical to the spiritual and religious traits. We have only presented examples from the Mediterranean and Western European culture areas, but the thesis is universal and also applies to the political forms in the East. The political community is always integrated in the overall context of human experience of world and God, irrespective of whether the political sphere occupies a subordinate level in the divine order of the hierarchy of being or whether it is deified itself. The language of politics is always interspersed with the ecstasies of religiosity and, thus, becomes a symbol in the concise sense by letting experiences concerned with the contents of the world be permeated with transcendental-divine experiences. Elements of the symbolic expressive forms that we have worked out on the basis of the Mediterranean and European examples can be found in all very advanced civilizations: the hierarchy, in which the sacral substance branches out from a transcendent God to the community of creatures; the ecclesia as the sacral communal substance; the apocalypse as the revelation of the empire; the holy kings as God's mediators and personality carriers of the community.

If we now enter into the religious space itself, the Christian determination becomes evident. The mystic of Frankfurt writes in the *German Theology*:[6] "If the human creature attributes something good to itself, such as being [*Wesen*], essence, life, knowledge, skill, in short, all that one must deem good, as if he were that or had that, as if it belonged to him or came from him, then he goes astray. What else did Satan do? What else was his fall and abandonment than his assumption he were something too, and his wish to be someone and to have his own. This assumption and his 'I' and 'my,' his 'me' and 'mine' were his abandonment and his fall. And it is that way still." It is not indifferent how the sphere of human-political organization is integrated in the order of being. The inner-worldly religiosity experienced by the collective body—be it humanity, the people, the class, the race, or the state—as the *realissimum* is abandonment of God; and some Christian thinkers, therefore, refuse—even with regard to language—to put the inner-worldly political religion on the same level with the spiritual religion of Christianity. They speak of demonologies in contrast to belief in God or of a belief that is man-made, a "*mystique humaine*," to distinguish true faith. According to the *German Theology* the belief that man is the source of good and of improvement of the world, as it is held by the Enlightenment, and the belief that the collective body is a mysterious, divine substance, which has been spreading since the nineteenth century, is anti-Christian renunciation. And within the meaning of the undogmatic *vita contemplativa*, the representation of being within the wealth of the stages extending from nature to God, the inner-worldly religiosity and its symbolism conceals the most essential parts of reality. It blocks the path to the reality of God and distorts the circumstances of the levels of being subordinate to God.

Neither knowledge nor Christian determination can solve the mystery of God and being. God's creation contains evil, the splendor of Being is clouded by human misery, the order of the community is built upon hate and blood, with misery and the apostasy of God. Schelling's fundamental question—"Why is there something; why is there not nothing?"—is followed by the other question, "Why is it the way it is?"—the question of theodicy.

6. *German Theology*, a work published by an unknown author in Frankfurt in the fourteenth century.

A Note on Sources

The actual, historical contents of this essay are based, almost without any exceptions, on the sources themselves. The theoretical assumptions and historical interpretations are not new but reflect the current state of the science. Below I have listed some of the main works discussing the problems studied herein for readers who would like to gain deeper understanding of individual questions.

The theological assumptions in general follow the work of Erich Przywara, S.J., "Religionsphilosophie katholischer Theologie," in *Handbuch der Philosophie*, ed. A. Bäumler and M. Schröter, sec. 2, "Nature-Spirit-God" (Munich: Verlag R. Oldenbourg, 1927).

A treasure trove for examples of the new mass religiosity at the end of the nineteenth century is the work by William James, *The Varieties of Religious Experience: A Study in Human Nature* (London: Longmans, Green, and Co., 1902) [Recent edition: Harmondsworth: Penguin Books, 1982].

With respect to the knowledge of current political-religious manifestations, the following treatise is important: Etienne de Greeff, "Le drame humain et la psychologie des 'mystiques' humaines," in *Foi et 'Mystiques' Humaines*, Etudes Carmélitaines, 22d year, vol. 1, April 1937.

The philosophical-anthropological fundamental views of the author are based on the general current literature available on this subject, e.g., Max Scheler, *Die Stellung des Menschen im Kosmos* (Darmstadt: Otto Reichl Verlag, 1928) [English edition: *Man's Place in Nature*, trans. Hans Meyerhoff (1928; New York: Noonday Press, 1962)].

The chapter on Akhenaton is based on J. H. Breasted, *Geschichte Ägyptens*, 2d ed. (Vienna: Phaidon Verlag, 1936) [Original edition,

A History of Egypt from the Earliest Times to the Persian Conquest (New York: Charles Scribner's Sons, 1909)].

For more information on the European Middle Ages, in particular on Joachim of Fiore, please refer to the following work: Alois Dempf, *Sacrum Imperium: Geschichts und Staatsphilosophie des Mittelalters und der politischen Renaissance* (Munich: Verlag R. Oldenbourg, 1929).

The problems of the twelfth and thirteenth centuries are also discussed in the work by Georges de Lagarde, *La Naissance de l'Esprit laique au déclin du Moyen-Age*, vols. 1 and 2 (Editions Béatrice, 1934) [Recent edition: *La naissance de l'esprit laïque au déclin du Moyen-Age*, 5 vols. (Louvaine: E. Nauwelaerts, 1956–1970)]. Also, Ernst Kantorowicz, *Kaiser Friedrich der Zweite* (Berlin: Georg Bondi, 1928) [English edition, *Frederick the Second, 1194–1250* (New York: Ungar, 1957)].

As far as major new attempts to understand the political problem as a religious problem are concerned, the author knows only of the following work: Alexander Ular, "Die Politik: Untersuchung über die völkerpsychologischen Bedingungen gesellschaftlicher Organisation," in *Die Gesellschaft. Sammlung sozialpsychologischer Monographien*, ed. Martin Buber, vol. 3 (Frankfurt: Rütten und Loening, 1906).

[For the writings of the fourteenth-century mystic known as "the Frankfurter," see the following: *Der Frankforter (Eyn deutsch Theologia)*, ed. Willo Uhl (Bonn: Marcus and Weber, 1912); *Der Frankforter, eine deutsch Theologie* (Leipzig: Im Insel-Verlag, 1920); English editions: *Theologia Germanica*, ed. Susanna Winkworth, pref. Charles Kingsley, 4th ed., Golden Treasury Series (1874; London: Macmillan and Co., 1907); *Theologica Germanica: The Way to a Sinless Life*, trans. and ed. Thomas S. Kepler (Cleveland: World Publishing Co., 1952); *The Theologica Germanica of Martin Luther*, trans. and intro. Bengt Hoffman, pref. Bengt Hägglund, Classics of Western Spirituality (New York: Paulist Press, 1980).]

The
New Science
of Politics

An Introduction

Posterity may know we have not loosely through silence
permitted things to pass away as in a dream.
RICHARD HOOKER

CONTENTS

Foreword

During the last thirty years or more there have arisen among the students in the field of politics those who would challenge the traditional approach to government and politics—an approach stemming from the days of Aristotle. The statistical, the psychological, and the sociological bases of a political science have each had adherents. Propounders of the new theories have either pushed aside or rejected the consideration of any system of values in their theories of the scientific approach to politics. While this type of approach has widespread acceptance today, it is being vigorously challenged in many quarters, particularly on the very home ground of the scientific school, the University of Chicago. Professor Voegelin in the present work makes an interesting and challenging contribution to the scope and method of politics. His position as an outstanding scholar in the field of political theory is a guaranty of his thoroughness and objectivity in handling his topic.

Under the sponsorship of the Charles R. Walgreen Foundation these lectures were given at the University of Chicago during the winter quarter, 1951. The co-operation of the author and the University of Chicago enables the Foundation to publish this series.

Jerome G. Kerwin
Chairman, Charles R. Walgreen Foundation
for the Study of American Institutions

Acknowledgments

On occasion of this book I should like to express my gratitude to the John Simon Guggenheim Memorial Foundation for enabling me to bring the state of the problems up to date through studies in Europe in the summer of 1950. These studies were, furthermore, facilitated by a grant-in-aid from the Research Council of Louisiana State University. My colleague, Professor Nelson E. Taylor, had the kindness to read the manuscript; I have gratefully availed myself of his advice in matters of style. My thanks for excellent secretarial help go to Miss Josephine Scurria. The Viking Press has kindly permitted the quotation of passages from a book published by it.

This book has grown from six lectures on "Truth and Representation" given in 1951 under the auspices of the Charles R. Walgreen Foundation. It is a pleasant opportunity to extend my thanks again to the Foundation as well as to its distinguished chairman, Professor Jerome G. Kerwin.

ERIC VOEGELIN
Baton Rouge, Louisiana

CONTENTS

Introduction

The existence of man in political society is historical existence; and a theory of politics, if it penetrates to principles, must at the same time be a theory of history. The following lectures on the central problem of a theory of politics, on representation, will, therefore, carry the inquiry beyond a description of the conventionally so-called representative institutions into the nature of representation as the form by which a political society gains existence for action in history. Moreover, the analysis will not stop at this point but will proceed to an exploration of the symbols by which political societies interpret themselves as representatives of a transcendent truth. And the manifold of such symbols, finally, will not form a flat catalogue but prove amenable to theoretization as an intelligible succession of phases in a historical process. An inquiry concerning representation, if its theoretical implications are unfolded consistently, will in fact become a philosophy of history.

To pursue a theoretical problem to the point where the principles of politics meet with the principles of a philosophy of history is not customary today. Nevertheless, the procedure cannot be considered an innovation in political science; it will rather appear as a restoration, if it be remembered that the two fields which today are cultivated separately were inseparably united when political science was founded by Plato. This integral theory of politics was born from the crisis of Hellenic society. In an hour of crisis, when the order of a society flounders and disintegrates, the fundamental problems of political existence in history are more apt to come into view than in periods of comparative stability. Ever since, one may say, the contraction of political science to a description of existing institutions and the apology of their principles, that is, the degradation of political science to a handmaid of the powers that be, has been typical for stable situations, while its expansion to its full grandeur as the science of human existence in society and history, as well as of the principles of order in general, has been typical for the great epochs of a revolutionary and critical nature. On the largest scale of Western history three such epochs occurred. The foundation of political science through Plato and Aristotle marked the Hellenic crisis; Saint Augustine's *Civitas Dei* marked the crisis of Rome and Christianity; and Hegel's philosophy of law and history marked the first major earthquake of the Western crisis. These are only the great epochs and the great restorations; the millennial periods between them are marked by minor epochs and secondary restorations; for the modern period, in particular, one should remember the great attempt of Bodin in the crisis of the sixteenth century.

By restoration of political science is meant a return to the consciousness of principles, not perhaps a return to the specific content of an earlier attempt. One cannot restore political science today through Platonism, Augustinianism, or Hegelianism. Much can be learned, to be sure, from the earlier philosophers concerning the range of problems, as well as concerning their theoretical treatment; but the very historicity of human existence, that is, the unfolding of the typical in meaningful concreteness, precludes a valid reformulation of principles through return to a former concreteness. Hence, political science cannot be restored to the dignity of a theoretical science in the strict sense by means of a literary renaissance of philosophical achievements of the past; the principles must be regained by a work of theoretization that starts from the concrete, historical situation of the age, taking into account the full amplitude of our empirical knowledge.

Formulated in such terms, the task looks formidable under any circumstances; and it may look hopeless in view of the enormous amounts of material that the empirical sciences of society and history put at our disposition today. In fact, however, this impression is deceptive. While the difficulties should by no means be underrated, the task begins to become feasible in our time because of the preparatory work that has been done during the last half-century. For two generations, now, the sciences of man and society have been engaged in a process of retheoretization. The new development, slow at first, gained momentum after the first World War; and today it is moving at a breathtaking speed. The task is approaching feasibility because, to a considerable extent, it is accomplished through convergent theoretization of the relevant materials in monographic studies. The title for these lectures on representation, *The New Science of Politics,* indicates the intention of introducing the reader to a development of political science that as yet is practically unknown to the general public as well as of showing that the monographic exploration of problems has reached the point where the application of results to a basic theoretical problem in politics can at least be attempted.

2

The movement toward retheoretization is not too well known, either in its range or in its accomplishments. And this is not the occasion for a description that, in order to be adequate, would have to run to considerable length. Nevertheless, a few indications must be given concerning its causes and intentions in order to answer some of the questions that inevitably will occur to the reader of the following lectures.

A restoration of political science to its principles implies that the restorative work is necessary because the consciousness of principles is lost. The movement toward retheoretization must be understood, indeed, as a recovery from the destruction of science that characterized the positivistic era in the second half of the nineteenth century. The destruction worked by positivism is the consequence of two fundamental assumptions. In the first place, the splendid unfolding of the natural sciences was co-responsible with other factors for the assumption that the methods used in the mathematizing sciences of the external world were possessed of some inherent virtue and that all other sciences would achieve comparable success if they followed the example and accepted these methods as their model. This belief by itself was a harmless idiosyncrasy that would have died out when the enthusiastic admirers of the model method set to work in their own science and did not achieve the expected successes. It became dangerous because it combined with the second assumption that the methods of the natural sciences were a criterion for theoretical relevance in general. From the combination of the two assumptions followed the well-known series of assertions that a study of reality could qualify as scientific only if it used the methods of the natural sciences, that problems couched in other terms were illusionary problems, that in particular metaphysical questions that do not admit of answers by the methods of the sciences of phenomena should not be asked, that realms of being that are not accessible to exploration by the model methods were irrelevant, and, in the extreme, that such realms of being did not exist.

The second assumption is the real source of danger. It is the key to the understanding of positivistic destructiveness, and it has by far not received the attention that it deserves. For this second assumption subordinates theoretical relevance to method and thereby perverts the meaning of science. Science is a search for truth concerning the nature of the various realms of being. Relevant in science is whatever contributes to the success of this search. Facts are relevant in so far as their knowledge contributes to the study of essence, while methods are adequate in so far as they can be effectively used as a means for this end. Different objects require different methods. A political scientist who tries to understand the meaning of Plato's *Republic* will not have much use for mathematics; a biologist who studies a cell structure will not have much use for methods of classical philology and principles of hermeneutics. This may sound trivial, but disregard for elementary verities happens to be one of the characteristics of the positivistic attitude; and hence it becomes necessary to elaborate the obvious. It is perhaps a consolation to remember that such disregard is a perennial problem in the history of science, for even Aristotle had to remind certain pests of his time that an "educated man" will not expect exactness of the mathematical type in a treatise on politics.

If the adequacy of a method is not measured by its usefulness to the purpose of science, if on the contrary the use of a method is made the criterion of science, then the meaning of science as a truthful account of the structure of reality, as the theoretical orientation of man in his world, and as the great instrument for man's understanding of his own position in the universe is lost. Science starts from the prescientific existence of man, from his participation in the world with his body, soul, intellect, and spirit, from his primary grip on all the realms of being that is assured to him because his own nature is their epitome. And from this primary cognitive participation, turgid with passion, rises the arduous way, the *methodos,* toward the dispassionate gaze on the order of being in the theoretical attitude. The question whether in the concrete case the way was the right one, however, can be decided only by looking back from the end to the beginning. If the method has brought to essential clarity the dimly seen, then it was adequate; if it has failed to do so, or even if it has brought to essential clarity something in which concretely we were not interested, then it has proved inadequate. If, for instance, in our prescientific participation in the order of a society, in our prescientific experiences of right and wrong, of justice and injustice, we should feel the desire to penetrate to a theoretical understanding of the source of order and its validity, we may arrive in the course of our endeavors at the theory that the justice of human order depends on its participation in the Platonic Agathon, or the Aristotelian Nous, or the Stoic Logos, or the Thomistic *ratio aeterna.* For one reason or another, none of these theories may satisfy us completely; but we know that we are in search for an answer of this type. If, however, the way should lead us to the notion that social order is motivated by will to power and fear, we know that we have lost the essence of the problem somewhere in the course of our inquiry—however valuable the results may be in clarifying other essential aspects of social order. In looking back from the answer to the question, we know, therefore, that the methods of a psychology of motivations are not adequate for the exploration of the problem and that in this concrete case it would be better to rely on the methods of metaphysical speculation and theological symbolization.

The subordination of theoretical relevance to method perverts the meaning of science on principle. Perversion will result whatever method should happen to be chosen as the model method. Hence, the principle must be carefully distinguished from its special manifestation. Without the distinction it is hardly possible to understand the historical phenomenon of positivism in its nature and range; and probably, because the distinction is not made, an adequate study of this important phase of Western intellectual history is still a desideratum. While such an analysis cannot be supplied on this occasion, the rules that would have to be followed must be set forth in order to bring the variety of positivistic phenomena into view. The analysis would inevitably come to a wrong start if positivism were defined as the doctrine of this or that outstanding positivistic thinker—if it were defined, for instance, in terms of the system of Comte. The special form of the perversion would obscure the principle; and related phenomena could not be recognized as such, because on the level of doctrine the adherents of different model methods are apt to oppose each other. Hence, it would be advisable to start from the impression that the Newtonian system made on Western intellectuals like Voltaire; to treat this impact as an emotional center from which the principle of perversion, as well as the special form of the model of physics, can radiate independently or in combination; and to trace the effects whatever form they may assume. This procedure recommends itself especially because a transfer of methods of mathematical physics in any strict sense of the word to the social sciences has hardly ever been attempted, for the good reason that the attempt would be too patently doomed to failure. The idea of finding a "law" of social phenomena that functionally would correspond to the law of gravitation in Newtonian physics never went beyond the stage of wild talk in the Napoleonic era. By the time of Comte the idea had already simmered down to the "law" of the three phases, that is, to a piece of fallacious speculation on the meaning of history, which interpreted itself as the discovery of an empirical law. Characteristic for the early diversification of the problem is the fate of the term *physique sociale.* Comte wanted to use it for his positivistic speculation but was thwarted in his intention because Quetelet appropriated the term for his own statistical investigations; the area of social phenomena that are indeed amenable to quantification began to separate from the area where toying with an imitation of physics is a pastime for dilettantes in both sciences. Hence, if positivism should be construed in a strict sense as meaning the development of social science through the use of mathematizing methods, one might arrive at the conclusion that positivism has never existed; if, however, it is understood as the intention of making the social sciences "scientific" through the use of methods that as closely as possible resemble the methods employed in sciences of the external world, then the results of this intention (though not intended) will be rather variegated.

The theoretical issue of positivism as a historical phenomenon had to be stated with some care; the variety of manifestations themselves can be listed briefly, now that their uniting bond is understood. The use of method as the criterion of science abolishes theoretical relevance. As a consequence, all propositions concerning facts will be promoted to the dignity of science, regardless of their relevance, as long as they result from a correct use of method. Since the ocean of facts is infinite, a prodigious expansion of science in the sociological sense becomes possible, giving employment to scientistic technicians and leading to the fantastic accumulation of irrelevant knowledge through huge "research projects" whose most interesting feature is the quantifiable expense that has gone into their production. The temptation is great to look more closely at these luxury flowers of late positivism and to add a few reflections on the garden of Academus in which they grow; but theoretical asceticism will not allow such horticultural pleasures. The present concern is with the principle that all facts are equal—as on occasion it has been formulated—if they are methodically ascertained. This equality of facts is independent of the method used in the special case. The accumulation of irrelevant facts does not require the application of statistical methods; it may quite as well occur under the pretext of critical methods in political history, description of institutions, history of ideas, or in the various branches of philology. The accumulation of theoretically undigested, and perhaps undigestible, facts, the excrescence for which the Germans have coined the term *Materialhuberei*, thus, is the first of the manifestations of positivism; and because of its pervasiveness, it is of much greater importance than such attractive oddities as the "unified science."

The accumulation of irrelevant facts, however, is inextricably interwoven with other phenomena. Major research enterprises that contain nothing but irrelevant materials are rare, indeed, if they exist at all. Even the worst instance will contain a page here and there of relevant analysis, and there may be grains of gold buried in them that wait for accidental discovery by a scholar who recognizes their value. For the phenomenon of positivism occurs in a civilization with theoretical traditions; and a case of complete irrelevance is practically impossible because, under environmental pressure, the most bulky and worthless collection of materials must hang on a thread, however thin, that connects it with the tradition. Even the staunchest positivist will find it difficult to write a completely worthless book about American constitutional law as long as with any conscientiousness he follows the lines of reasoning and precedents indicated by the decisions of the Supreme Court; even though the book be a dry reportage, and not relate the reasoning of the judges (who are not always the best of theorists) to a critical theory of politics and law, the material will compel submission at least to its own system of relevance.

Much deeper than by the easily recognizable accumulation of trivialities has science been destroyed by the second manifestation of positivism, that is, by the operation on relevant materials under defective theoretical principles. Highly respectable scholars have invested an immense erudition into the digestion of historical materials, and their effort has gone largely to waste because their principles of selection and interpretation had no proper theoretical foundation but derived from the *Zeitgeist,* political preferences, or personal idiosyncrasies. Into this class belong the histories of Greek philosophy that from their sources primarily extracted a "contribution" to the foundation of Western science; the treatises on Plato that discovered in him a precursor of Neo-Kantian logic or, according to the political fashions of the time, a constitutionalist, a utopian, a socialist, or a Fascist; the histories of political ideas that defined politics in terms of Western constitutionalism and then were unable to discover much political theory in the Middle Ages; or the other variant that discovered in the Middle Ages a good deal of "contribution" to constitutional doctrine but completely ignored the block of political sectarian movements that culminated in the Reformation; or a giant enterprise like Gierke's *Genossenschafts-recht* that was badly vitiated by its author's conviction that the history of political and legal thought was providentially moving toward its climax in his own theory of the *Realperson.* In cases of this class the damage is not due to an accumulation of worthless materials; on the contrary, the treatises of this type quite frequently are still indispensable because of their reliable informations concerning facts (bibliographical references, critical establishment of texts, etc.). The damage is rather done through interpretation. The content of a source may be reported correctly as far as it goes, and nevertheless the report may create an entirely false picture because essential parts are omitted. And they are omitted because the uncritical principles of interpretation do not permit recognizing them as essential. Uncritical opinion, private or public (*doxa* in the Platonic sense), cannot substitute for theory in science.

The third manifestation of positivism was the development of methodology, especially in the half-century from 1870 to 1920. The movement was distinctly a phase of positivism in so far as the perversion of relevance, through the shift from theory to method, was the very principle by which it lived. At the same time, however, it was instrumental in overcoming positivism because it generalized the relevance of method and thereby regained the understanding of the specific adequacy of different methods for different sciences. Thinkers like Husserl or Cassirer, for instance, were still positivists of the Comtean persuasion with regard to their philosophy of history; but Husserl's critique of psychologism and Cassirer's philosophy of symbolic forms were important steps toward the restoration of theoretical relevance. The movement as a whole, therefore, is far too complex to admit of generalizations without careful and extensive qualifications. Only one problem can, and must, be selected because it has a specific bearing on the destruction of science, that is, the attempt at making political science (and the social sciences in general) "objective" through a methodologically rigorous exclusion of all "value-judgments."

In order to arrive at clarity about the issue, it must first of all be realized that the terms "value-judgment" and "value-free" science were not part of the philosophical vocabulary before the second half of the nineteenth century. The notion of a value-judgment (*Werturteil*) is meaningless in itself; it gains its meaning from a situation in which it is opposed to judgments concerning facts (*Tatsachenurteile*). And this situation was created through the positivistic conceit that only propositions concerning facts of the phenomenal world were "objective," while judgments concerning the right order of soul and society were "subjective." Only propositions of the first type could be considered "scientific," while propositions of the second type expressed personal preferences and decisions, incapable of critical verification and therefore devoid of objective validity. This classification made sense only if the positivistic dogma was accepted on principle; and it could be accepted only by thinkers who did not master the classic and Christian science of man. For neither classic nor Christian ethics and politics contain "value-judgments" but elaborate, empirically and critically, the problems of order that derive from philosophical anthropology as part of a general ontology. Only when ontology as a science was lost, and when consequently ethics and politics could no longer be understood as sciences of the order in which human nature reaches its maximal actualization, was it possible for this realm of knowledge to become suspect as a field of subjective, uncritical opinion.

In so far as the methodologists accepted the positivistic dogma, they participated in the destruction of science. At the same time, however, they tried valiantly to save the historical and social sciences from the disrepute into which they were liable to fall because of the destruction in which they participated. When the *episteme* is ruined, men do not stop talking about politics; but they now must express themselves in the mode of *doxa*. The so-called value-judgments could become a serious concern for methodologists because, in philosophical language, they were *doxai*, uncritical opinions concerning the problem of order; and the methodologists' attempt to make the social sciences again respectable by eliminating current uncritical opining did at least awaken the consciousness of critical standards, even though it could not re-establish a science of order. Hence, the theory of "value-judgments" as well as the attempt to establish a "value-free" science were ambivalent in their effects. In so far as the attack on value-judgments was an attack on uncritical opinion under the guise of political science, it had the wholesome effect of theoretical purification. In so far as under the concept of value-judgments was subsumed the whole body of classic and Christian metaphysics, and especially of philosophical anthropology, the attack could result in nothing less than a confession that a science of human and social order did not exist.

The variety of concrete attempts has to a large part lost its interest now that the great methodological battles have subsided. They were generically governed by the principle of pushing the "values" out of science into the position of unquestioned axioms or hypotheses. Under the assumption, for instance, that the "state" was a value, political history and political science would be legitimated as "objective" in so far as they explored motivations, actions, and conditions that had a bearing on creation, preservation, and extinction of states. Obviously, the principle would lead to dubious results if the legitimating value was put at the discretion of the scientist. If science was defined as exploration of facts in relation to a value, there would be as many political histories and political sciences as there were scholars with different ideas about what was valuable. The facts that are treated as relevant because they have a bearing on the values of a progressivist will not be the same facts that are considered relevant by a conservative; and the relevant facts of a liberal economist will not be the relevant facts of a Marxist. Neither the most scrupulous care in keeping the concrete work "value-free" nor the most conscientious observation of critical method in establishing facts and causal relations could prevent the sinking of historical and political sciences into a morass of relativism. As a matter of fact, the idea was advanced, and could find wide consent, that every generation would have to write history anew because the "values" that determined the selection of problems and materials had changed. If the resulting mess was not worse than it actually was, the reason must again be sought in the pressure of a civilizational tradition that held the diversification of uncritical opinion within its general frame.

3

The movement of methodology, as far as political science is concerned, ran to the end of its immanent logic in the person and work of Max Weber. A full characterization cannot be attempted in the present context. Only a few of the lines that mark him as a thinker between the end and a new beginning will be traced.

A value-free science meant to Weber the exploration of causes and effects, the construction of ideal types that would permit distinguishing regularities of institutions as well as deviations from them, and especially the construction of typical causal relations. Such a science would not be in a position to tell anybody whether he should be an economic liberal or a socialist, a democratic constitutionalist or a Marxist revolutionary, but it could tell him what the consequences would be if he tried to translate the values of his preference into political practice. On the one side, there were the "values" of political order beyond critical evaluation; on the other side, there was a science of the structure of social reality that might be used as technical knowledge by a politician. In sharpening the issue of a "value-free" science to this pragmatic point, Weber moved the debate beyond methodological squabbles again to the order of relevance. He wanted science because he wanted clarity about the world in which he passionately participated; he was headed again on the road toward essence. The search for truth, however, was cut short at the level of pragmatic action. In the intellectual climate of the methodological debate the "values" had to be accepted as unquestionable, and the search could not advance to the contemplation of order. The *ratio* of science extended, for Weber, not to the principles but only to the causality of action.

The new sense of theoretical relevance could express itself, therefore, only in the creation of the categories of "responsibility" and "demonism" in politics. Weber recognized the "values" for what they were, that is, as ordering ideas for political action, but he accorded them the status of "demonic" decisions beyond rational argument. Science could grapple with the demonism of politics only by making politicians aware of the consequences of their actions and awakening in them the sense of responsibility. This Weberian "ethics of responsibility" is not at all negligible. It was calculated to put a damper on the revolutionary ardor of opinionated political intellectuals, especially after 1918; to bring it home that ideals justify neither the means nor the results of action, that action involves in guilt, and that the responsibility for political effects rests squarely on the man who makes himself a cause. Moreover, by the diagnosis as "demonic" it revealed that unquestionable "values" cannot be traced to rational sources of order and that the politics of the age had indeed become a field of demonic disorder. The accomplished smoothness by which this aspect of Weber's work was, and is, ignored by those whom it might concern is perhaps the best proof of its importance.

If Weber had done nothing but revealed that a "value-free" political science is not a science of order and that "values" are demonic decisions, the grandeur of his work (that is more sensed than understood) might be open to doubt. The ascent toward essence would have stopped at the point at which the side road branches off which conventionally is marked as "existentialism"—an escape for the bewildered that in recent years has become internationally fashionable through the work of Sartre. Weber, however, went much further—though the interpreter finds himself in the difficult position of extracting the achievement from the intellectual conflicts and contradictions in which Weber involved himself. The approach to the problem of a value-free science that was just described compels more than one question. Weber's conception of science, for instance, assumed a social relation between scientist and politician, activated in the institution of a university, where the scientist as teacher will inform his students, the prospective *homines politici*, about the structure of political reality. The question may be asked: What purpose should such information have? The science of Weber supposedly left the political values of the students untouched, since the values were beyond science. The political principles of the students could not be formed by a science that did not extend to principles of order. Could it perhaps have the indirect effect of inviting the students to revise their values when they realized what unsuspected, and perhaps undesired, consequences their political ideas would have in practice? But in that case the values of the students would not be quite so demonically fixed. An appeal to judgment would be possible, and what could a judgment that resulted in reasoned preference of value over value be but a value-judgment? Were reasoned value-judgments possible after all? The teaching of a value-free science of politics in a university would be a senseless enterprise unless it were calculated to influence the values of the students by putting at their disposition an objective knowledge of political reality. In so far as Weber was a great teacher, he gave the lie to his idea of values as demonic decisions.

To what extent his method of teaching could be effective is another matter. In the first place, it was a teaching by indirection because he shunned an explicit statement of positive principles of order; and, in the second place, the teaching even through direct elaboration of principles could not be effective if the student was indeed demonically fixed in his attitudes. Weber, as an educator, could rely only on shame (the Aristotelian *aidos*) in the student as the sentiment that would induce rational consideration. But what if the student was beyond shame? If the appeal to his sense of responsibility would only make him uncomfortable without producing a change of attitude? Or if it would not even make him uncomfortable but rather fall back on what Weber called an "ethics of intention" (*Gesinnungsethik*), that is, on the thesis that his creed contained its own justification, that the consequences did not matter if the intention of action was right? This question, again, was not clarified by Weber. As the model case for his "ethics of intention" he used a not-too-well-defined Christian "other-worldly" morality; he never touched the problem whether the demonic values were not perhaps demonic precisely because they partook of his "ethics of intention" rather than of his "ethics of responsibility," because they had arrogated the quality of a divine command to a human velleity. A discussion of such questions would have been possible only on the level of a philosophical anthropology from which Weber shied away. Nevertheless, while he shied away from a discussion, he had made his decision for entering into rational conflict with values through the mere fact of his enterprise.

The rational conflict with the unquestionable values of political intellectuals was inherent in his enterprise of an objective science of politics. The original conception of a value-free science was dissolving. To the methodologists preceding Max Weber, a historical or social science could be value-free because its object was constituted by "reference to a value" (*wertbeziehende Methode*); within the field thus constituted the scientist was then supposed to work without value-judgments. Weber recognized that there was a plurality of conflicting "values" current in the politics of his time; each of them might be used to constitute an "object." The result would be the aforementioned relativism, and political science would be degraded to an apology for the dubious fancies of political intellectuals, as at the time it was and as to a very considerable extent it still is. How did he escape such degradation?—for escape he certainly did. If none of the conflicting values constituted for him the field of science, if he preserved his critical integrity against the current political values, what then were the values that constituted his science? An exhaustive answer to these questions lies beyond the present purpose. Only the principle of his technique will be illustrated. The "objectivity" of Weber's science, such as there was, could be derived only from the authentic principles of order as they had been discovered and elaborated in the history of mankind. Since in the intellectual situation of Weber the existence of a science of order could not be admitted, its content (or as much of it as was possible) had to be introduced by recognizing its historical expressions as facts and causal factors in history. While Weber as a methodologist of value-free science would profess to have no argument against a political intellectual who had "demonically" settled on Marxism as the "value" of his preference, he could blandly engage in a study of Protestant ethics and show that certain religious convictions rather than the class struggle played an important role in the formation of capitalism. In the preceding pages it has been repeatedly stressed that the arbitrariness of method did not degenerate into complete irrelevance of scientific production, because the pressure of theoretical traditions remained a determining factor in the selection of materials and problems. This pressure, one might say, was erected by Weber into a principle. The three volumes, for instance, of his sociology of religion threw a massive bulk of more or less clearly seen verities about human and social order into the debate about the structure of reality. By pointing to the undisputable fact that verities about order were factors in the order of reality—and not perhaps only lust for power and wealth or fear and fraud—a tentative objectivity of science could be regained, even though the principles had to be introduced by the back door of "beliefs" in competition, and in rationally insoluble conflict, with Weber's contemporary "values."

Again, Weber ignored the theoretical difficulties into which this procedure involved him. If the "objective" study of historical processes showed that, for instance, the materialistic interpretation of history was wrong, then obviously there existed a standard of objectivity in science that precluded the constitution of the object of science by "referring" facts and problems to the "value" of a Marxist; or—without methodological jargon—a scholar could not be a Marxist. But if critical objectivity made it impossible for a scholar to be a Marxist, could then any man be a Marxist without surrendering the standards of critical objectivity that he would be obliged to observe as a responsible human being? There are no answers to such questions in Weber's work. The time had not yet come to state flatly that "historical materialism" is not a theory but a falsification of history or that a "materialistic" interpreter of politics is an ignoramus who had better bone up on elementary facts. As a second component in the "demonism" of values there begins to emerge, not acknowledged as such by Weber, a goodly portion of ignorance. And the political intellectual who "demonically" decides himself for his "value" begins to look suspiciously like a megalomaniac ignoramus. It would seem that "demonism" is a quality that a man possesses in inverse proportion to the radius of his relevant knowledge.

The whole complex of ideas—of "values," "reference to values," "value-judgments," and "value-free science"—seemed on the point of disintegration. An "objectivity" of science had been regained that plainly did not fit into the pattern of the methodological debate. And, yet, even the studies on sociology of religion could not induce Weber to take the decisive step toward a science of order. The ultimate reason for his hesitation, if not fear, is perhaps impenetrable; but the technical point at which he stopped can be clearly discerned. His studies on sociology of religion have always aroused admiration as a tour de force, if not for other reasons. The amount of materials he mastered in these voluminous studies on Protestantism, Confucianism, Taoism, Hinduism, Buddhism,

Jainism, Israel, and Judaism, to be completed by a study on Islam, is indeed awe-inspiring. In the face of such impressive performance it has perhaps not been sufficiently observed that the series of these studies receives its general tone through a significant omission, that is, of pre-Reformation Christianity. The reason of the omission seems to be obvious. One can hardly engage in a serious study of medieval Christianity without discovering among its "values" the belief in a rational science of human and social order and especially of natural law. Moreover, this science was not simply a belief, but it was actually elaborated as a work of reason. Here Weber would have run into the fact of a science of order, just as he would if he had seriously occupied himself with Greek philosophy. Weber's readiness to introduce verities about order as historical facts stopped short of Greek and medieval metaphysics. In order to degrade the politics of Plato, Aristotle, or Saint Thomas to the rank of "values" among others, a conscientious scholar would first have to show that their claim to be science was unfounded. And that attempt is self-defeating. By the time the would-be critic has penetrated the meaning of metaphysics with sufficient thoroughness to make his criticism weighty, he will have become a metaphysician himself. The attack on metaphysics can be undertaken with a good conscience only from the safe distance of imperfect knowledge. The horizon of Weber's social science was immense; all the more does his caution in coming too close to its decisive center reveal his positivistic limitations.

Hence, the result of Weber's work was ambiguous. He had reduced the principle of a value-free science *ad absurdum.* The idea of a value-free science whose object would be constituted by "reference to a value" could be realized only under the condition that a scientist was willing to decide on a "value" for reference. If the scientist refused to decide on a "value," if he treated all "values" as equal (as Max Weber did), if, moreover, he treated them as social facts among others—then there were no "values" left that could constitute the object of science, because they had become part of the object itself. This abolition of the "values" as the constituents of science led to a theoretically impossible situation because the object of science has a "constitution" after all, that is, the essence toward which we are moving in our search for truth. Since the positivistic hangover, however, did not permit the admission of a science of essence, of a true *episteme,* the principles of order had to be introduced as historical facts. When Weber built the great edifice of his "sociology" (i.e., the positivistic escape from the science of order), he did not seriously consider "all values" as equal. He did not indulge in a worthless trash collection but displayed quite sensible preferences for phenomena that were "important" in the history of mankind; he could distinguish quite well between major civilizations and less important side developments and equally well between "world religions" and unimportant religious phenomena. In the absence of a reasoned principle of theoretization he let himself be guided not by "values" but by the *auctoritas majorum* and his own sensitiveness for excellence.

Thus far the work of Weber can be characterized as a successful attempt to disengage political science from the irrelevances of methodology and to restore it to theoretical order. The new theory toward which he was moving, however, could not become explicit because he religiously observed the positivistic taboo on metaphysics. Instead, something else became explicit; for Weber wanted to be explicit on his principles, as a theorist should be. Throughout his work he struggled with an explication of his theory under the title of construction of "types." The various phases through which this struggle passed cannot be considered on this occasion. In the last phase he used types of "rational action" as the standard types and constructed the other types as deviations from rationality. The procedure suggested itself because Weber understood history as an evolution toward rationality and his own age as the hitherto highest point of "rational self-determination" of man. In various degrees of completeness he carried this idea out for economic, political, and religious history, most completely for the history of music. The general conception obviously derived from Comte's philosophy of history; and Weber's own interpretation of history might justly be understood as the last of the great positivistic systems. In Weber's execution of the plan, however, there can be sensed a new tone. The evolution of mankind toward the rationality of positive science was for Comte a distinctly progressive development; for Weber it was a process of disenchantment (*Entzauberung*) and de-divinization (*Entgöttlichung*) of the world. By the overtones of his regret that divine enchantment had seeped out of the world, by his resignation to rationalism as a fate to be borne but not desired, by the occasional complaint that his soul was not attuned to the divine (*religiös unmusikalisch*), he rather betrayed his brotherhood in the sufferings of Nietzsche—though, in spite of his confession, his soul was sufficiently attuned to the divine not to follow Nietzsche into his tragic revolt. He knew what he wanted but somehow could not break through to it. He saw the promised land but was not permitted to enter it.

4

In the work of Max Weber positivism had come to its end, and the lines on which the restoration of political science would have to move became visible. The correlation between a constituent "value" and a constituted "value-free" science had broken down; the "value-judgments" were back in science in the form of the "legitimating beliefs" that created units of social order. The last stronghold was Weber's conviction that history moved toward a type of rationalism that relegated religion and metaphysics into the realm of the "irrational." And that was not much of a stronghold as soon as it was understood that nobody was obliged to enter it; that one simply could turn around and rediscover the rationality of metaphysics in general and of philosophical anthropology in particular, that is, the areas of science from which Max Weber had kept studiously aloof.

The formula for the remedy is simpler than its application. Science is not the singlehanded achievement of this or that individual scholar; it is a cooperative effort. Effective work is possible only within a tradition of intellectual culture. When science is as thoroughly ruined as it was around 1900, the mere recovery of theoretical craftsmanship is a considerable task, to say nothing of the amounts of materials that must be reworked in order to reconstruct the order of relevance in facts and problems. Moreover, the personal difficulties must not be overlooked; the exposition of apparently wild, new ideas will inevitably meet with resistance in the environment. An example will help to understand the nature of these various difficulties.

Weber, as has just been set forth, still conceived history as an increase of rationalism in the positivistic sense. From the position of a science of order, however, the exclusion of the *scientia prima* from the realm of reason is not an increase but a decrease of rationalism. What Weber, in the wake of Comte, understood as modern rationalism would have to be reinterpreted as modern irrationalism. This inversion of the socially accepted meaning of terms would arouse a certain hostility. But a reinterpretation could not stop at this point. The rejection of sciences that were already developed and the return to a lower level of rationality obviously must have experientially deep-seated motivations. A closer inquiry would reveal certain religious experiences at the bottom of the unwillingness to recognize the *ratio* of ontology and philosophical anthropology; and, as a matter of fact, in the 1890s began the exploration of socialism as a religious movement, an exploration that later developed into the extensive study of totalitarian movements as a new "myth" or religion. The inquiry would, furthermore, lead to the general problem of a connection between types of rationality and types of religious experience. Some religious experiences would have to be classified as higher, others as lower, by the objective criterion of the degree of rationality that they admit in the interpretation of reality. The religious experiences of the Greek mystic philosophers and of Christianity would rank high because they allow the unfolding of metaphysics; the religious experiences of Comte and Marx would rank low because they prohibit the asking of metaphysical questions. Such considerations would radically upset the positivistic conception of an evolution from an early religious or theological phase of mankind to rationalism and science. Not only would the evolution go from a higher to a lower degree of rationalism, at least for the modern period, but, in addition, this decline of reason would have to be understood as the consequence of religious retrogression. An interpretation of Western history that had grown over centuries would have to be revolutionized; and a revolution of this magnitude would meet the opposition of "progressives" who all of a sudden would find themselves in the position of retrogressive irrationalists.

The possibilities of a reinterpretation of rationalism, as well as of the positivistic conception of history, were put in the subjunctive in order to indicate the hypothetical character of a restoration of political science at the turn of the century. Ideas of the suggested type were afloat; but from the certainty that something was badly wrong in the state of science to a precise understanding of the nature of the evil there was a long way; and equally long was the way from intelligent surmises about the direction in which one had to move to the attainment of the goal. A good number of conditions had to be fulfilled before the propositions in this case could be translated into the indicative mood. The understanding of ontology as well as the craftsmanship of metaphysical speculation had to be regained, and especially philosophical anthropology as a science had to be re-established. By the standards thus regained it was possible to define with precision the technical points of irrationality in the positivistic position. For this purpose the works of the leading positivistic thinkers had to be analyzed with care in order to find their critical rejections of rational argument; one had, for instance, to show the passages in the works of Comte and Marx where these thinkers recognized the validity of metaphysical questions but refused to consider them because such consideration would make their irrational opining impossible. When the study proceeded further to the motivations of irrationalism, positivistic thinking had to be determined as a variant of theologizing, again on the basis of the sources; and the underlying religious experiences had to be diagnosed. This diagnosis could be conducted successfully only if a general theory of religious phenomena was sufficiently elaborated to allow the subsumption of the concrete case under a type. The further generalization concerning the connection of degrees of rationality with religious experiences, and the comparison with Greek and Christian instances, required a renewed study of Greek philosophy that would bring out the connection between the unfolding of Greek metaphysics and the religious experiences of the philosophers who developed it; and a further study of medieval metaphysics had to establish the corresponding connection for the Christian case. It had, moreover, to demonstrate the characteristic differences between Greek and Christian metaphysics that could be attributed to the religious differences. And when all these preparatory studies were made, when critical concepts for treatment of the problems were formed, and the propositions were supported by the sources, the final task had to be faced of searching for a theoretically intelligible order of history into which these variegated phenomena could be organized.

This task of restoration has, indeed, been undertaken; and today it has reached the point where one can say that at least the foundations for a new science of order have been laid. A detailed description of the far-flung enterprise lies beyond the present purpose—and besides it would have to grow into a compendious history of science in the first half of the twentieth century.[1] The following lectures on the problem of representation intend to introduce the reader to this movement as well as to the promise that it holds for a restoration of political science.

---

1. The intellectual history of the first half of the twentieth century is extremely complex because it is the history of a slow recovery (with many trials that have ended in impasses) from the thorough destruction of intellectual culture in the late nineteenth century. A critical study of this process would be perhaps premature as long as the dust of the struggle is still flying; and in fact, no such comprehensive study has hitherto been attempted. There exists, however, a recent introduction to contemporary philosophy that (in spite of certain technical shortcomings) demonstrates how much can be done even today; it is I. M. Bochenski's *Europäische Philosophie der Gegenwart* (Bern, 1947). In his interpretation the author is guided by the two mottoes on the title page of his book: Marcus Aurelius's "The philosopher, this priest and helper of the Gods" and Bergson's "Philosophy, too, has its scribes and pharisees." The various philosophies are ranked according to their value as ontologies, from the lowest to the highest, under the chapter headings of "Matter," "Idea," "Life," "Essence," "Existence," "Being." The last chapter, on the philosophies of being, deals with the English and German metaphysicians (Samuel Alexander, Alfred N. Whitehead, Nicolai Hartmann) and the neo-Thomists. The first chapter deals with the lowest-ranking philosophies, from the bottom up with Bertrand Russell, neo-positivism, and dialectical materialism.

1

Representation and Existence

I

Political science is suffering from a difficulty that originates in its very nature as a science of man in historical existence. For man does not wait for science to have his life explained to him, and when the theorist approaches social reality he finds the field pre-empted by what may be called the self-interpretation of society. Human society is not merely a fact, or an event, in the external world to be studied by an observer like a natural phenomenon. Although it has externality as one of its important components, it is as a whole a little world, a cosmion, illuminated with meaning from within by the human beings who continuously create and bear it as the mode and condition of their self-realization. It is illuminated through an elaborate symbolism, in various degrees of compactness and differentiation—from rite, through myth, to theory—and this symbolism illuminates it with meaning in so far as the symbols make the internal structure of such a cosmion, the relations between its members and groups of members, as well as its existence as a whole, transparent for the mystery of human existence. The self-illumination of society through symbols is an integral part of social reality, and one may even say its essential part, for through such symbolization the members of a society experience it as more than an accident or a convenience; they experience it as of their human essence. And, inversely, the symbols express the experience that man is fully man by virtue of his participation in a whole that transcends his particular existence, by virtue of his participation in the *xynon*, the common, as Heraclitus called it, the first Western thinker who differentiated this concept. As a consequence, every human society has an understanding of itself through a variety of symbols, sometimes highly differentiated language symbols, independent of political science; and such self-understanding precedes historically by millenniums the emergence of political science, of the *episteme politike* in the Aristotelian sense. Hence, when political science begins, it does not begin with a *tabula rasa* on which it can inscribe its concepts; it will inevitably start from the rich body of self-interpretation of a society and proceed by critical clarification of socially pre-existent symbols. When Aristotle wrote his *Ethics* and *Politics,* when he constructed his concepts of the polis, of the constitution, the citizen, the various forms of government, of justice, of happiness, etc., he did not invent these terms and endow them with arbitrary meanings; he took rather the symbols that he found in his social environment, surveyed with care the variety of meanings that they had in common parlance, and ordered and clarified these meanings by the criteria of his theory.[1]

These preliminaries by no means exhaust the peculiar situation of political science, but they have gone far enough for the more immediate purpose. They will allow a few theoretical conclusions that, in their turn, can be applied to the topic of representation.

When a theorist reflects on his own theoretical situation, he finds himself faced with two sets of symbols: the language symbols that are produced as an integral part of the social cosmion in the process of its self-illumination and the language symbols of political science. Both are related with each other in so far as the second set is developed out of the first one through the process that provisionally was called critical clarification. In the course of this process some of the symbols that occur in reality will be dropped because they cannot be put to any use in the economy of science, while new symbols will be developed in theory for the critically adequate description of symbols that are part of reality. If the theorist, for instance, describes the Marxian idea of the realm of freedom, to be established by a Communist revolution, as an immanentist hypostasis of a Christian eschatological symbol, the symbol "realm of freedom" is part of reality; it is part of a secular movement of which the Marxist movement is a subdivision, while such terms as "immanentist," "hypostasis," and "eschatology" are concepts of political science. The terms used in the description do not occur in the reality of the Marxist movement, while the symbol "realm of freedom" is useless in critical science. Hence, neither are there two

1. Aristotle *Politics* 1280a7 ff.

sets of terms with different meanings nor is there one set of terms with two distinct sets of meanings; there exist rather two sets of symbols with a large area of overlapping phonemes. Moreover, the symbols in reality are themselves to a considerable extent the result of clarifying processes so that the two sets will also approach each other frequently with regard to their meanings and sometimes even achieve identity. This complicated situation inevitably is a source of confusion; in particular, it is the source of the illusion that the symbols used in political reality are theoretical concepts.

This confusing illusion unfortunately has rather deeply corroded contemporary political science. One does not hesitate, for instance, to speak of a "contract theory of government," or of a "theory of sovereignty," or of a "Marxist theory of history," while in fact it is rather doubtful whether any of these so-called theories can qualify as theory in the critical sense; and voluminous histories of "political theory" bring an exposition of symbols that, for the larger part, have very little theoretical about them. Such confusion even destroys some of the gains that already were made in political science in antiquity. Take, for instance, the so-called contract theory. In this case the fact is ignored that Plato has given a very thorough analysis of the contract symbol. He not only established its nontheoretical character but also explored the type of experience that lies at its root. Moreover, he introduced the technical term *doxa* for the class of symbols of which the "contract theory" is an instance in order to distinguish them from the symbols of theory.[2] Today theorists do not use the term *doxa* for this purpose, nor have they developed an equivalent—the distinction is lost. Instead the term "ideology" has come into vogue and in some respects is related to the Platonic *doxa*. But precisely this term has become a further source of confusion because under the pressure of what Mannheim has called the *allgemeine Ideologieverdacht*, the general suspicion of ideology, its meaning has been extended so far as to cover all types of symbols used in propositions on politics, including the symbols of theory themselves; there are numerous political scientists today who would even call the Platonic-Aristotelian *episteme* an ideology.

A further symptom of such confusion is certain discussion habits. More than once in a discussion of a political topic it has happened that a student—and for that matter not always a student—would

2. Plato *Republic* 358e–367e.

ask me how I defined fascism, or socialism, or some other ism of that order. And more than once I had to surprise the questioner—who apparently as part of a college education had picked up the idea that science was a warehouse of dictionary definitions—by my assurance that I did not feel obliged to indulge in such definitions, because movements of the suggested type, together with their symbolisms, were part of reality, that only concepts could be defined but not reality, and that it was highly doubtful whether the language symbols in question could be critically clarified to such a point that they were of any cognitive use in science.

The ground is now prepared for approaching the topic of representation proper. The foregoing reflections will have made it clear that the task will not be quite simple if the inquiry is conducted in accordance with critical standards of a search for truth. Theoretical concepts and the symbols that are part of reality must be carefully distinguished; in the transition from reality to theory the criteria employed in the process of clarification must be well defined; and the cognitive value of the resulting concepts must be tested by placing them in larger theoretical contexts. The method thus outlined is substantially the Aristotelian procedure.

2

It will be appropriate to begin with the elemental aspects of the topic. In order to determine what is theoretically elemental, it will be well to recall the beginning of this lecture. A political society was characterized as a cosmion illuminated from within; this characterization, however, was qualified by stressing externality as one of its important components. The cosmion has its inner realm of meaning; but this realm exists tangibly in the external world in human beings who have bodies and through their bodies participate in the organic and inorganic externality of the world. A political society can dissolve not only through the disintegration of the beliefs that make it an acting unit in history; it can also be destroyed through the dispersion of its members in such a manner that communication between them becomes physically impossible or, most radically, through their physical extermination; it also can suffer serious damage, partial destruction of tradition, and prolonged paralysis through extermination or suppression of the active members who constitute the political and intellectual ruling minorities of a society. External existence of society in this sense is intended when, for reasons that will appear presently, we speak of the theoretically elemental aspect of our topic.

In political debate, in the press, and in the publicist literature, countries like the United States, the United Kingdom, France, Switzerland, the Low Countries, or the Scandinavian kingdoms are habitually referred to as countries with representative institutions. In such contexts the term occurs as a symbol in political reality. When a man who uses the symbol would be requested to explain what he means by it, he would almost certainly respond by saying that the institutions of a country will qualify as representative when the members of the legislative assembly hold their membership by virtue of popular election. When the questioning is extended to the executive, he will accept the American election of a chief executive by the people, but he will also agree to the English system of a committee of the parliamentary majority as the ministry, or to the Swiss system of having the executive elected by the two houses in common session; and probably he will not find the representative character impaired by a monarch, as long as the monarch can act only with the countersignature of a responsible minister. When he is urged to be a bit more explicit about what he means by popular election, he will primarily consider the election of a representative by all persons of age who are resident in a territorial district; but he will probably not deny the representative character when women are excluded from suffrage or when, under a system of proportional representation, the constituencies are personal instead of territorial. He, finally, may suggest that elections should be reasonably frequent, and he will mention parties as the organizers and mediators of the election procedure.

What can the theorist do with an answer of this type in science? Does it have any cognitive value?

Obviously, the answer is not negligible. To be sure, the existence of the enumerated countries must be taken for granted without too many questions about what makes them exist or what existence means. Nevertheless, light falls on an area of institutions within an existential framework, even though that framework itself remains in the shadow. There exist, indeed, several countries whose institutions can be subsumed under the adumbrated type; and if the exploration of institutions is relevant at all, this answer certainly suggests a formidable body of scientific knowledge. Moreover, this body of knowledge exists as a massive fact of science in the form of numerous monographic studies on the institutions of single countries, describing the ramifications and auxiliary institutions that are necessary for the operation of a modern representative government, as well as in the form of comparative studies that elaborate the type and its variants. There can, furthermore, be no doubt about the theoretical relevance of such studies, at least on principle, because the external existence of a political society is part of its ontological structure. Whatever their relevance may prove to be when they are placed in a larger theoretical context, the types of external realization of a society will have at least some relevance.

In the theoretization of representative institutions on this level, the concepts that enter into the construction of the descriptive type refer to simple data of the external world. They refer to geographical districts, to human beings who are resident in them, to men and women, to their age, to their voting, which consists in placing check marks on pieces of paper by the side of names printed on them, to operations of counting and calculation that will result in the designation of other human beings as representatives, to the behavior of representatives that will result in formal acts recognizable as such through external data, etc. Because the concepts on this level are unproblematic in terms of the internal self-interpretation of a society, this aspect of our topic may be considered elemental; and the descriptive type of representation that can be developed on this level, therefore, shall be called the elemental type.

The relevance of the elemental approach to the topic is established on principle. The actual extent of its cognitive value, however, can be measured only by placing the type into the previously suggested larger theoretical context. The elemental type, as we said, casts light only on an area of institutions within an existential framework, to be taken for granted without questions. Hence, a few questions must now be raised with regard to the area that hitherto remained in shadow.

3

In raising these questions, again the Aristotelian procedure of examining symbols as they occur in reality will be followed. A suitable subject for such questioning is the representative character of the Soviet institutions. The Soviet Union has a constitution, even beautifully written, providing for institutions that, on the whole, can be subsumed under the elemental type. Nevertheless, opinion concerning its representative character is sharply divided between Western democrats and Communists. Westerners will say that the mechanism of representation alone will not do, that the voter must have a genuine choice, and that the party monopoly provided by the Soviet constitution makes a choice impossible. Communists will say that the true representative must have the interest of the people at heart, that the exclusion of parties representing special interests is necessary in order to make the institutions truly representative, and that only countries where the monopoly of representation is secured for the Communist party are genuine people's democracies. The argument, thus, hinges on the mediatory function of the party in the process of representation.

The issue is too unclear for rendering immediate judgment. The situation rather invites a little deeper stirring, and, indeed, one can easily add to the confusion by recalling that at the time of the foundation of the American Republic eminent statesmen were of the opinion that true representation was possible only when there were no parties at all. Other thinkers, furthermore, will attribute the functioning of the English two-party system to the fact that originally the two parties were, indeed, two factions of the English aristocracy; and still others will find in the American two-party system an ulterior homogeneousness that lets the two parties appear as factions of one party. In summarizing the variety of opinion, hence, one can form the series: a representative system is truly representative when there are no parties, when there is one party, when there are two or more parties, when the two parties can be considered factions of one party. In order to complete the picture, there may be, finally, added the type concept of the pluralistic party state that came into vogue after the first World War with its implication that a representative system will not work if there are two or more parties that disagree on points of principle.

From this variety of opinions it will be possible to draw the following conclusions. The elemental type of representative institutions does not exhaust the problem of representation. Through the conflict of opinions there can be discerned the consensus that the procedure of representation is meaningful only when certain requirements concerning its substance are fulfilled and that the establishment of the procedure does not automatically provide the desired substance. There is, furthermore, a consensus that certain mediatory institutions, the parties, have something to do with securing or corrupting this substance. Beyond this point, however, the issue becomes confused. The substance in question is vaguely associated with the will of the people, but what precisely is meant by the symbol "people" does not become clear. This symbol must be stored away for later examination. Moreover, the disagreement on the number of parties that will, or will not, guarantee the flow of the substance suggests an insufficiently analyzed ulterior issue that will not come into grasp by counting parties. Hence, a type concept like the "one-party state" must be considered as theoretically of dubious value; it may have some practical use for brief reference in current political debate, but it is obviously not sufficiently clarified to be of relevance in science. It belongs to the elemental class like the elemental type concept of representative institutions.

These first methodical questions have not led into an impasse, but the gain is inconclusive because too much was netted at a time. The issue must be narrowed down for clarification; and for this purpose further reflection on the tempting subject of the Soviet Union is indicated.

4

While there may be radical disagreement on the question whether the Soviet government represents the people, there can be no doubt whatsoever that the Soviet government represents the Soviet society as a political society in form for action in history. The legislative and administrative acts of the Soviet government are domestically effective in the sense that the governmental commands find obedience with the people, making allowance for the politically irrelevant margin of failure; and the Soviet Union is a power on the historical scene because the Soviet government can effectively operate an enormous military machine fed by the human and material resources of the Soviet society.

At first glance it appears that with such propositions the argument has advanced to theoretically much more fertile ground. For under the title of political societies in form for action, the clearly distinguishable power units in history come into view. Political societies, in order to be in form for action, must have an internal structure that will enable some of its members—the ruler, the government, the prince, the sovereign, the magistrate, etc., according to the varying terminology of the ages—to find habitual obedience for their acts of command; and these acts must serve the existential necessities of a society, such as the defense of the realm and administration of justice—if a medieval classification of purposes will be allowed. Such societies with their internal organization for action, however, do not exist as cosmic fixtures from eternity but grow in history; this process in which human beings form themselves into a society for action shall be called the articulation of a society. As the result of political articulation we find human beings, the rulers, who can act for the society, men whose acts are not imputed to their own persons but to the society as a whole—with the consequence that, for instance, the pronunciation of a general rule regulating an area of human life will not be understood as an exercise in moral philosophy but will be experienced by the members of the society as the declaration of a rule with obligatory force for themselves. When his acts are effectively imputed in this manner, a person is the representative of a society.

If the meaning of representation in this context shall be based on effective imputation, it will be necessary, however, to distinguish representation from other types of imputation; it will be necessary to clarify the difference between an agent and a representative. By an agent, therefore, shall be understood a person who is empowered by his principal to transact a specific business under instructions, while by a representative shall be understood a person who has power to act for a society by virtue of his position in the structure of the community, without specific instructions for a specified business, and whose acts will not be effectively repudiated by the members of the society. A delegate to the United Nations, for instance, is an agent of his government acting under instructions, while the government that has delegated him is the representative of the respective political society.

5

Obviously, the representative ruler of an articulated society cannot represent it as a whole without standing in some sort of relationship to the other members of the society. Here is a source of difficulties for political science in our time because, under pressure of the democratic symbolism, the resistance to distinguishing between the two relations terminologically has become so strong that it has also affected political theory. Ruling power is ruling power even in a democracy, but one is shy of facing the fact. The government represents the people, and the symbol "people" has absorbed the two meanings that, in medieval language, for instance, could be distinguished without emotional resistance as the "realm" and the "subjects."

This pressure of the democratic symbolism, now, is the last phase of a series of terminological complications that commence in the high Middle Ages with the very beginnings of the articulation of Western political societies. The Magna Carta, for instance, refers to Parliament as the *commune consilium regni nostri*, as "the common council of our realm."[3] Let us examine this formula. It designates Parliament as the council of the realm, not perhaps as a representation of the people, while the realm itself is possessively the king's. The formula is characteristic for an epoch where two periods of social articulation meet. In a first phase the king alone is the representative of the realm, and the sense of this monopoly of representation is preserved in the possessive pronoun attached to the symbol "realm." In a second phase, communes within the realm, the shires, boroughs, and cities, begin to articulate themselves to the point where they are capable of representing themselves for action; and the barons themselves cease to be individual feudatories and also form themselves into the *baronagium*, a commune capable of action as it appears in the *forma securitatis* of the Magna Carta. The details of this complicated process need not be traced; the point of theoretical interest is that the representatives of the articulate communes when they meet in council form communes of a higher order, ultimately the Parliament of two houses, which understands itself as the representative council of a still larger society, of the realm as a whole. With advancing articulation of society, thus, develops a peculiar composite representative, along with a symbolism expressing its internal hierarchical structure.

The weight of representation remained with the king in the centuries following the Magna Carta. The writs of summons of the thirteenth and fourteenth centuries reveal a consistent terminology, recognizing the articulation of society but still drawing the new

3. Magna Carta, chap. 12.

participants of representation into the royal representation itself. Not only is the realm the king's, but the prelates, the magnates, and the cities are also his. Individual merchants, on the other hand, are not included in the representative symbolism; they are not the king's but always "of the realm" or "of the city," that is, of the whole or of an articulate subdivision.[4] Ordinary individual members of the society are plainly "inhabitants" or "fellow-citizens of the realm."[5] The symbol "people" does not appear as signifying a rank in articulation and representation; it is only used, on occasion, as a synonym for realm in a phrase like the "common welfare of the realm."[6]

The melting of this representative hierarchy into one single representative, the king in Parliament, took a considerable time; that such a melting process was under way became theoretically tangible only centuries later, in a famous passage in the address of Henry VIII to Parliament in Ferrers' case. On that occasion, in 1543, the king said: "We be informed by our judges that we at no time stand so highly in our estate royal as in the time of Parliament, wherein we as head and you as members are conjoined and knit together into one body politic, so as whatsoever offence or injury (during that time) is offered to the meanest member of the House is to be judged as done against our person and the whole Court of Parliament." The difference of rank between king and Parliament is still preserved, but it can now be symbolized through the relationship of head and members within one body; the composite representative has become "one body politic," the royal estate being enhanced by its participation in parliamentary representation, the Parliament by its participation in the majesty of royal representation.

The direction in which the symbols shift will have become clear from this passage: When articulation expands throughout society, the representative will also expand until the limit is reached where the membership of the society has become politically articulate down to the last individual and, correspondingly, the society becomes the representative of itself. Symbolically this limit is reached with the masterful, dialectical concentration of Lincoln's "government of the people, by the people, for the people." The symbol

4. *Writ of Summons to a 'Colloquium' of Merchants* (1303), in Stubbs, *Select Charters* (8th ed.), 500.
5. *Summons of the Archbishop and Clergy to Parliament* (1295), ibid., 485.
6. *Summons to the Parliament of Lincoln* (1301), ibid., 499.

"people" in this formula means successively the articulated political society, its representative, and the membership that is bound by the acts of the representative. The unsurpassable fusion of democratic symbolism with theoretical content in this formula is the secret of its effectiveness. The historical process in which the limit of articulation is reached that expresses itself in the symbolism of the "people" will occupy us in greater detail in a later part of these lectures. For the present it should be noted that the transition to the dialectical limit presupposes an articulation of society down to the individual as a representable unit. This peculiar type of articulation does not occur everywhere; in fact, it occurs only in Western societies. It is by far not an appurtenance of the nature of man but cannot be separated from certain historical conditions that, again, are given only in the Occident. In the Orient, where the specific conditions are historically not present, this type of articulation does not occur at all—and the Orient is the larger part of mankind.

6

Articulation, thus, is the condition of representation. In order to come into existence, a society must articulate itself by producing a representative that will act for it. The clarification of these concepts can now be continued. Behind the symbol "articulation" there hides nothing less than the historical process in which political societies, the nations, the empires, rise and fall, as well as the evolutions and revolutions between the two terminal points. This process is historically not so individualized for each instance of a political society that it would be impossible to bring the manifold of varieties under a few general types. But this is a vast topic (Toynbee has already filled six volumes with its exposition), and it must be set aside. The present concern will rather be whether the implications of the concept of articulation can be differentiated still further. This can, indeed, be done, and there exist several interesting attempts at further theoretization. In the nature of the case such attempts will be made when the articulation of a society has arrived at a critical juncture; the problem will attract attention when a society is about to come into existence, when it is about to disintegrate, or when it is in an epochal phase of its career. Such an epochal phase in the growth of Western societies occurred about the middle of the fifteenth century with the consolidation of the Western national realms after the Hundred Years' War. At this critical epoch one of the finest English political thinkers, Sir John Fortescue, tried to theorize the problem of articulation. It will be worth while to examine what he had to say.

The political reality that interested Fortescue primarily was the kingdoms of England and France. His beloved England was a *dominium politicum et regale*, what today would be called a constitutional government; the bad France of Louis XI was a *dominium tantum regale*, something like a tyranny—good only for exile when the constitutional paradise became too inhospitable.[7] It was the merit, now, of Fortescue not to have stopped at a static description of the two types of government. To be sure, he used the static analogy of the organism when he insisted that a realm must have a ruler like a body a head, but then, in a brilliant page of his *De laudibus legum Anglie,* he made the analogy dynamic by comparing the creation of a realm with the growth of the articulate body out of the embryo.[8] A politically inarticulate social state breaks out into the articulation of the realm, *ex populo erumpit regnum.* Fortescue coined the term "eruption" as a technical term for designating the initial articulation of a society, and he coined the further term "proruption" for designating advances of articulation, such as the transition from a merely royal to a political realm. This theory of the eruption of a people is not a theory of a state of nature from which a people through contract will emerge into order under law. Fortescue was keenly aware of the difference. In order to make his point clear, he criticized Saint Augustine's definition of the people as a multitude associated through consent to a right order and a communion of interests. Such a people, Fortescue insisted, would be *acephalus*, headless, the trunk of a body without a head; a realm will be achieved only when a head is erected, *rex erectus est,* that will rule the body.

To have created the concepts of eruption and proruption is no mean theoretical achievement in itself, because it allows us to distinguish the component in representation that is almost forgotten wherever the legal symbolism of the following centuries came to

7. Fortescue, *The Governance of England,* ed. Plummer (Oxford, 1885), chaps. 1, 2.

8. Fortescue, *De laudibus legum Anglie,* ed. S. B. Chrimes (Cambridge, 1942), chap. 13.

predominate in the interpretation of political reality. But Fortescue went even further. He understood that the organic analogy could be a scaffold for building his concept of eruption but that otherwise it was of little cognitive use. There was something about an articulated realm, an inner substance that provided the binding force of society, and this something could not be grasped by organic analogy. In order to come closer to this mysterious substance, he transferred the Christian symbol of the *corpus mysticum* to the realm. This was a momentous step in his analysis, of interest in more than one respect. In the first place, the fact that it could be taken at all was symptomatic of the decline of the Christian society, articulated into church and empire; and it was symptomatic, correspondingly, of the increasing consolidation of the national realms, of their closure as self-centered societies. The step indicated, second, that the realms had acquired a peculiar ultimacy of meaning. In the transfer of the *corpus mysticum* to the realm we can sense the evolution toward a type of political society that will succeed not only to the empire but also to the church. To be sure, these implications were not envisaged by Fortescue even vaguely; but the transfer, nevertheless, pointed toward a representative who will represent the society with regard to the whole range of human existence, including its spiritual dimension. Fortescue himself, on the contrary, was rather aware that the realm could even be called a *corpus mysticum* only analogically. The *tertium comparationis* would be the sacramental bond of the community, but the sacramental bond would be neither the Logos of Christ that lives in the members of the Christian *corpus mysticum* nor a perverted Logos as it lives in modern totalitarian communities. Nevertheless, while he was not clear about the implications of his search for an immanent Logos of society, he found a name for it; he called it the *intencio populi*. This *intencio populi* is the center of the mystical body of the realm; again in an organic analogy he described it as the heart from which is transmitted into the head and members of the body as its nourishing bloodstream the political provision for the well-being of the people. Please note the function of the organic analogy in this context: It does not serve as the identification of some member of a society with a corresponding organ of the body, but, on the contrary, it strives to show that the animating center of a social body is not to be found in any of its human members. The *intencio populi* is located neither in the royal representative nor in the people as a multitude of subjects but is the intangible living center of the realm as a whole. The word "people" in this formula does not signify an external multitude of human beings but the mystical substance erupting in articulation; and the word "intention" signifies the urge or drive of this substance to erupt and to maintain itself in articulate existence as an entity that, by means of its articulation, can provide for its well-being.

When Fortescue applied his conception concretely, in *The Governance of England,* he clarified his idea of the royal representative a bit further by contrasting it with the feudal, hierarchical conception of the royal estate. In the feudal conception the king was "the highest temporal estate on the earth," lower in rank than the ecclesiastical estate, but higher than the feudatories within the realm.[9] Fortescue accepted the order of estates in the *Christianitas;* he was far from conceiving the idea of a sovereign closed state; but he intruded the new *corpus mysticum* into the mystical body of Christ by attributing a double function to the royal representative. In the order of the *Christianitas* the king remained the highest temporal estate; but at the same time, the estate royal was to be understood as an office that ministers defense and justice to the realm. Fortescue quotes Saint Thomas: "The king is given for the realm, and not the realm for the king"; and then he goes on to conclude: The king is in his realm what the pope is in the church, a *servus servorum Dei;* and, as a consequence, "all that the king does ought to be referred to his kingdom"—the most concentrated formulation of the problem of representation.[10]

7

The elaboration of this symbolism was Fortescue's personal achievement as a theorist. The realms of England and France impressed the age convincingly with their existence as power units once the Hundred Years' War had disentangled the feudal power field and resulted in the territorial fixation of the realms. Fortescue tried to clarify what these curious new entities, the realms, really were; and his theory was the original solution of a problem that presented itself in reality. In his solution he was aided, however, by a tradition of political articulation that had survived into his age from the period of the Great Migration, preceding the foundation

9. Fortescue, *The Governance of England,* chap. 8.
10. Ibid.

of the Western Empire. In a not sufficiently observed section of the *Governance of England* he used as his model of political articulation one of the many versions of the foundation of the migration kingdoms by a group of Trojan refugees. The myth of the foundation of Western kingdoms by a band of Trojans under the leadership of a son or grandson of Aeneas was fairly widespread; and, in the early Western centuries, it served the purpose of arrogating to the new establishments a dignity of foundation, of the same rank as the Roman. In Fortescue's model it was such a band under Brutus, the eponymos of the Britains, that stood at the beginning of the world for England. When such a "great commonalty," he writes, "as was the fellowship that came into this land with Brute [was] willing to unite and made a body politic called a realm, having a head to govern it . . . they chose the same Brute to be their head and king. And they and he upon this incorporation, institution, and uniting of themselves into a realm, ordained the same realm to be ruled and justified by such laws as they all would assent to."[11]

The Trojan component of the myth, the rivalry with Rome, is only of secondary interest for the present purpose; but under the guise of the myth there is recorded the actual articulation of migration bands into political societies. The myth points toward the initial phase of articulation itself, and it suggests a brief glance at the original accounts of such foundations as well as at the terminology in which the articulation is described. I shall select for this purpose a few passages from the *History of the Lombards* of Paulus Diaconus, written in the second half of the eighth century.

In the account of Paul the active history of the Lombards begins when, after the death of two dukes, the people decided that they no longer wanted to live in small federated groups under dukes and "set themselves a king like the other nations."[12] The language is influenced by the Israelitic desire, in the Book of Samuel, for a king like the other nations, but the actual process of the articulation of tribes into a realm is recorded quite clearly. When in the course of the migration the loose tribal federation proved too weak, a king was elected for the purpose of a more effective military and administrative conduct of affairs; and this king was selected from a family "which was considered among them particularly noble."

11. Ibid., chap. 3; also Fortescue, *De laudibus*, chap. 13.
12. *Pauli Historia Langobardorum* (Hanover, 1878), 1:14.

The account reaches down to the historically concrete, initial articulation. In this situation there was present what may be called a social raw material, consisting of groupings on the tribal level, homogeneous enough to articulate themselves into a larger society. There can be discerned, furthermore, a pressure of circumstances, providing the stimulus for articulation; and, finally, there were members of the group sufficiently distinguished by blood charisma and personal charisma to have become successful representatives.

But let us now follow the historian of the Lombards a bit further. Subsequent to the election of a king the victorious wars began. First the Herules were defeated and their power broken to the degree that "they no longer had a king."[13] Then followed the war with the Gepids, the decisive event being the death of the son of the Gepid king "who had been mainly instrumental in bringing the war about."[14] After the death of the young prince the Gepids fled, and, again, they "finally sank so deep that they no longer had a king." Similar passages could be accumulated from other historians of the migration period. Let us give just one good example: Isidorus tells how the Alans and Suebes lost the independence of their kingdom through the Goths but, oddly enough, preserved their kingship in Spain for a long time, "though they had no need for it in their undisturbed quiet." Throughout the historiography of the migration, from the fifth to the eighth centuries, the historical existence of a political society was consistently expressed in terms of acquisition, possession, or loss of the *rex*, of the royal representative. To be articulate for action meant to have a king; to lose the king meant to lose fitness for action; when the group did not act, it did not need a king.[15]

8

The theoretizations just examined belonged to the period of foundation and to the late medieval consolidation of the Western political societies. The problem of representative articulation became of absorbing interest again when a society moved into the danger zone of disintegration. The malaise of the Third Republic was the climate

13. Ibid., 20.
14. Ibid., 23.
15. For a survey of the problem, see Alfred Dove, *Der Wiedereintritt des nationalen Prinzips in die Wetgeschichte* (1890), in *Ausgewählte Schriften* (1898).

in which Maurice Hauriou developed his theory of representation. I shall give a brief summary of the theory as it was developed by Hauriou in his *Précis de droit constitutionnel.*[16]

The power of a government is legitimate, according to Hauriou, by virtue of its functioning as the representative of an institution, specifically of the state. The state is a national community in which the ruling power conducts the business of the *res publica.* The first task of a ruling power is the creation of a politically unified nation by transforming the pre-existent, unorganized manifold into a body organized for action. The nucleus of such an institution will be the idea, the *idée directrice,* of realizing and expanding it and of increasing its power; and the specific function of a ruler is the conception of this idea and its realization in history. The institution is successfully perfected when the ruler has become subordinate to the idea and when at the same time the *consentement coutumier* of the members is achieved. To be a representative means to guide, in a ruling position, the work of realizing the idea through institutional embodiment; and the power of a ruler has authority in so far as he is able to make his factual power representative of the idea.

From this conception Hauriou then derives a set of propositions concerning the relations between power and law: (1) The authority of a representative power precedes existentially the regulation of this power by positive law. (2) Power itself is a phenomenon of law by virtue of its basis in the institution; in so far as a power has representative authority, it can make positive law. (3) The origin of law cannot be found in legal regulations but must be sought in the decision that replaces a litigious situation by ordered power.

The theory just summarized as well as the set of propositions were pointed against certain well-known weaknesses of the Third Republic; the lesson of Hauriou's analysis may be concentrated in the thesis: In order to be representative, it is not enough for a government to be representative in the constitutional sense (our elemental type of representative institutions); it must also be representative in the existential sense of realizing the idea of the institution. And the implied warning may be explicated in the thesis: If a government is nothing but representative in the constitutional sense, a representative ruler in the existential sense will sooner or later make an end of it; and quite possibly the new existential ruler will not be too representative in the constitutional sense.

16. Maurice Hauriou, *Précis de droit constitutionnel,* 2d ed. (1929).

9

The analysis of representation on this level has come to its end. The summary of results can be brief.

We dealt successively with representation in the elemental and the existential sense. The transition from the one type to the other was necessary because the mere description of external realization of a political society did not touch the fundamental question of its existence. The inquiry into the conditions of existence, then, led to the problems of articulation as well as to an understanding of the close correspondence between types of articulation and representation. The result of this analysis can be expressed by the definition that a political society comes into existence when it articulates itself and produces a representative. If this definition be accepted, it follows that the elemental type of representative institutions covers the external realization of one special type of articulation and representation. In critical science it will, therefore, be advisable to restrict the use of the term "representation" to its existential sense. Only when its use is restricted in this manner will social articulation come into clear view as the existentially overriding problem; and only then will there be gained a clear understanding of the very special historical conditions under which the conventionally so-called representative institutions can develop. It was hinted already that they occur in the Greco-Roman and Western civilizations only; and the condition of their development was formulated in a preliminary fashion as the articulation of the individual as a representable unit. Incidental to the analysis, then, emerged a number of problems that could not be pursued further at the moment—such as the symbol of the "people," Fortescue's *intencio populi* with its immanentist implications, and the relation of such a closed realm to the spiritual representation of man in the church. These loose ends will be gathered up in the later course of these lectures.

The adequate differentiation of concepts, however, proved to be not merely a matter of theoretical concern. The insufficient distinction between elemental and existential problems could be observed as a fact in political reality. As an occurrence in reality this confusion raises a problem of its own. The persistent arrogation of the symbol "representation" for a special type of articulation is a symptom of political and civilizational provincialism. And provincialisms of this kind, when they obscure the structure of reality, may become dangerous. Hauriou very strongly suggested that representation in the elemental sense is no insurance against existential disintegration and rearticulation of a society. When a representative does not fulfil his existential task, no constitutional legality of his position will save him; when a creative minority, in Toynbee's language, has become a dominant minority, it is in danger of being replaced by a new creative minority. The practical disregard for this problem has been an important contributive factor in our time in the serious internal upheavals of Western political societies as well as in their tremendous international repercussions. Our own foreign policy was a factor in aggravating international disorder through its sincere but naïve endeavor of curing the evils of the world by spreading representative institutions in the elemental sense to areas where the existential conditions for their functioning were not given. Such provincialism, persistent in the face of its consequences, is in itself an interesting problem for the scientist. One cannot explain the odd policies of Western democratic powers leading to continuous warfare, with weaknesses of individual statesmen—though such weaknesses are strongly in evidence. They are rather symptomatic of a massive resistance to face reality, deeply rooted in the sentiments and opinion of the broad masses of our contemporary Western societies. Only because they are symptoms of a mass phenomenon is it justified to speak of a crisis of Western civilization. The causes of this phenomenon will receive careful attention in the course of these lectures; but their critical exploration presupposes a clearer understanding of the relation between theory and reality. We must, therefore, resume the description of the theoretical situation that was left incomplete at the opening of the present lecture.

2

Representation and Truth

I

In a first approach, the analysis used the Aristotelian method of examining language symbols as they occur in political reality, in the hope that the procedure of clarification would lead to critically tenable concepts. Society was a cosmion of meaning, illuminated from within by its own self-interpretation; and since this little world of meaning was precisely the object to be explored by political science, the method of starting from the symbols in reality seemed at least to assure the grip on the object.

To assure the object, however, is no more than a first step in an inquiry, and before venturing further on the way it must be ascertained whether there is a way at all and where it leads. A number of assumptions were made that cannot remain unchallenged. It was taken for granted that one could speak of social reality and of a theorist who explored it; of critical clarification and theoretical contexts; of symbols of theory that did not seem to be symbols in reality; and of concepts that referred to reality while, at the same time, their meaning was derived from reality through the mysterious critical clarification. Obviously a whole series of questions imposes itself. Is it possible that a theorist be a person outside social reality, or is he not rather a part of it? And if he be himself a part of reality, in what sense can this reality be his object? And what does he actually do when he clarifies the symbols that occur in reality? If he does no more than introduce distinctions, remove equivocations, extract a true core from propositions that were too sweeping, make symbols and propositions logically consistent, etc., would then not everybody who participates in the self-interpretation of society be at least a tentative theorist, and would theory in a technical sense be anything but a better reflected self-interpretation? Or does the theorist perhaps possess standards of interpretation of his own by which he measures the self-interpretation of society, and does clarification mean that he develops an interpretation of superior quality on occasion of the symbols in reality? And, if this should be the case, will there not arise a conflict between two interpretations?

The symbols in which a society interprets the meaning of its existence are meant to be true; if the theorist arrives at a different interpretation, he arrives at a different truth concerning the meaning of human existence in society. And then one would have to inquire: What is this truth that is represented by the theorist, this truth that furnishes him with standards by which he can measure the truth represented by society? What is the source of this truth that apparently is developed in critical opposition to society? And if the truth represented by the theorist should be different from the truth represented by society, how can the one be developed out of the other by something that looks as innocuous as a critical clarification?

2

Certainly these questions cannot be answered all at once; but the catalogue should indicate the complexities of the theoretical situation. The analysis will suitably concentrate on the point where the catalogue apparently comes closest to the present topic, that is, in the questions concerning a conflict of truth. A truth represented by the theorist was opposed to another truth represented by society. Is such language empty, or is there really something like a representation of truth to be found in political societies in history? If this should be the case, the problem of representation would not be exhausted by representation in the existential sense. It would then become necessary to distinguish between the representation of society by its articulated representatives and a second relation in which society itself becomes the representative of something beyond itself, of a transcendent reality. Is such a relation to be found concretely in historical societies?

As a matter of fact, this relation is to be found as far back as the recorded history of major political societies beyond the tribal level goes. All the early empires, Near Eastern as well as Far Eastern, understood themselves as representatives of a transcendent order, of the order of the cosmos; and some of them even understood this order as a "truth." Whether one turns to the earliest Chinese sources in the *Shû King* or to the inscriptions of Egypt, Babylonia, Assyria, or Persia, one uniformly finds the order of the empire interpreted as a representation of cosmic order in the medium of human society. The empire is a cosmic analogue, a little world reflecting the order of the great, comprehensive world. Rulership becomes the task of securing the order of society in harmony with cosmic order; the territory of the empire is an analogical representation of the world with its four quarters; the great ceremonies of the empire represent the rhythm of the cosmos; festivals and sacrifices are a cosmic liturgy, a symbolic participation of the cosmion in the cosmos; and the ruler himself represents the society, because on Earth he represents the transcendent power that maintains cosmic order. The term "cosmion," thus, gains a new component of meaning as the representative of the cosmos.

Inevitably such an enterprise of representative order is exposed to resistance from enemies within and without; and the ruler is no more than a human being and may fail through circumstance or mismanagement, with the result of internal revolutions and external defeats. The experience of resistance, of possible or actual defeat now, is the occasion on which the meaning of truth comes into clearer view. In so far as the order of society does not exist automatically but must be founded, preserved, and defended, those who are on the side of order represent the truth, while their enemies represent disorder and falsehood.

This level of self-interpretation of an empire was reached by the Achaemenides. In the Behistun Inscription, celebrating the feats of Darius I, the king was victorious because he was the righteous tool of Ahuramazda; he "was not wicked, nor a liar"; neither he nor his family were servants of Ahriman, of the Lie, but "ruled according to righteousness."[1] With regard to the enemies, on the other hand, the inscription assures us that "lies made them revolt, so that they deceived the people. Then Ahuramazda delivered them into my hand."[2] The expansion of empire and the submission of its enemies become, in this conception, the establishment of a terrestrial realm of peace, through the king who acts as the representative

1. L. W. King and R. C. Thompson, *The Sculptures and Inscriptions of Darius the Great on the Rock of Behistun* (London, 1907), § LXIII, p. 72.
2. Ibid., § LIV, p. 65.

of the divine Lord of Wisdom. Moreover, the conception has its ramifications into the ethos of political conduct. The rebels against Truth, to be sure, are recognizable as such by their resistance to the king, but they also are recognizable as representatives of the Lie by the propaganda lies that they spread in order to deceive the people. On the king, on the other hand, is incumbent the duty of being scrupulously correct in his own pronouncements. The Behistun Inscription contains the touching passage: "By the grace of Ahuramazda there is also much else that has been done by me which is not graven in this inscription; it has not been inscribed lest he who should read this inscription hereafter should then hold that which has been done by me to be too much and should not believe it, but should take it to be lies."[3] No fibs for a representative of the truth; he must even lean over backward.

When faced with such ostentatiously virtuous conduct, one begins to wonder what the other side would have to say if it had a chance to talk back. And one would like to know what sort of amenities would be exchanged when two or more such representatives of truth were to become competitors in establishing the one true order of mankind. In the nature of the case, such clashes are rare; nevertheless, there occurred a fine instance on occasion of the Mongol expansion in the thirteenth century, which threatened the Western Empire with extinction. Both the pope and the king of France sent embassies to the Mongol court in order to feel out the intentions of the dangerous conquerors and generally to form contacts; the notes carried by the ambassadors, as well as their oral presentations, must have contained complaints about the Mongol massacres in eastern Europe, suggestions concerning the immorality of such conduct, especially when the victims were Christians, and even the request that the Mongols should receive baptism and submit to the authority of the pope. The Mongols, however, turned out to be masters of political theology. There is preserved a letter from Kuyuk Khan to Innocent IV, in which the presentations of the ambassadors are carefully answered. Let me quote a passage:

> You have said it would be good if I received baptism;
> You have informed me of it, and you have sent me the request.
> This your request, we do not understand it.

3. Ibid., § LVIII, p. 68.

Another point: You have sent me these words "You have taken all the
   realms of the Magyars and the Christians altogether; I am surprised
   at that. Tell us what has been the fault of these?"
These your words we did not understand them.
(In order to avoid, however, any appearance that we pass over this
   point in silence, we speak in answer to you thus:)
The Order of God, both Genghis Khan and the Kha Khan have sent it
   to make it known,
But the Order of God they did not believe.
Those of whom you speak did even meet in a great council,
They showed themselves arrogant and have killed our envoy-
   ambassadors.
The eternal God has killed and destroyed the men in those realms.
Save by order of God, anybody by his own force, how could he kill,
   how could he take?
And if you say: "I am a Christian; I adore God; I despise the others,"
How shall you know whom God forgives and to whom He grants His
   mercy?
How do you know that you speak such words?

By the virtue of God,
From the rising of the sun to its setting,
All realms have been granted to us.
Without the Order of God
How could anyone do anything?

Now, you ought to say from a sincere heart:
"We shall be your subjects;
We shall give unto you our strength."
You in person, at the head of the kings, all together, without exception,
   come and offer us service and homage;
Then shall we recognize your submission.
And if you do not observe the Order of God,
And disobey our orders,
We shall know you to be our enemies.

That is what we make known to you.
If you disobey,
What shall we know then?
God will know it.[4]

4. The Persian original and a French translation of this letter are to be found
in Paul Pellior, "Les Mongols et la papauté," *Revue de l'Orient Chrétien* 3, 3d
ser. (1923). The passage in parentheses is taken from a Latin version of the same
letter, published in *Chronica Fratris Salimbene*, ed. O. Holder-Egger, *Monumenta
Germanica Historica*, SS, 32:208. The extant Mongol documents are collected and
edited in Eric Voegelin, "The Mongol Orders of Submission to European Powers,
1245–1255," *Byzantion* 15 (1940–1941).

This meeting of truth with truth has a familiar ring. And the ring will become even more familiar when a few corollaries of Mongol legal theory are taken into account. The Order of God on which the imperial construction was based is preserved in the edicts of Kuyuk Khan and Mangu Khan:

> By order of the living God
> Genghis Khan, the sweet and venerable Son of God, says:
> God is high above all, He, Himself, the immortal God,
> And on earth, Genghis Khan is the only Lord.[5]

The empire of the Lord Genghis Khan is *de jure* in existence even if it is not yet realized *de facto*. All human societies are part of the Mongol empire by virtue of the Order of God, even if they are not yet conquered. The actual expansion of the empire, therefore, follows a very strict process of law. Societies whose turn for actual integration into the empire has come must be notified by ambassadors of the Order of God and requested to make their submission. If they refuse, or perhaps kill the ambassadors, then they are rebels, and military sanctions will be taken against them. The Mongol empire, thus, by its own legal order has never conducted a war but only punitive expeditions against rebellious subjects of the empire.[6]

It will have become clear by now that the Behistun Inscription and the Mongol Orders are not oddities of a remote past but instances of a structure in politics that may occur at any time, and especially in our own. The self-understanding of a society as the representative of cosmic order originates in the period of the cosmological empires in the technical sense, but it is not confined to this period. Not only does cosmological representation survive in the imperial symbols of the Western Middle Ages or in continuity into the China of the twentieth century; its principle is also recognizable where the truth to be represented is symbolized in an entirely different manner. In Marxian dialectics, for instance, the truth of cosmic order is replaced by the truth of a historically immanent order. Nevertheless, the Communist movement is a representative of this differently symbolized truth in the same sense in which a Mongol Khan was the representative of the truth contained in the Order of God; and the consciousness of this representation leads to

5. From the Edict of Kuyuk Khan, in Vincent of Beauvais, *Speculum Historiale* (s.l., 1474), book 31, chaps. 51, 52; Voegelin, *The Mongol Orders,* 389.
6. Voegelin, *The Mongol Orders,* 404 ff.

the same political and legal constructions as in the other instances of imperial representation of truth. Its order is in harmony with the truth of history; its aim is the establishment of the realm of freedom and peace; the opponents run counter to the truth of history and will be defeated in the end; nobody can be at war with the Soviet Union legitimately but must be a representative of untruth in history, or, in contemporary language, an aggressor; and the victims are not conquered but liberated from their oppressors and therewith from the untruth of their existence.

3

Political societies as representatives of truth, thus, actually occur in history. But as soon as the fact is recognized new questions impose themselves. Are all political societies monadic entities, expressing the universality of truth by their universal claim of empire? Can the monadism of such representation not be broken by questioning the validity of the truth in each case? Is the clash of empires the only test of truth, with the result that the victorious power is right? Obviously, the mere raising of these questions is in part the answer. In the very act of raising them the spell of monadic representation is broken; with our questioning we have set up ourselves as the representatives of the truth in whose name we are questioning—even though its nature and source should be only dimly discerned. Beyond this point, however, the difficulties begin. The challenge to imperial truth and the establishment of the challenging theoretical truth are a rather complex affair requiring a more detailed examination.

The discovery of the truth that is apt to challenge the truth of the cosmological empires is itself a historical event of major dimensions. It is a process that occupies about five centuries in the history of mankind, that is, roughly the period from 800 to 300 B.C.; it occurs simultaneously in the various civilizations but without apparent mutual influences. In China it is the age of Confucius and Lao-tse as well as of the other philosophical schools; in India, the age of the *Upanishads* and the Buddha; in Persia, of Zoroastrianism; in Israel, of the Prophets; in Hellas, of the philosophers and of tragedy. The period around 500 B.C. when Heraclitus, the Buddha, and Confucius were contemporaries may be recognized as a specifically characteristic phase in this long-drawn-out process. This simultaneous outbreak of the truth of the mystic philosophers and prophets has attracted the attention of historians and philosophers ever since it came into full view with the enlargement of the historical horizon in the eighteenth and nineteenth centuries. Some are inclined to recognize it as the decisive epoch in the history of mankind. Karl Jaspers, in a recent study on *Vom Ursprung und Ziel der Geschichte,* has called it the axis time of human history, the one great epoch that is relevant for all mankind, as distinguished from the epoch of Christ, which supposedly is relevant for Christians only.[7] And in the classic masterpiece of contemporary philosophy of society, in his *Les deux sources de la morale et de la religion,* Henri Bergson has formed the concepts of a closed and an open society for the purpose of characterizing the two social states in the development of mankind that are created by this epoch.[8] No more than such brief hints are possible for the general orientation of the problem; we must turn to the more special form that this outbreak has assumed in the West. Only in the West, owing to specific historical circumstances that were not present in other civilizations, has the outbreak culminated in the establishment of philosophy in the Greek sense and in particular of a theory of politics.

4

You are familiar with Plato's often-quoted phrase that a polis is man written large.[9] This formula, one may say, is the creed of the new epoch. To be sure, it is Plato's first word in the matter and by far not his last. But, however much this principle must be limited by the introduction of other ones, and even though concessions must be made to cosmological interpretation and to the truth that, after all, it contains, this is the dynamic core of the new theory. The wedge of this principle must be permanently driven into the idea that society represents nothing but cosmic truth, today quite as much as in the time of Plato. A political society in existence will have to be an ordered cosmion, but not at the price of man; it should be not only a microcosmos but also a macroanthropos. This principle of Plato will briefly be referred to as the anthropological principle.

7. Karl Jaspers, *Vom Ursprung und Ziel der Geschichte* (Zurich, 1949), 18 ff.
8. Henri Bergson, *Les deux sources de la morale et de la religion* (Paris, 1932), passim, esp. 287 ff.
9. Plato *Republic* 368c–d.

Two aspects of the principle must be distinguished. Under the first aspect it is a general principle for the interpretation of society; under a second aspect it is an instrument of social critique.

As a general principle it means that in its order every society reflects the type of men of whom it is composed. One would have to say, for instance, that cosmological empires consist of a type of men who experience the truth of their existence as a harmony with the cosmos. That in itself is, of course, a heuristic principle of the first importance; whenever the theorist wants to understand a political society, it will be one of his first tasks, if not the very first, to ascertain the human type that expresses itself in the order of this concrete society. Plato used his principle under this first aspect when he described the Athenian society in which he lived as the sophist written large, explaining the peculiarities of Athenian order by referring them to the socially predominant sophistic type;[10] he, furthermore, used it in this sense when he developed his Polis of the Idea as the paradigmatic construction of a social order in which should find expression his philosophical type of man;[11] and he, finally, used it under this first aspect when in *Republic* viii–ix he interpreted the successive changes of political order as the expression of corresponding changes in the socially predominant human types.[12]

Inseparably connected with this first aspect is the use of the principle as an instrument of social critique. That differences of social order come into view as differences of human types at all is due to the discovery of a true order of the human psyche and to the desire of expressing the true order in the social environment of the discoverer. Now, truth is never discovered in empty space; the discovery is a differentiating act in a tightly packed environment of opinion; and if the discovery concerns the truth of human existence, it will shock the environment in its strongest convictions on a broad front. As soon as the discoverer begins to communicate, to invite acceptance, to persuade, he will inevitably run into a resistance that may prove fatal, as in the case of Socrates. Just as in the cosmological empires the enemy is discovered as the representative of the Lie, so is now, through the experience of resistance and conflict, the opponent discovered as the representative of untruth,

10. Ibid., 492b.
11. Ibid., 435e.
12. Ibid., 544d–e.

of falsehood, of the *pseudos*,[13] with regard to the order of the soul. Hence, the several Platonic types do not form a flat catalogue of human varieties but are distinguished as the one type of true humanity and the several types of disorder in the psyche. The true type is the philosopher, while the sophist becomes the prototype of disorder.[14]

The identification of the true type with the philosopher is a point that must be well understood, because today its meaning is obscured by modernistic prejudices. Today, in the retrospect of a history of philosophy, Plato's philosophy has become one among others. In Plato's intention, his theory did not develop *a* philosophy of man; Plato was engaged concretely in the exploration of the human soul, and the true order of the soul turned out to be dependent on philosophy in the strict sense of the love of the divine *sophon*.[15] It is the meaning that was still alive in Saint Augustine when he translated the Greek philosopher into his Latin as the *amator sapientiae*.[16] The truth of the soul would be achieved through its loving orientation toward the *sophon*. The true order of man, thus, is a constitution of the soul, to be defined in terms of certain experiences that have become predominant to the point of forming a character. The true order of the soul in this sense furnishes the standard for measuring and classifying the empirical variety of human types as well as of the social order in which they find their expression.

5

This is the crucial point on which the meaning of theory depends. Theory is not just any opining about human existence in society; it rather is an attempt at formulating the meaning of existence by explicating the content of a definite class of experiences. Its argument is not arbitrary but derives its validity from the aggregate of experiences to which it must permanently refer for empirical control. Aristotle was the first thinker to recognize this condition of theorizing about man. He coined a term for the man whose character is formed by the aggregate of experiences in question, and

13. Ibid., 382a.
14. *Philosophos* and *philodoxos* distinguished, ibid., 480.
15. Plato *Phaedrus* 278d–e; cf. the complex of Heraclitean fragments B 35, B 40, B 50, B 108 [Diels-Kranz, *Fragmente der Vorsokratiker*, 5th ed. (Berlin, 1934–1938)].
16. Augustine *Civitas Dei* viii.1.

he called him the *spoudaios*, the mature man.[17] The *spoudaios* is the man who has maximally actualized the potentialities of human nature, who has formed his character into habitual actualization of the dianoetic and ethical virtues, the man who at the fullest of his development is capable of the *bios theoretikos*. Hence, the science of ethics in the Aristotelian sense is a type study of the *spoudaios*.[18] Moreover, Aristotle was acutely aware of the practical corollaries of such a theory of man. In the first place, theory cannot be developed under all conditions by everybody. The theorist need perhaps not be a paragon of virtue himself, but he must, at least, be capable of imaginative re-enactment of the experiences of which theory is an explication; and this faculty can be developed only under certain conditions such as inclination, an economic basis that will allow the investment of years of work into such studies, and a social environment that does not suppress a man when he engages in them. And, second, theory as an explication of certain experiences is intelligible only to those in whom the explication will stir up parallel experiences as the empirical basis for testing the truth of theory. Unless a theoretical exposition activates the corresponding experiences at least to a degree, it will create the impression of empty talk or will perhaps be rejected as an irrelevant expression of subjective opinions. A theoretical debate can be conducted only among *spoudaioi* in the Aristotelian sense; theory has no argument against a man who feels, or pretends to feel, unable of re-enacting the experience. Historically, as a consequence, the discovery of theoretical truth may not at all find acceptance in the surrounding society. Aristotle had no illusions on this point. To be sure, like Plato, he attempted a paradigmatic construction of a social order that would express the truth of the *spoudaios*, in *Politics* vii–viii; but he also asserted with firm regret that in none of the Hellenic poleis of his time could there be found a hundred men who were able to form the ruling nucleus of such a society; any attempt at realizing it would be utterly futile. A practical impasse seems to be the result.[19]

A study of the experiences is impossible in the present context. In view of the vastness of the subject, even a lengthy sketch would be pitiably inadequate. No more than a brief catalogue can be given

17. Aristotle *Nicomachean Ethics* 1113a, 29–35.
18. Ibid., 1176a, 17 ff.
19. Aristotle *Politics* 1286b, 8–21, and 1302a, 2.

that will appeal to your historical knowledge. To the previously mentioned love of the *sophon* may now be added the variants of the Platonic Eros toward the *kalon* and the *agathon,* as well as the Platonic Dike, the virtue of right superordination and subordination of the forces in the soul, in opposition to the sophistic *polypragmosyne;* and, above all, there must be included the experience of Thanatos, of death as the cathartic experience of the soul which purifies conduct by placing it into the longest of all long-range perspectives, into the perspective of death. Under the aspect of death the life of the philosophical man becomes for Plato the practice of dying; the philosophers' souls are dead souls—in the sense of the *Gorgias*— and when the philosopher speaks as the representative of truth, he does it with the authority of death over the shortsightedness of life. To the three fundamental forces of Thanatos, Eros, and Dike should be added, still within the Platonic range, the experiences in which the inner dimension of the soul is given in height and depth. The dimension in height is scaled through the mystical ascent, over the *via negativa,* toward the border of transcendence—the subject of the *Symposion.* The dimension in depth is probed through the anamnetic descent into the unconscious, into the depth from where are drawn up the "true logoi" of the *Timaeus* and *Critias.*

The discovery and exploration of these experiences started centuries before Plato and continued after him. The Platonic descent into the depth of the soul, for instance, differentiated experiences that were explored by Heraclitus and Aeschylus. And the name of Heraclitus reminds us that the Ephesian had already discovered the triad of love, hope, and faith that reappeared in the experiential triad of Saint Paul. For the *via negativa* Plato could draw on the mysteries as well as on the description of the way toward truth that Parmenides had given in his didactic poem. And there should be mentioned, as close to the Platonic range, the Aristotelian *philia,* the experiential nucleus of true community between mature men; and again the Aristotelian love of the noetic self is hearkening back to the Heraclitean followership of the common Logos of mankind.

6

Brief and incomplete as these hints are, they should be sufficient to evoke the class of experiences that form the basis of theory in the

Platonic-Aristotelian sense. It must now be ascertained why they should become the carriers of a truth about human existence in rivalry with the truth of the older myth, and why the theorist, as the representative of this truth, should be able to pit his authority against the authority of society.

The answer to this question must be sought in the nature of the experience under discussion. The discovery of the new truth is not an advancement of psychological knowledge in the immanentist sense; one would rather have to say that the psyche itself is found as a new center in man at which he experiences himself as open toward transcendental reality. Moreover, this center is not found as if it were an object that had been present all the time and only escaped notice. The psyche as the region in which transcendence is experienced must be differentiated out of a more compact structure of the soul; it must be developed and named. With due regard for the problem of compactness and differentiation, one might almost say that before the discovery of the psyche man had no soul. Hence, it is a discovery that produces its experiential material along with its explication; the openness of the soul is experienced through the opening of the soul itself. This opening, which is as much action as it is passion, we owe to the genius of the mystic philosophers.[20]

These experiences become the source of a new authority. Through the opening of the soul the philosopher finds himself in a new relation with God; he not only discovers his own psyche as the instrument for experiencing transcendence but at the same time discovers the divinity in its radically nonhuman transcendence. Hence, the differentiation of the psyche is inseparable from a new truth about God. The true order of the soul can become the standard for measuring both human types and types of social order because it represents the truth about human existence on the border of transcendence. The meaning of the anthropological principle must, therefore, be qualified by the understanding that what becomes the instrument of social critique is, not an arbitrary idea of man as a world-immanent being, but the idea of a man who has found his true nature through finding his true relation to God. The new measure that is found for the critique of society is, indeed, not man himself

20. On the evolution of the meaning of psyche, see Werner Jaeger, *The Theology of the Early Greek Philosophers* (Oxford, 1947), esp. chap. 5; and Bruno Snell, *Die Entdeckung des Geistes: Studien zur Entstehung des europäischen Denkens bei den Griechen* (Hamburg, 1948).

but man in so far as through the differentiation of his psyche he has become the representative of divine truth.

The anthropological principle, thus, must be supplemented by a second principle for the theoretical interpretation of society. Plato expressed it when he created his formula "God is the Measure," in opposition to the Protagorean "Man is the Measure."[21] In formulating this principle, Plato drew the sum of a long development. His ancestor Solon already had been in search of the truth that could be imposed with authority on the factions of Athens, and with a sigh he admitted, "It is very hard to know the unseen measure of right judgment—and yet it alone contains the right boundaries of all things."[22] As a statesman he lived in the tension between the unseen measure and the necessity of incarnating it in the eunomia of society; on the one hand: "The mind of the immortals is all unseen to men";[23] and on the other hand: "At the behest of the gods have I done what I did."[24] Heraclitus, then, who always looms as the great shadow behind the ideas of Plato, went deeper into the experiences leading toward the invisible measure. He recognized its overruling validity: "The invisible harmony is better (or: greater, more powerful) than the visible."[25] But this invisible harmony is difficult to find, and it will not be found at all unless the soul be animated by an anticipating urge in the right direction: "If you do not hope you will not find the unhoped-for, since it is hard to be found and the way is all but impassable,"[26] and: "Through lack of faith (apistie) the divine(?) escapes being known."[27] And, finally, Plato has absorbed the Xenophantic critique of unseemly symbolization of the gods. As long as men create gods in their image, is the argument of Xenophanes, the true nature of the one God who is "greatest among gods and men, not like mortals in body or thought," must remain hidden;[28] and only when the one God is understood in his formless transcendence as the same God for every man will the nature of every man be understood as the same by virtue of the sameness of his relation to the transcendent

21. Plato Laws 716c.
22. Elegy and Iambus (Loeb Classical Library), vol. 1, Solon 16.
23. Ibid., Solon 17.
24. Ibid., Solon 34, vs. 6.
25. Diels-Kranz, Fragmente der Vorsokratiker, Heraclitus B 54.
26. Ibid., Heraclitus B 18.
27. Ibid., Heraclitus B 86.
28. Ibid., Xenophanes B 23.

divinity. Of all the early Greek thinkers, Xenophanes had perhaps the clearest insight into the constitution of a universal idea of man through the experience of universal transcendence.[29]

The truth of man and the truth of God are inseparably one. Man will be in the truth of his existence when he has opened his psyche to the truth of God; and the truth of God will become manifest in history when it has formed the psyche of man into receptivity for the unseen measure. This is the great subject of the *Republic*; at the center of the dialogue Plato placed the Parable of the Cave, with its description of the *periagoge*, the conversion, the turning-around from the untruth of human existence as it prevailed in the Athenian sophistic society to the truth of the Idea.[30] Moreover, Plato understood that the best way of securing the truth of existence was proper education from early childhood; for that reason, in *Republic* ii, he wanted to remove unseemly symbolizations of the gods, as they were to be found in the poets, from the education of the young and have them replaced by seemly symbols.[31] On this occasion he developed the technical vocabulary for dealing with such problems. In order to speak of the various types of symbolization, he coined the term "theology" and called them types of theology, *typoi peri theologias*.[32] On the same occasion Plato, furthermore, distinguished the gnoseological component of the problem. If the soul is exposed in its youth to the wrong type of theology, it will be warped at its decisive center where it knows about the nature of God; it will fall a prey to the "arch-lie," the *alethos pseudos*, of misconception about the gods.[33] This lie is not an ordinary lie in daily life for which there may be extenuating circumstances; it is the supreme lie of "ignorance, of *agnoia*, within the soul."[34] If now the Platonic terminology be adopted, one may say, therefore, that the anthropological principle in a theoretical interpretation of society requires the theological principle as its correlate. The validity of the standards developed by Plato and Aristotle depends on the conception of a man who can be the measure of society because God is the measure of his soul.

29. Jaeger, *Theology of the Early Greek Philosophers*, chap. 3: "Xenophanes' Doctrine of God."
30. Plato *Republic* 518d–e.
31. Ibid., 378–79.
32. Ibid., 379a.
33. Ibid., 382a.
34. Ibid., 382b.

7

The theorist is the representative of a new truth in rivalry with the truth represented by society. So much is secured. But there seems to be left the difficulty of the impasse that the new truth has little chance of becoming socially effective, of forming a society in its image.

This impasse, in fact, never existed. Its appearance was created through Plato's disappointment with Athens. The polis of his time was indeed no longer capable of a great spiritual reform—but the polis had not always been so sterile as it looks when attention is focused on its resistance to Socrates and Plato. The Platonic-Aristotelian elaboration of the new truth marked the end of a long history; it was the work of Athenian thinkers who hardly could have accomplished their theoretical generalization without the preceding concrete practice of Athenian politics. The paradigmatic constructions of Plato and Aristotle would have appeared as odd fancies to their contemporaries unless the Athens of Marathon and the tragedy had been the living memory of an ephemeral representation of the new truth. Here, for a golden hour in history, the miracle had happened of a political society articulated down to the individual citizen as a representable unit, the miracle of a generation that individually experienced the responsibility of representing the truth of the soul and expressed this experience through the tragedy as a public cult. We must examine one such tragedy in order to understand the new type of representation; and the purpose will be served best by the *Suppliants* of Aeschylus.

The plot of the *Suppliants* turns on a legal problem and its solution through political action. The daughters of Danaus come with their father on their flight from Egypt to Argos because the sons of Aegyptus try to force them into an unwanted marriage. In Argos, the home of their ancestor Io, they hope to find asylum. Pelasgus, the king of Argos, appears, and the case is presented to him by the fugitives. Immediately he sees the dilemma: Either he must deny asylum and let the suppliants be taken by the Egyptians who are near in pursuit, and thereby incur the wrath of Zeus, or he will become involved in a war with the Egyptians that at best will be a costly affair for his polis. He states the alternatives: "Without harm I do not know how to help you; and yet again it is not advisable to slight such supplications." Frankly he describes himself as being in a state of perplexed indecision; his soul is gripped by fear whether "to act, or not to act and take what fortune brings."[35]

The decision is not easy. By the law, the *nomos* of their country, the damsels in distress have no case against the Egyptians who want them in marriage; but the suppliants are quick to remind the king that there is a higher justice, *dike*, that the marriage is offensive to them, and that Zeus is the god of suppliants. On the one side, the king is admonished to take Dike as his ally in deciding the case; on the other side, he must consider the interests of the Argivian polis. If he involves his city in a war, he will be charged with honoring aliens at the expense of his country; if he abandons the suppliants, his children and his house will have to pay measure for measure for this violation of Dike. Gravely he reflects: "There is need of deep and saving counsel, like a diver's, descending to the depths, with keen eye and not too much perturbed."[36] We are reminded of the Heraclitean "deep-knowing," of the conception of the soul whose border cannot be reached because its Logos is too deep.[37] The lines of Aeschylus translate the Heraclitean conception of depth into the action of descent.[38]

At this juncture, however, there enters the problem of constitutional government as a complicating factor. As far as the king himself is concerned, the descent brings the desired judgment in favor of the suppliants; but Pelasgus is a constitutional king, not a tyrant. The people, the *demos*, who will have to bear the burden of the inevitable war must be consulted and their consent reached. The king leaves the suppliants in order to assemble the people and to submit the case to the general body, the *koinon*; he will try to persuade them to agree with the decision that he has reached in his own soul. The speech of the prince is successful; the proper decrees, the *psephismata*, are passed unanimously. The people enter into the argument of the subtly winding speech, following the royal descent into the depth of the soul. The Peitho, the persuasion of the king, forms the souls of his listeners, who are willing to let themselves be formed, and makes the Dike of Zeus prevail against passion, so that the mature decision represents the truth of the God. The chorus

35. Aeschylus *Suppliants* v.380.
36. Ibid., 407–8.
37. Diels-Kranz, *Fragmente der Vorsokratiker*, Heraclitus B 45.
38. On the genesis of a conception of "depth" of the soul, see Snell, *Die Entdeckung des Geistes*, esp. 32 ff.

summarizes the meaning of the event in the line: "It is Zeus who brings the end to pass."[39]

The tragedy was a public cult—and a very expensive one. It presupposed as its audience a people who would follow the performance with a keen sense of *tua res agitur*. They would have to understand the meaning of action, of drama, as action in obedience to Dike, and to consider the escape into the easy way out as nonaction. They would have to understand the Athenian *prostasia* as the organization of a people under a leader—in which the leader tries to represent the Jovian Dike and uses his power of persuasion to create the same state of the soul in the people on occasion of concrete decisions, while the people are willing to follow such persuasive leadership into the representation of truth, through action in battle against a demonically disordered world, symbolized in the *Suppliants* by the Egyptians. The tragedy in its great period is a liturgy that re-enacts the great decision for Dike. Even if the audience is not an assembly of heroes, the spectators must at least be disposed to regard tragic action as paradigmatic; the heroic soul-searching and suffering of consequences must be experienced as holding a valid appeal; the fate of the hero must arouse the shudder of his own fate in the soul of the spectator. The meaning of tragedy as a state cult consists in representative suffering.[40]

8

The miracle of tragic Athens was short-lived; its glory was submerged in the horrors of the Peloponnesian War. With the decline of Athens the problems of tragedy changed. In a late work of Euripides, in the *Troads* of *ca.* 415, the issue is the mass of filth, abuse, vulgarity, and atrocity displayed by the Greeks on occasion of the fall of Troy; the heroic adventure slides into a morass that will suck down the Greeks themselves. Ominous is the opening scene, the conversation between Athena and Poseidon; Athena, who formerly protected the Greeks, will now switch sides because her temple has been insulted and will combine with Poseidon for the destruction of the victors on their homeward trip. The tragedy falls into the year

39. The analysis of the *Suppliants* in Erik Wolf, *Griechisches Rechtsdenken*, vol. 1, *Vorsokratiker und frühe Dichter* (Frankfurt a.M., 1950), 345–56, was too recent to be used in the present lectures.

40. On representative suffering through descent to the depth, see especially Aeschylus *Prometheus* 1026 ff.

after the butchery at Melos that revealed the corruption of Athenian ethos, as we know it from Thucydides' unforgettable Melian dialogue; and it falls into the very year of the Sicilian expedition that was to end disastrously. It was the year in which the doom of Athens was sealed; the gods, indeed, had switched sides.[41]

The representation of truth passed on from the Athens of Marathon to the philosophers. When Aristophanes complained that the tragedy died from philosophy, he had at least an inkling of what actually took place, that is, of the *translatio* of truth from the people of Athens to Socrates. The tragedy died because the citizens of Athens no longer were representable by the suffering heroes. And the *drama*, the action in the Aeschylean sense, found now its hero in the new representative of truth, in its Suffering Servant Socrates—if we may use the symbol of Deutero-Isaiah. The tragedy as a literary genus was followed by the Socratic dialogue. Nor was the new theoretical truth ineffective in the social sense. Athens, to be sure, could be no longer its representative; but Plato and Aristotle themselves created the new type of society that could become the carrier of their truth, that is, the philosophical schools. The schools outlived the political catastrophe of the polis and became formative influences of the first order, not in Hellenistic and Roman society only, but through the ages in Islamic and Western civilizations. Again, the illusion of an impasse is created only by the fascination with the fate of Athens.

9

The result of the inquiry can now be summarized. To the existential meaning of representation must be added the sense in which society is the representative of a transcendent truth. The two meanings refer to aspects of one problem in so far as, first, the existential representative of a society is its active leader in the representation of truth; and in so far as, second, a government by consent of the citizen-body presupposes the articulation of the individual citizens to the point where they can be made active participants in the representation of truth through Peitho, through persuasion. The precise nature of this many-sided problem, furthermore, came historically into the range of reflective consciousness through the

41. On the political implications of the *Troads*, see Alfred Weber, *Das Tragische und die Geschichte* (Hamburg, 1943), 385 ff.

discovery of the psyche as the sensorium of transcendence. The discoverer, the mystic philosopher, became as a consequence the representative of the new truth; and the symbols in which he explicated his experience formed the nucleus of a theory of social order. And, finally, it was possible to penetrate the mystery of critical clarification. Genetically it proved to consist in the discovery of the psyche and of its anthropological and theological truth, while critically it consisted in the measuring of the symbols in reality by the standards of the new truth.

3

The Struggle for Representation
in the Roman Empire

I

The preceding lecture has shown that the problems of representation were not exhausted by internal articulation of a society in historical existence. Society as a whole proved to represent a transcendent truth; and, hence, the concept of representation in the existential sense had to be supplemented by a concept of transcendental representation. And on this new level of the problem, then, arose a further complication through the development of theory as a truth about man in rivalry with the truth represented by society. Even this complication, however, is not the last one. The field of competitive types of truth is historically broadened by the appearance of Christianity. All three of these types enter into the great struggle for the monopoly of existential representation in the Roman Empire. This struggle will form the subject matter of the present lecture; but, before approaching the subject itself, a few terminological and general theoretical points must be clarified. This procedure of bracketing out the general issues will avoid awkward digressions and explanations that otherwise would have to interrupt the political study proper when the questions become acute.

Terminologically, it will be necessary to distinguish between three types of truth. The first of these types is the truth represented by the early empires; it shall be designated as "cosmological truth." The second type of truth appears in the political culture of Athens and specifically in tragedy; it shall be called "anthropological truth"—with the understanding that the term covers the whole range of problems connected with the psyche as the sensorium of transcendence. The third type of truth that appears with Christianity shall be called "soteriological truth."

The terminological differentiation between the second and third types is theoretically necessary because the Platonic-Aristotelian complex of experiences was enlarged by Christianity in a decisive point. This point of difference can be established perhaps best by reflecting for a moment on the Aristotelian conception of *philia politike*, of political friendship.[1] Such friendship is for Aristotle the substance of political society; it consists in *homonoia*, in spiritual agreement between men; and it is possible between men only in so far as these men live in agreement with the nous, that is, the divinest part in themselves. All men participate in the nous, though in varying degrees of intenseness; and, hence, the love of men for their own noetic self will make the nous the common bond between them.[2] Only in so far as men are equal through the love of their noetic self is friendship possible; the social bond between unequals will be weak. On this occasion, now, Aristotle formulated his thesis that friendship was impossible between God and man because of their radical inequality.[3]

The impossibility of *philia* between God and man may be considered typical for the whole range of anthropological truth. The experiences that were explicated into a theory of man by the mystic philosophers had in common the accent on the human side of the orientation of the soul toward divinity. The soul orients itself toward a God who rests in his immovable transcendence; it reaches out toward divine reality, but it does not meet an answering movement from beyond. The Christian bending of God in grace toward the soul does not come within the range of these experiences— though, to be sure, in reading Plato one has the feeling of moving continuously on the verge of a breakthrough into this new dimension. The experience of mutuality in the relation with God, of the *amicitia* in the Thomistic sense, of the grace that imposes a supernatural form on the nature of man, is the specific difference of Christian truth.[4] The revelation of this grace in history, through the incarnation of the Logos in Christ, intelligibly fulfilled the adventitious movement of the spirit in the mystic philosophers. The

---

1. Aristotle *Nicomachean Ethics* 1167b3–4.
2. Ibid., 1166a1 ff., 1167a22 ff., 1177a12–18, 1177b27–1178a8.
3. Ibid., 1158b29–1159a13.
4. Thomas Aquinas *Contra Gentiles* iii.91.

critical authority over the older truth of society that the soul had gained through its opening and its orientation toward the unseen measure was now confirmed through the revelation of the measure itself. In this sense, then, it may be said that the fact of revelation is its content.[5]

In speaking in such terms about the experiences of the mystic philosophers and their fulfillment through Christianity, an assumption concerning history is implied that must be explicated. It is the assumption that the substance of history consists in the experiences in which man gains the understanding of his humanity and together with it the understanding of its limits. Philosophy and Christianity have endowed man with the stature that enables him, with historical effectiveness, to play the role of rational contemplator and pragmatic master of a nature that has lost its demonic terrors. With equal historical effectiveness, however, limits were placed on human grandeur; for Christianity has concentrated demonism into the permanent danger of a fall from the spirit—that is man's only by the grace of God—into the autonomy of his own self, from the *amor Dei* into the *amor sui*. The insight that man in his mere humanity, without the *fides caritate formata*, is demonic nothingness has been brought by Christianity to the ultimate border of clarity that by tradition is called revelation.

This assumption about the substance of history, now, entails consequences for a theory of human existence in society that, under the pressure of a secularized civilization, even philosophers of rank sometimes hesitate to accept without reservation. You have seen, for instance, that Karl Jaspers considered the age of the mystic philosophers the axis time of mankind, in preference to the Christian epoch, disregarding the ultimate clarity concerning the *conditio humana* that was brought by Christianity. And Henri Bergson had hesitations on the same issue—though in his last conversations, published posthumously by Sertillanges, he seemed inclined to accept the consequence of his own philosophy of history.[6] This consequence can be formulated as the principle that a theory of human existence in society must operate within the medium of experiences that have differentiated historically. There is a strict

5. This conception of revelation as well as of its function in a philosophy of history is more fully elaborated in H. Richard Niebuhr, *The Meaning of Revelation* (New York, 1946), esp. 93, 109 ff.
6. A. D. Sertillanges, *Avec Henri Bergson* (Paris, 1941).

correlation between the theory of human existence and the historical differentiation of experiences in which this existence has gained its self-understanding. Neither is the theorist permitted to disregard any part of this experience for one reason or another; nor can he take his position at an Archimedean point outside the substance of history. Theory is bound by history in the sense of the differentiating experiences. Since the maximum of differentiation was achieved through Greek philosophy and Christianity, this means concretely that theory is bound to move within the historical horizon of classic and Christian experiences. To recede from the maximum of differentiation is theoretical retrogression; it will result in the various types of derailment that Plato has characterized as *doxa*.[7] Whenever in modern intellectual history a revolt against the maximum of differentiation was undertaken systematically, the result was the fall into anti-Christian nihilism, into the idea of the superman in one or the other of its variants—be it the progressive superman of Condorcet, the positivistic superman of Comte, the materialistic superman of Marx, or the Dionysiac superman of Nietzsche. This problem of the antitheoretical derailments, however, will be dealt with in greater detail in the second part of these lectures, in the study of modern political mass movements. The principle of correlation between theory and the maximal experiential differentiation that will govern the following analysis should have become sufficiently clear for the present purpose.

2

The analysis will again be conducted in accordance with the Aristotelian procedure. It will start from the self-interpretation of

7. The dependence of a progress of theorizing on the differentiating experiences of transcendence has become a major problem in intellectual history. Theoretical superiority as a factor in the victory of Christianity over paganism in the Roman Empire, for instance, is strongly stressed in Charles N. Cochrane, *Christianity and Classical Culture: A Study of Thought and Action from Augustus to Augustine* (New York, 1944), esp. chaps. 11 and 12. The technical superiority of Christian over Greek metaphysics has, furthermore, received careful treatment in Étienne Gilson, *L'Esprit de la philosophie médiévale*, 2d ed. (Paris, 1948), esp. chaps. 3, 4, and 5. The continuity of development from Greek into Christian theoretical explication of experiences of transcendence, on the other hand, was clarified by Jaeger's *Theology of the Early Greek Philosophers*. In this contemporary debate comes to life again the great problem of the *praeparatio evangelica* that had been understood by Clement of Alexandria when he referred to Hebrew Scripture and Greek philosophy as the two Old Testaments of Christianity (*Stromates* vi). On this question see also Serge Boulgakof, *Le Paraclet* (Paris, 1946), 10 ff.

society—with the understanding, however, that self-interpretation now includes the interpretations by theorists and saints.

The various types of truth, the Platonic *typoi peri theologias*, that entered into competition became the subject of formal classification. The earliest extant classification precedes the Christian Era; it was made by Varro in his *Antiquities*, a work that was completed about 47 B.C. A reclassification was undertaken toward the end of the Roman period by Saint Augustine in his *Civitas Dei*. The two works are related to each other in so far as the Varronic classification is preserved through the account and criticism of Saint Augustine.[8]

According to the Augustinian account, Varro distinguished three kinds (*genera*) of theology—the mythical, the physical, and the civil.[9] The mythical is the theology of the poets, the physical of the philosophers, the civil of the peoples[10] or, in another version, of the *principes civitatis*.[11] The Greek terminology as well as the formulation in detail indicates that Varro had not invented the classification but had taken it from a Greek, probably a Stoic source.

Saint Augustine in his turn adopted the Varronic types with certain modifications. In the first place, he translated the mythical and physical theologies into his Latin as fabulous and natural, thereby giving currency to the term "natural theology," which has remained in use to this day.[12] Second, he treated the fabulous as part of civil theology because of the cult character of dramatic poetry about the gods.[13] As a consequence, the Varronic kinds would be reduced to civil and natural theologies. The reduction is not without interest, because quite probably it is due, through various intermediaries, to the influence of a saying of Antisthenes that "according to *nomos* there are many gods, while according to *physis* there is one." In opposition to *physis*, *nomos* would embrace culture both poetic and political as the work of man—an accentuation of the human origin of pagan gods that must have appealed to Saint Augustine.[14]

---

8. A partial reconstruction of Varro's work on the basis of the Augustinian account is to be found in R. Agahd, *De Varronis rerum divinarum libris*, I, XIV, XV, XVI (Leipzig, 1896).

9. Augustine *Civitas Dei* (ed. Dombart) vi.5.

10. Ibid., 5.

11. Ibid., iv.27.

12. Ibid., vi.5. On Augustine's use of the term "natural theology," see Jaeger, *Theology of the Early Greek Philosophers*, 2 ff.

13. Augustine *Civitas Dei* vi.6.

14. See on this question Jaeger, *Theology of the Early Greek Philosophers*, 3 nn 8–10. The classification of Antisthenes, together with its quotations in Minucius

And since, finally, Christianity and its supernatural truth had to be included in the kinds of theology, the result was again a tripartite division of the types into civil, natural, and supernatural theologies.

3

The classifications arose incidental to the struggle for representation; they were loaded with the tensions of self-consciousness and opposition. The analysis of these tensions may profitably be opened by reflecting on an oddity of the *Civitas Dei*. The book, as far as its political function is concerned, was a *livre de circonstance*. The conquest of Rome by Alaric in A.C. 410 had aroused the pagan population of the empire; the fall of Rome was considered a punishment by the gods for the neglect of their cult. The dangerous wave of resentment seemed to require a comprehensive critique and refutation of pagan theology in general and of the arguments against Christianity in particular. The Augustinian solution of the task was curious, because it assumed the form of a critical attack on Varro's *Antiquities*, a work that had been written almost five hundred years earlier for the purpose of bolstering the waning enthusiasm of the Romans for their civil religion. The enthusiasm had not markedly increased since Varro, and the non-Roman population could hardly be suspected of more zeal than the Romans themselves. At the time of Saint Augustine the vast majority of pagans in the empire were, in fact, adherents of the mysteries of Eleusis, of Isis, of Attis, and of Mithra rather than of the cult divinities of republican Rome; and, nevertheless, he barely mentioned the mysteries while he submitted the civil theology to the detailed criticism of books vi–vii.

The answer to the puzzle cannot be found in a statistics of religious affiliation; it must rather be sought in the issue of public representation of transcendent truth. The loyalists of the Roman civil religion were, indeed, a comparatively small group, but the Roman cult had remained the state cult of the empire well into the second half of the fourth century. Neither Constantine nor his Christian successors had considered it advisable to abandon their function as the *pontifex maximus* of Rome. Serious inroads were made, to be sure, into the freedom of the pagan cults under the sons

---

Felix, Lactantius, and Clement of Alexandria, is to be found in Eduard Zeller, *Die Philosophie der Griechen*, II/1, 5th ed. (Leipzig, 1922), 329 n 1.

of Constantine, but the great blow came only under Theodosius with the famous law of 380 that made orthodox Christianity the obligatory creed for all subjects of the empire, branded all dissidents as foolish and demented, and threatened them with the eternal wrath of God as well as with the punishment of the emperor.[15] Up to this date the enforcement of imperial legislation in religious matters had been rather spotty, as might well be expected in the predominantly pagan environment; and judging by the number of repetitious laws, it cannot have been overly effective even after 380. Anyway, in the city of Rome the laws were simply set aside, and the official cult had remained pagan. Now, however, the attack was seriously concentrated on this sensitive center. In 382 Gratianus, the emperor of the West, abandoned his title of *pontifex maximus*, rejecting thereby the responsibility of the government for the sacrifices of Rome; at the same time, furthermore, the cult endowment was abolished, so that the expensive sacrifices and festivals could no longer be continued; and, most decisively, the image and the Altar of Victoria were removed from the assembly room of the Senate. The gods of Rome were no longer represented even in the capital of the empire.[16]

Most gratifyingly—from the pagan point of view—Gratianus was murdered in 383, the city was threatened by the anti-emperor Maximus, and a poor harvest was causing a famine. The gods obviously showed their anger, and the time seemed propitious to request rescinding of the measures, and in particular restoration of the Altar of Victoria, from the young Valentinian II. The petition of the Pagan party in the Senate was handed to the emperor in 384 by Symmachus; regrettably, though, the harvest of 384 was excellent and thus furnished a cheap argument to Saint Ambrose, who defended the Christian side.[17]

The memorandum of Symmachus was a noble plea for the Roman tradition, based on the ancient principle of *do-ut-des*. Neglect of

15. *Codex Theodosianus* xvi.i.2.

16. On the affair of the Altar of Victoria see Hendrik Berkhof, *Kirche und Kaiser: Eine Untersuchung der Entstehung der byzantinischen und der theokratischen Staatsauffassung im vierten Jahrhundert*, trans. Gottfried W. Locher (Zollikon-Zurich, 1947), 174 ff.; Gaston Boissier, *La Fin du paganisme*, vol. 2, 2d ed. (Paris, 1894).

17. Ambrosius *Epistolae* xvii and xviii. The *Relatio Symmachi urbis praefecti* is appended to Ambrosius' Letter XVII (Migne, Pl. XVI).

the cult will lead to disaster; Victoria especially has benefited the empire and should not be despised;[18] and then, with a touch of tolerance, the author pleads that everybody should be permitted to venerate the one divinity in his own way.[19] Saint Ambrose in his answer could easily dispose, as we have hinted, of the *do-ut-des* principle;[20] and it was not difficult to show that the noble tolerance of Symmachus was less impressive if one considered that in practice it implied compulsion for Christian senators to participate in the sacrifices for Victoria.[21] The decisive argument, however, was contained in the sentence that formulated the principle of representation: "While all men who are subject to Roman rule serve (*militare*) you emperors and princes of the earth, you yourselves serve (*militare*) the omnipotent God and holy faith."[22] It almost sounds like the Mongol Order of God that was discussed in the preceding lecture, but, in fact, it is its inversion. The formulation of Saint Ambrose does not justify the imperial monarchy by pointing to the monarchical rule of God—though this problem also became acute in the Roman Empire, as will be seen a bit later on. It does not speak of any rule at all but of service. The subjects serve the prince on earth as their existential representative, and Saint Ambrose had no illusions about the source of the imperial position: The legions make Victoria, he remarked contemptuously, not Victoria the empire.[23] Political society in historical existence begins to show the hue of temporality as distinguished from spiritual order. Above this temporal sphere of service on the part of the subjects, then, rises the emperor, who serves only God. The appeal of Saint Ambrose does not go to the imperial ruler but to the Christian who happens to be the incumbent of the office. The Christian ruler is admonished not to pretend ignorance and let things drift; if he does not show his zeal in the faith positively as he should, he must at least not give his assent to idolatry and pagan cults.[24] A Christian emperor knows that he should honor only the altar of Christ, and "the voice of our Emperor be the echo of Christ."[25] In barely veiled language the

18. *Relatio Symmachi* 3–4.
19. Ibid., 6 and 10.
20. Ambrosius *Epistolae* xviii.4 ff.
21. Ibid., xvii.9.
22. Ibid., 1.
23. Ibid., xviii.30.
24. Ibid., xvii.2.
25. Ibid., xviii.10.

bishop threatens the emperor with excommunication if he should grant the petition of the Senate.[26] The truth of Christ cannot be represented by the *imperium mundi* but only by the service of God.

These are the beginnings of a theocratic conception of rulership in the strict sense, theocracy not meaning a rule by the priesthood but the recognition by the ruler of the truth of God.[27] The conception unfolded fully in the next generation in the Augustinian image of the *imperator felix* in *Civitas Dei* v. 24–26. The happiness of the emperor cannot be measured by the external successes of his rule; Saint Augustine makes a special point of the successes of pagan and the misfortunes and murderous ends of some Christian rulers; the true happiness of the emperor can be measured only by his conduct as a Christian on the throne. The chapters on the *imperator felix* are the first "Mirror of the Prince"; they stand at the beginning of the medieval literary genus and have immeasurably influenced the idea and practice of Western rulership ever since Charlemagne made them his guidebook.

In the affair of the Altar of Victoria, Saint Ambrose won. In the following years the situation tightened still further. In 391 a law of Theodosius prohibited all pagan ceremonies in the city of Rome;[28] a law of his sons, in 396, removed the last immunities of pagan priests and hierophants;[29] a law of 407 for Italy suppressed all allocations for *epula sacra* and ritual games, ordered the removal of statues from the temples, the destruction of altars, and the return of the temples *ad usum publicum*.[30] When in 410 Rome fell to the Gothic invaders, the cult of Rome was indeed a living issue for the victims of the recent antipagan legislation; and the fall of the city could well be propagandized as the revenge of the gods for the specific insults to the civil religion of Rome.

4

The curiosity has been cleared up only to give way to another one. The Christian protagonists in this struggle were not concerned with the salvation of pagan souls; they were engaged in a political

26. Ibid., xvii.14.
27. On the struggle for theocracy in this sense, see Berkhof, *Kirche und Kaiser*, chap. 7, "Um die Theokratie."
28. *Codex Theodosianus* xvi.x.10.
29. Ibid., x.14.
30. Ibid., 19.

struggle about the public cult of the empire. To be sure, the appeal of Saint Ambrose went to the Christian on the throne; and about the sincerity of his intentions there can be no doubt when we remember his clash with Theodosius in 390, on occasion of the massacre of Thessalonica. Nevertheless, when the Christian is an emperor, his Christian conduct will put the pagans into the same position in which the Christians were under pagan emperors. It is curious that both Saint Ambrose and Saint Augustine, while bitterly engaged in the struggle for existential representation of Christianity, should have been almost completely blind to the nature of the issue. Nothing seemed to be at stake but the truth of Christianity versus the untruth of paganism. This does not mean that they were quite unaware of the existential issue involved; on the contrary, the *Civitas Dei* has its peculiar fascination because Saint Augustine, while obviously not understanding the existential problem of paganism, was rather worried that something eluded him. His attitude toward Varro's civil theology resembled that of an enlightened intellectual toward Christianity—he simply could not understand that an intelligent person would seriously maintain such nonsense. He escaped from his difficulty by assuming that Varro, the Stoic philosopher, could not have believed in the Roman divinities but that, under cover of a respectful account, he wanted to expose them to ridicule.[31] It will be necessary to hear Varro himself, as well as his friend Cicero, in order to find the point that eluded Saint Augustine.

The elusive point was reported by Saint Augustine himself with great care; it obviously disconcerted him. Varro, in his *Antiquities*, had treated first of "human things" and then only of the "divine things" of Rome.[32] First, the city must exist; then it can proceed to institute its cults. "As the painter is prior to the painting, and the architect prior to the building, so are the cities prior to the institutions of the cities."[33] This Varronic conception that the gods were instituted by political society aroused the incomprehending irritation of Saint Augustine. On the contrary, he insisted, "true religion is not instituted by some terrestrial city," but the true God, the inspirator of true religion, "has instituted the celestial

31. Augustine *Civitas Dei* vi.2.
32. Ibid., 3.
33. Ibid., 4.

city."[34] Varro's attitude seemed particularly reprehensible because the things human to which he gave priority were not even universally human but just Roman.[35] Moreover, Saint Augustine suspected him of deception because Varro admitted that he would have put the things divine first if he had intended to treat of the nature of the gods exhaustively;[36] and because he, furthermore, suggested that in matters of religion much is true that the people ought not to know and much false that the people ought not to suspect.[37]

What Saint Augustine could not understand was the compactness of Roman experience, the inseparable community of gods and men in the historically concrete *civitas*, the simultaneousness of human and divine institution of a social order. For him the order of human existence had already separated into the *civitas terrena* of profane history and the *civitas coelestis* of divine institution. Nor was the understanding facilitated by the apparently somewhat primitive formulations of the encyclopedist Varro. The more supple Cicero voiced the same convictions as his friend with more conceptual refinement through the figures of his *De natura deorum*, especially through the *princeps civis* and *pontifex* Cotta. In the debate about the existence of the gods there stand against each other the opinions of the philosopher and of the Roman social leader. Subtly Cicero suggests the different sources of authority when he opposes the *princeps philosophiae* Socrates[38] to the *princeps civis* Cotta;[39] the *auctoritas philosophi* clashes with the *auctoritas majorum*.[40] The dignitary of the Roman cult is not inclined to doubt the immortal gods and their worship whatever anybody may say. In matters of religion he will follow the pontiffs who preceded him in the office and no Greek philosophers. The auspices of Romulus and the rites of Numa laid the foundations of the state that never could have achieved its greatness without the ritual conciliation of the immortals in its favor.[41] He accepts the gods on the authority of the forebears, but he is willing to listen to the opinion of others; and not without irony he invites Balbus to give the reasons, *rationem*, for

34. Ibid.
35. Ibid.
36. Ibid., iv.31, vi.4.
37. Ibid., iv.31.
38. Cicero *De natura deorum* ii.167.
39. Ibid., 168.
40. Ibid., iii.5.
41. Ibid.

his religious beliefs that as a philosopher he ought to have, while he the pontiff is compelled to believe the forebears without reason.[42]

The Varronic and Ciceronian expositions are precious documents for the theorist. The Roman thinkers live firmly in their political myth but at the same time have been made aware of the fact through contact with Greek philosophy; the contact has not affected the solidity of their sentiments but only equipped them with the means of elucidating their position. The conventional treatment of Cicero is apt to overlook that in his work something considerably more interesting is to be found than a variant of Stoicism—something that no Greek source can give us, that is, the archaic experience of social order before its dissolution through the experience of the mystic philosophers. In the Greek sources this archaic stratum never can really be touched, because the earliest literary documents, the poems of Homer and Hesiod, are already magnificently free reorganizations of mythical material—in the case of Hesiod even with the conscious opposition of a truth found by him as an individual to the lie, the *pseudos,* of the older myth. It was perhaps the unsettlement in the wake of the Doric invasion that broke the compactness of Greek social existence so much earlier, a type of shock that never disturbed Rome. Anyway, Rome was an archaic survival in the Hellenistic civilization of the Mediterranean and still more so with its advancing Christianization; one might compare the situation with the role of Japan in a civilizational environment that is dominated by Western ideas.

Romans like Cicero understood the problem quite well. In his *De re publica,* for instance, he deliberately opposed the Roman style of dealing with matters of political order to the Greek style. In the debate about the best political order (*status civitatis*), again a *princeps civis,* Scipio, takes his stand against Socrates. Scipio refuses to discuss the best order in the manner of the Platonic Socrates; he will not build up a "fictitious" order before his audience but will rather give an account of the origins of Rome.[43] The order of Rome is superior to any other—this dogma is heavily put down as the condition of debate.[44] The discussion itself may freely range through all topics of Greek learning, but this learning will have

42. Ibid., 6.
43. Cicero *De re publica* ii.3.
44. Ibid., i.70, ii.2.

meaning only in so far as it can be brought usefully to bear on problems of Roman order. The highest rank, to be sure, is held by the man who can add the "foreign learning" to his ancestral customs; but if a choice must be made between the two ways of life, the *vita civilis* of the statesman is preferable to the *vita quieta* of the sage.[45]

The thinker who can speak of philosophy as a "foreign learning," to be respected but nevertheless to be considered as a spice that will add perfection to superiority, has, one may safely say, understood neither the nature of the spiritual revolution that found its expression in philosophy nor the nature of its universal claim upon man. The peculiar way in which Cicero mixes his respect for Greek philosophy with amused contempt indicates that the truth of theory, while sensed as an enlargement of the intellectual and moral horizon, could have no existential meaning for a Roman. Rome was the Rome of its gods into every detail of daily routine; to participate experientially in the spiritual revolution of philosophy would have implied the recognition that the Rome of the ancestors was finished and that a new order was in the making into which the Romans would have to merge—as the Greeks had to merge, whether they liked it or not, into the imperial constructions of Alexander and the Diadochi and finally of Rome. The Rome of the generation of Cicero and Caesar was simply not so far gone as was the Athens of the fourth century B.C. that engendered Plato and Aristotle. The Roman substance preserved its strength well into the empire, and it really petered out only in the troubles of the third century A.D. Only then had come the time for Rome to merge into the empire of its own making; and only then did the struggle among the various types of alternative truth, among philosophies, oriental cults, and Christianity, enter into the crucial phase where the existential representative, the emperor, had to decide which transcendental truth he would represent now that the myth of Rome had lost its ordering force. For a Cicero such problems did not exist, and when he encountered them in his "foreign learning" he emasculated the inexorable threat: The Stoic idea that every man had two countries, the polis of his birth and the cosmopolis, he transformed deftly into the idea that every man had indeed two

45. Ibid., iii.5–6.

fatherlands, the countryside of his birth, for Cicero his Arpinum, and Rome.[46] The cosmopolis of the philosophers was realized in historical existence; it was the *imperium Romanum.*[47]

5

The strength of its archaic compactness secured for Rome the survival in the struggle for empire. This successful survival, however, raises one of the great questions of history, that is, the question how the institutions of republican Rome—which in themselves were no more fit for the organization of an empire than the institutions of Athens or any other Greek polis—could be adapted in such a manner that an emperor would emerge from them as the existential representative of the Mediterranean *orbis terrarum*. The process of transformation is obscure in many details and will remain so forever because of the scarcity of sources. Nevertheless, the careful analysis and evaluation of the scanty materials by two generations of scholars has resulted in a coherent picture of the process, as it can be found in the penetrating study of the principate by Anton von Premerstein.[48]

The main burden of adaptation to imperial rule was not carried by the republican constitution at all. To be sure, the number of senators could be increased by appointment of provincials in order to make it more representative of the empire, as it had been done already by Caesar; and citizenship could be extended to Italy and successively to other provinces. But a development of representation through elections on a popular basis from the provinces of the empire was impossible in face of the constitutional inflexibility that Rome shared with the other poleis. The adaptation had to rely on social institutions outside the constitution proper; and the main institution, which developed into the imperial office, was that of the *princeps civis* or *princeps civitatis*, of the social and political leader.

In earlier republican history the term "princeps" designated any leading citizen. At the core of the institution was the patronate,

46. Cicero *De legibus* ii.5.
47. A tendency toward this identification is discernible before Cicero, especially in Polybius (see Harry A. Wolfson, *Philo* [Cambridge, Mass., 1947], 2:419 ff.).
48. Anton von Premerstein, *Vom Werden und Wesen des Prinzipats*, ed. Hans Volkmann ("Abhandlungen der Bayerischen Akademie der Wissenschaften, Phil.-hist. Abt., Neue Folge," Heft 15 [Munich, 1937]).

a relationship created through the fact of various favors—political aid, loans, personal gifts, etc.—between a man of social influence and a man of lesser social rank in need of such favors. Through tendering and accepting such favors a sacred bond under the sanction of the gods was created between the two men; the accepting man, the client, became the follower of the patron, and their relationship was governed by *fides*, by loyalty. In the nature of the case, the patron had to be a man of social rank and wealth. The formation of a considerable clientele would be the privilege of members of the patricio-plebeian nobility; and the most important senators of consular rank would at the same time be the most powerful patrons. Such patrons of highest official rank were the *principes civitatis*; and of their number one could be a leader of unquestioned superiority if he belonged to one of the old patrician families and held the position of a *princeps senatus* and perhaps, in addition, that of the *pontifex maximus*. Roman society, thus, was a complicated network of personal followerships—hierarchically organized in so far as the clients of a powerful patron might themselves be patrons of a numerous clientele, and competitively organized in so far as the principes were rivals in the struggle for high offices and for political power in general.[49] The substance of Roman politics in the late republican period was the struggle for power among wealthy leaders of personal parties, based on the patrocinial relationship. Among such leaders, then, agreements were possible, the so-called *amicitiae*; and the breach of agreement led to formal feuds, the *inimicitiae*, preceded by mutual accusations, the *altercatio*, which in the period of the civil wars assumed the form of propaganda pamphlets to the public detailing the infamous conduct of the opponent. Such *inimicitiae* were distinguished from formal wars, from a *bellum justum* of the Roman people against a public enemy. The last war of Octavianus against Antony and Cleopatra, for instance, was juridically conducted with great care as a formal war against Cleopatra and as an *inimicitia* against Antony and his Roman clientele.[50]

The transformation of the original principate into a few giant party organizations was caused by the military expansion of Rome and the ensuing social changes. The wars of the third century,

49. Ibid., 15–16.
50. Ibid., 37.

with their conquests in Greece, Africa, and Spain, had raised an insolvable problem of logistics. The overseas territories could not be conquered and held by armies that were to be renewed by annual levies; it proved impossible to transport the old contingents home every year and to replace them with new ones. The provincial armies of necessity had to become professional, with ten and twenty years of service. The returning veterans were a homeless mass that had to be taken care of by land allotments, by colonization, or by permission to reside within the city of Rome with the attendant privileges. For obtaining such benefits the veterans had to rely on their military commanders who were principes, with the result that whole armies became part of the clientele of a princeps. If anything is significant for the evolution of late republican Rome, it is the fact that the class discipline of the nobility held out for a whole century before the powerful new party leaders turned against the Senate and transformed the political life of Rome into a private contest among themselves. Moreover, with the enormous enlargement of the clienteles, and their increase by armed forces for warfare and street fights, it became necessary to formalize the previously formless relationships through special oaths by which the client was bound in *fides* to his patron. On this point the sources are particularly scanty, but it is possible nevertheless to trace such oaths in increasing numbers and varieties after 100 B.C.[51] And, finally, the structure of the system was determined by the hereditary character of the clientele. The inheritance of the clientele was a factor of considerable importance in the course of the civil wars of the first century B.C. In his early struggle with Antony, for instance, Octavianus had the great asset of Caesar's veteran colonies in Campania, which had become his clientele as Caesar's heir.[52] And the settlement of inherited soldier clienteles even determined the theater of war. The Pompeians, for instance, had to be fought down in Spain because the Magnus had colonized his soldiers in the Iberian Peninsula.[53]

The emergence of the principate, thus, may be described as an evolution of the patronate—which for the rest continued to exist in its modest form well into the imperial period. When the patron was a *princeps civis*, the clientele would become an instrument of

51. Ibid., 26 ff.
52. Ibid., 24.
53. Ibid., 16 ff.

political power, and with the inclusion of veteran armies it would become an instrument of military power in rivalry with the constitutional armed forces. Political influence, wealth, and military clientele determined and increased one another mutually in so far as the political position secured the military command, necessary for the conquest of provinces and their profitable exploitation, while the exploitation of the provinces was necessary for supporting the clientele with spoils and land, and the clientele was necessary to hold political influence. With the reduction of the competitors to a few great party leaders the breaking point of constitutional legality was reached, especially when the Senate and the magistrates themselves were divided between the clienteles of the protagonists. In the life of each of the great party leaders of the first century there came the time when he had to decide upon his transgression of the line between legality and illegality—the most famous of these decisions being Caesar's crossing of the Rubicon.[54] And Octavianus, a cool and calculating politician, chose to conduct his last war with Antony as an *inimicitia* because a declaration of Antony as public enemy could have provoked the same declaration against himself, since both consuls and part of the Senate were in Antony's camp. The mutual declaration as public enemies would have split Rome, as it were, into two hostile states fighting each other; and the shaking of the Republic to its constitutional foundations might have had the same disastrous results as the parallel situation in the death struggle between Caesar and Pompey—with the murder of the victorious leader in the year after his triumph at the hands of republican sentimentalists. The principate, thus, evolved through the reduction of the great patrocinial principes to the three of the triumvirates, then to Antony and Octavianus, and finally to the monopolization of the position by the victor of Actium.[55]

The representative order of Rome after Actium was a skillful combination of the old republican constitution with the new existential representation of the empire people by the princeps. The direct relationship between the princeps and the people was secured through the extension of the clientele oath to the people at large. In 32 B.C. Octavianus, before entering on his struggle with Antony, had exacted such an oath from Italy and the western provinces,

54. Ibid., 24 ff.
55. Ibid., 37.

the so-called conjuration of the West; it was an oath of loyalty rendered to Octavianus *pro partibus suis*, that is, to him as the leader of a party.[56] Concerning the extension of the oath to the eastern provinces, which must have taken place after Actium, no sources are available.[57] Nevertheless, the oath to the princeps in the form of 32 B.C. became a permanent institution. It was sworn again to the successors of Augustus on occasion of their ascent to power,[58] and beginning with Caius Caligula it was renewed annually.[59] The patrocinial articulation of a group into leader and followers had expanded into the form of imperial representation.

6

The patrocinial, expanded into the imperial, principate was the institution that made the new ruler the existential representative for the vast agglomeration of conquered territories and peoples. Obviously, the instrument was brittle. Its effectiveness depended on the experience of the patrocinial relation as a sacramental bond in the Roman sense. The new Augustus saw the problem; and his legislation for moral and religious reform must be understood, at least in part, as the attempt of reinforcing sacramental sentiments that had been waning even among the Romans at the time of Varro's *Antiquities*. In face of the vast oriental population the task was hopeless, especially since the Easterners streamed into Rome in ever increasing numbers and were clinging to their non-Roman cults in spite of all prohibitions; and the task became still more hopeless when the emperors themselves ceased to be Romans, when the Julian dynasty was followed by the provincial Flavians, by the Spaniards, the Syrians, and the Illyrians.

The remedy for the sacramental deficiency in the position of the emperor was found only gradually, on a tortuous path of experimentation and failure. The divinization of the emperor, following the model of Hellenistic kingship, proved insufficient. It also had to be determined which divine power he represented among the mass of cult divinities in the empire. Under the pressure of this problem the religious culture of the Roman Mediterranean underwent a process

56. Ibid., 42 ff.
57. Ibid., 52.
58. Ibid., 56 ff.
59. Ibid., 60 ff.

that usually is called syncretism, or *theokrasia*, mixture of the gods. The evolution is not singular; it is in substance the same process that the Near Eastern empires had undergone at an earlier time, the process of reinterpreting the multitude of local cult divinities in the politically unified area as the aspects of one highest god who then became the empire-god. Under the peculiar conditions of the civilizationally mixed Roman area, experimentation with such a highest god was not easy. On the one hand, the god could not be a conceptual abstraction but had to have an intelligible relationship to one or more concretely experienced gods who were known as high; on the other hand, if the relationship to a concretely existing god became too close, his value as a god above all known special gods was in danger. The attempt of Elagabalus (218–222) to introduce the Baal of Emesa as the *highest* god to Rome miscarried. A circumcised Caesar who married a Vestal virgin in order to symbolize the union between Baal and Tanit proved too much of a strain on the Roman tradition. He was murdered by his praetorian guards. The Illyrian Aurelian (270–275) tried with better success when he declared a sufficiently nondescript sun god, the *Sol Invictus*, as the highest god of the empire and himself as his descendant and representative. With some variation under Diocletian (284–305) the system lasted until A.D. 313.

The fact that the empire cult was a subject of experimentation should not deceive us, however, about the religious seriousness with which these experiments were undertaken. Spiritually the late Roman summodeism had approached closely enough to Christianity to make conversion almost a slight transition. There is extant the prayer of Licinius before his battle against Maximinus Daza in 313. An angel appeared to Licinius in the night and assured him of victory if he and the army would pray it:

> Highest God, we pray to thee,
> Holy God, we pray to thee.
> All justice we command to thee,
> Our weal we command to thee,
> Our realm we command to thee.
> By thee we live, by thee we are victorious and successful.
> Highest, Holy God, hear our prayers.
> We raise our arms to thee,
> Hear us, oh Holy, Highest God.

Story and prayer are reported by Lactantius,[60] with the understanding that the victory was due to a conversion similar to Constantine's in the year before. The Christianity of Licinius is at least doubtful in view of his anti-Christian policy in subsequent years, but the prayer, which could as well have been prayed by his pagan opponent Maximinus, appeared as a confession of Christianity to Lactantius.

The precise meaning of the surprising turn of events that in 311–313 gave freedom to Christianity is still a matter of debate. It seems, however, that the recent interpretation by the Dutch theologian Hendrik Berkhof has cleared up the mysterious affair as far as the sources allow.[61] The persistence and survival of the Christians under violent persecutions apparently convinced the regents Galerius, Licinius, and Constantinus that the Christian God was powerful enough to protect his followers in adversity; that he was a reality that should be treated with caution. The Edict of Galerius, of 311, explained that as a consequence of the persecutions the Christians neither fulfilled their cult obligations to the official gods nor worshiped their own God in proper form.[62] This observation apparently motivated the sudden change of policy. If the powerful God of the Christians were not worshiped by his own adherents, he might take his revenge and add to the troubles of the rulers who prevented his worship. It was the good, solid Roman *do-ut-des* principle.[63] In return for their new freedom the edict ordered the Christians to pray for the emperor, the public weal, and their own.[64] This was no conversion to Christianity but rather an inclusion of the Christian God into the imperial system of divinity.[65] The Edict of Licinius, of 313, stated that the former anti-Christian policy had been revised "so that all that is of *divinitas* in the celestial habitat be propitious to us and all who are under our rule."[66] The curious term *divinitas* was reconcilable with official polytheism and the recognition of the *Summus Deus* of the empire religion, and at the same time

60. Lactantius *De mortibus persecutorum* xlvi.
61. Premerstein, *Vom Werden und Wesen*, 47 ff.
62. Lactantius *De mortibus persecutorum* xxxiv: "cum . . . videremus nec diis eosdem cultum ac religionem debitam exhibere, nec Christianorum Deum observare."
63. Berkhof, *Kirche und Kaiser*, 48.
64. Lactantius *De mortibus persecutorum* xxxi *in fine*.
65. A similar interpretation is to be found in Joseph Vogt, *Constantin der Grosse und sein Jahrhundert* (Munich, 1949), 154 ff.
66. Ibid., xlviii. I am following the reading "quidquid est divinitatis in sede coelesti," as does Berkhof, *Kirche und Kaiser*, 51.

it sounded monotheistic enough to make Christians happy. The suspense of meaning was probably intended—one feels in it the deft hand of the Constantine, who later, in the christological debate, insisted on the sublimely meaningless *homo-ousios.*

7

The problems of imperial theology, however, could not be solved by a linguistic compromise. The Christians were persecuted for a good reason; there was a revolutionary substance in Christianity that made it incompatible with paganism. The new alliance was bound to increase the social effectiveness of this revolutionary substance. What made Christianity so dangerous was its uncompromising, radical de-divinization of the world. The problem had been formulated perhaps most clearly by Celsus in his *True Discourse,* of *ca.* A.D. 180, the most competent pagan critique of Christianity. The Christians, he complained, reject polytheism with the argument that one cannot serve two masters.[67] This was for Celsus the "language of sedition (*stasis*)."[68] The rule, he admitted, holds true among men; but nothing can be taken from God when we serve his divinity in the many manifestations of his kingdom. On the contrary, we honor and please the Most High when we honor many of those who belong to him,[69] while singling out one God and honoring him alone introduces factiousness into the divine kingdom.[70] That part will be taken only by men who stand aloof from human society and transfer their own isolating passions to God.[71] The Christians, thus, are factionals in religion and metaphysics, a sedition against the divinity that harmoniously animates the whole world in all its subdivisions. And since the various quarters of the earth were from the beginning allotted to various ruling spirits and superintending principalities,[72] the religious sedition is at the same time a political revolt. Who wishes to destroy the national cult wants to destroy the national cultures.[73] And since they all have found their place in the empire, an attack on the cults by radical monotheists is an attack on

67. Origenes *Contra Celsum* vii.68.
68. Ibid., viii.2.
69. Ibid.
70. Ibid., 11.
71. Ibid., 2.
72. Ibid., v.25.
73. Ibid., 26.

the construction of the *imperium Romanum*. Not that it were not desirable, even in the opinion of Celsus, if Asiatics, Europeans and Libyans, Hellenes and barbarians, would agree in one *nomos*, but, he adds contemptuously, "anyone who thinks this possible knows nothing."[74] The answer of Origen in his *Contra Celsum* was that it not only was possible but that it surely would come to pass.[75] Celsus, one may say, discerned the implications of Christianity even more clearly than Cicero the implications of Greek philosophy. He understood the existential problem of polytheism; and he knew that the Christian de-divinization of the world spelled the end of a civilizational epoch and would radically transform the ethnic cultures of the age.

8

The belief that Christianity could be used for bolstering the political theology of the empire, either alone or in combination with the pagan conception of a *Summus Deus*, was destined to experience a quick disappointment. Nevertheless, the belief could be entertained with reason because it found support from a Christian tendency of interpreting the one God of Christianity in the direction of a metaphysical monotheism.[76] To indulge in this experiment was an understandable temptation in the path of Eastern religions when they found themselves in the Hellenistic environment and began to express themselves in the language of Greek speculation. In fact, the Christian development in this direction was not original but followed the example of Philo Judaeus; and Philo had at his disposition already the preparatory peripatetic speculations of the first century B.C. In his *Metaphysics* Aristotle had formulated the principle: "The world does not have the will to be ruled badly; the rule of many is not good, one be the Lord."[77] In the peripatetic literature immediately preceding the time of Philo, of which the representative extant example is the pseudo-Aristotelian *De mundo*,

74. Ibid., viii.72.
75. Ibid.
76. On metaphysical monotheism and its function in the political theology of the Roman Empire see Erik Peterson, *Der Monotheismus als politisches Problem: Ein Beitrag zur Geschichte der politischen Theologie im Imperium Romanum* (Leipzig, 1935). Our own analysis follows Peterson's closely.
77. Aristotle *Metaphysics* 1076a.

this principle was elaborated into the great parallel constructions of imperial monarchy and divine world monarchy.[78] The divine monarchical ruler of the cosmos governs the world through his lesser messengers in the same manner in which the Persian great king governs his empire through the satraps in the provinces.[79] Philo adapted the construction to his Jewish monotheism with the purpose of forging a political propaganda instrument that would make Judaism attractive as a one-god cult in the empire.[80] Apparently following a peripatetic source he made the Jewish God a "king of kings" in the Persian sense, while all other gods were relegated to the rank of subrulers.[81] He carefully preserved the position of the Jews as the chosen people, but he skillfully extricated them from their metaphysical impasse by making the service of Yahve the service of the God that rules the cosmos in the peripatetic sense.[82] He even referred to Plato's *Timaeus* in order to make him the God who establishes the order, the *taxis*, of the world in a constitutional sense.[83] The Jews in serving this God serve him representatively for mankind. And when he quoted the passage from Aristotle's *Metaphysics* with its Homeric verse, he insisted that the verse be considered valid for cosmic as for political rulership.[84]

The Philonic speculation was taken over by Christian thinkers.[85] The adaptation to the Christian situation in the empire achieved its fullest development through Eusebius of Caesarea in the time of

78. The *De mundo* is to be dated in the first century A.D. Whether it still falls in the lifetime of Philo does not matter for our purpose, because we are interested only in its typical contents.

79. *De mundo* 6.

80. On Philo's political intentions see Peterson, *Der Monotheismus als politisches Problem*, 27; Erwin R. Goodenough, *The Politics of Philo Judaeus* (New Haven, 1938); and the same author's *An Introduction to Philo Judaeus* (New Haven, 1940), chap. 3.

81. Philo *De specialibus legibus* i.13.18.31; *De decalego* 61.

82. Peterson, *Der Monotheismus als politisches Problem*, 23 ff. In *De Abrahamo* 98 the Jews are described as the nation "dearest to God" and endowed with the gifts of priesthood and prophecy "on behalf of the whole race of men"; in *De spec. leg.* 167 the prayers of the Jews are representative for all mankind; in *De spec. leg.* 97 the high priest of the Jews prays and gives thanks not only for mankind but for the whole creation.

83. Philo *De fuga et inventione* 10. On the change of the Platonic meaning of *taxis* to the meaning of constitutional order see Peterson, *Der Monotheismus als politisches Problem*, 28–29.

84. Philo *De confusione linguarum* 170.

85. On the absorption of Philo's speculation on divine monarchy into the Christian apologetic literature, see Peterson, *Der Monotheismus als politisches Problem*, 34–42.

Constantine.[86] Eusebius, like many Christian thinkers before and after him, was attracted by the coincidence of the appearance of Christ with the pacification of the empire through Augustus. His elaborate historical work was motivated in part by his interest in the providential subjugation of formerly independent nations by the Romans. When the autonomous existence of the political entities in the Mediterranean area was broken by Augustus, the apostles of Christianity could roam unmolested through the whole empire and spread the Gospel; they could hardly have carried out their mission unless the wrath of the "superstitious of the polis" had been kept in check by fear of Roman power.[87] The establishment of the *pax Romana* was, furthermore, not only of pragmatic importance for the expansion of Christianity but to Eusebius it seemed intimately connected with the mysteries of the Kingdom of God. In the pre-Roman period, he opined, neighbors did not live in real community but were engaged in continuous warfare with each other. Augustus dissolved the pluralistic polyarchy; with his monarchy peace descended on the earth, thus fulfilling the scriptural predictions of Mic. 4:4 and Ps. 71:7. In brief, the eschatological prophecies concerning the peace of the Lord were politicized by Eusebius when he referred them to a *pax Romana* that coincided historically with the manifestation of the Logos.[88] And, finally, Eusebius considered the work that had been begun by Augustus to be fulfilled by Constantine. In his *Tricennial Speech* he praised Constantine because in his imperial he had imitated the divine monarchy: the one *basileus* on earth represents the one God, the one King in Heaven, the one Nomos and Logos.[89] It is a return, indeed, to the imperial representation of cosmic truth.

Such harmony, of course, could not last; it had to break as soon as somewhat more sensitive Christians would get hold of the problem. The issue came to a head through the struggle about the Christology. Celsus had railed at the Christians because they did not take their own monotheism seriously and had a second God in Christ.[90] This was indeed the crucial question that had to be settled

---

86. On Eusebius, see ibid., 71–76, and Berkhof, *Kirche und Kaiser*, 100–101.

87. Eusebius *Demonstratio evangelica* iii.7.30–35.

88. Ibid., vii.2.22, viii.3.13–15; Peterson, *Der Monotheismus als politisches Problem*, 75–77.

89. Eusebius *Laus Constantini* 1–10; Peterson, *Der Monotheismus als politisches Problem*, 78; Berkhof, *Kirche und Kaiser*, 102.

90. Origenes *Contra Celsum* viii.12–16.

in the christological debate when it was stirred up by the heresy of Arius. The symbols had to be found for interpreting the one God as three persons in one; and with the full understanding of trinitarianism the constructions of the Eusebian type would be finished. Understandably the emperors and court theologians were rather on the Arian side; the trinitarian debate was seriously disturbing the monotheistic ideology on which depended the conception of the emperor as the representative of the one God. When the resistance of Athanasius, supported by the Westerners, had carried the trinitarian symbolism to victory, the speculations on parallel monarchies in heaven and on earth could no longer be continued. The language of a divine monarchy did not disappear, but it acquired a new meaning. Gregory of Nazianzus, for instance, declared the Christians to be believers in the divine monarchy, but, he continued, they do not believe in the monarchy of a single person in the godhead, for such a godhead would be a source of discord; Christians believe in the triunity—and this triunity of God has no analogue in creation. The one person of an imperial monarch could not represent the triune divinity.[91] How impossible it had become to operate with the idea of a trinitarian God in politics may be illustrated by an incident from the reign of Constantine IV Pogonatus (668–85): The army demanded that he install his two brothers as co-emperors in order to have on earth a representation of the divine trinity.[92] It sounds more like a joke than like a serious suggestion; and it was perhaps inevitable that in the course of events the second and third persons of the imperial trinity got their noses cut off.

The other brilliant idea of Eusebius, the idea of recognizing in the *pax Romana* the fulfilment of eschatological prophecies (an idea strongly reminiscent of Cicero's inclination to see the perfect order of the philosophers realized through Rome), fell to pieces under the pressure of a troubled age. Nevertheless, the commentary of Saint Augustine on the prophecy of Ps. 46:9 may serve as a specific assertion of the orthodox counterposition. The text is: "He maketh

91. Peterson, *Der Monotheismus als politisches Problem*, 96 ff.

92. Karl Krumbacher, *Geschichte der byzantinischen Literatur*, 2d ed. (Munich, 1897), 954; E. W. Brooks, *The Successors of Heraclius to 717* (*CMH*, 11, 13), 405; Berkhof, *Kirche und Kaiser*, 144. The only other instance of an application of the Trinity to imperial rule, as far as I know, is the *Versus Paschales* of Ausonius, A.D. 368 or shortly thereafter. In this Easter poem the Trinity is seen figured on earth by Valentinian I and his co-emperors Valens and Gratianus (*Ausonius* [Loeb Classical Library], 1:34 ff).

wars to cease unto the end of the earth." Saint Augustine comments: "That we see not yet accomplished; hitherto we have wars. Between the nations there are the wars for domination. And there are also wars between the sects, between Jews, Pagans, Christians and heretics, and these wars even increase; one side fighting for truth, the other side for falsehood. In no way is there fulfilled the 'ceasing of the wars to the end of the earth'; but perhaps, we hope, it will be fulfilled."[93]

This is the end of political theology in orthodox Christianity. The spiritual destiny of man in the Christian sense cannot be represented on earth by the power organization of a political society; it can be represented only by the church. The sphere of power is radically de-divinized; it has become temporal. The double representation of man in society through church and empire lasted through the Middle Ages. The specifically modern problems of representation are connected with the re-divinization of society. The subsequent three lectures will deal with these problems.

93. Augustine *Enarratio in Psalmos* xlv.13.

4

Gnosticism

The Nature of Modernity

I

The clash between the various types of truth in the Roman Empire ended with the victory of Christianity. The fateful result of this victory was the de-divinization of the temporal sphere of power; and it was anticipated that the specifically modern problems of representation would have something to do with a re-divinization of man and society. Both of these terms are in need of further definition, especially since the concept of modernity and with it the periodization of history depend on the meaning of re-divinization. Hence, by de-divinization shall be meant the historical process in which the culture of polytheism died from experiential atrophy, and human existence in society became reordered through the experience of man's destination, by the grace of the world-transcendent God, toward eternal life in beatific vision. By re-divinization, however, shall not be meant a revival of polytheistic culture in the Greco-Roman sense. The characterization of modern political mass movements as neopagan, which has a certain vogue, is misleading because it sacrifices the historically unique nature of modern movements to a superficial resemblance. Modern re-divinization has its origins rather in Christianity itself, deriving from components that were suppressed as heretical by the universal church. The nature of this inner-Christian tension, therefore, will have to be determined more closely.

The tension was given with the historical origin of Christianity as a Jewish messianic movement. The life of the early Christian communities was experientially not fixed but oscillated between the eschatological expectation of the Parousia that would bring the Kingdom of God and the understanding of the church as the apocalypse of Christ in history. Since the Parousia did not occur, the church actually evolved from the eschatology of the realm in history toward the eschatology of trans-historical, supernatural perfection. In this evolution the specific essence of Christianity separated from its historical origin.[1] This separation began within the life of Jesus itself,[2] and it was on principle completed with the Pentecostal descent of the Spirit. Nevertheless, the expectation of an imminent coming of the realm was stirred to white heat again and again by the suffering of the persecutions; and the most grandiose expression of eschatological pathos, the Revelation of Saint John, was included in the canon in spite of misgivings about its compatibility with the idea of the church. The inclusion had fateful consequences, for with the Revelation was accepted the revolutionary annunciation of the millennium in which Christ would reign with his saints on this earth.[3] Not only did the inclusion sanction the permanent effectiveness within Christianity of the broad mass of Jewish apocalyptic literature but it also raised the immediate question how chiliasm could be reconciled with idea and existence of the church. If Christianity consisted in the burning desire for deliverance from the world, if Christians lived in expectation of the end of unredeemed history, if their destiny could be fulfilled only by the realm in the sense of chapter 20 of Revelation, the church was reduced to an ephemeral community of men waiting for the great event and hoping that it would occur in their lifetime. On the theoretical level the problem could be solved only by the tour de force of interpretation that Saint Augustine performed in the *Civitas Dei*. There he roundly dismissed the literal belief in the millennium as "ridiculous fables" and then boldly declared the realm of the thousand years to be the reign of Christ in his church in the present saeculum that would continue until the Last Judgment and the advent of the eternal realm in the beyond.[4]

1. On the transition from eschatological to apocalyptic Christianity see Alois Dempf, *Sacrum Imperium* (Munich, 1929), 71 ff.

2. Albert Schweitzer, *Geschichte der Leben Jesu Forschung* (Tübingen, 1920), 406 ff.; and Maurice Goguel, *Jesus*, 2d ed. (Paris, 1950), the chapter on "La Crise galiléenne."

3. On the tension in early Christianity, the reception of Revelation, and its subsequent role in Western revolutionary eschatology, see Jakob Taubes, *Abendländische Eschatologie* (Bern, 1947), esp. 69 ff.

4. Augustine *Civitas Dei* xx.7, 8, 9.

The Augustinian conception of the church, without substantial change, remained historically effective to the end of the Middle Ages. The revolutionary expectation of a Second Coming that would transfigure the structure of history on earth was ruled out as "ridiculous." The Logos had become flesh in Christ; the grace of redemption had been bestowed on man; there would be no divinization of society beyond the pneumatic presence of Christ in his church. Jewish chiliasm was excluded along with polytheism, just as Jewish monotheism had been excluded along with pagan, metaphysical monotheism. This left the church as the universal spiritual organization of saints and sinners who professed faith in Christ, as the representative of the *civitas Dei* in history, as the flash of eternity into time. And correspondingly it left the power organization of society as a temporal representation of man in the specific sense of a representation of that part of human nature that will pass away with the transfiguration of time into eternity. The one Christian society was articulated into its spiritual and temporal orders. In its temporal articulation it accepted the *conditio humana* without chiliastic fancies, while it heightened natural existence by the representation of spiritual destiny through the church.

This picture must be rounded out by remembering that the idea of the temporal order was historically concretized through the Roman Empire. Rome was built into the idea of a Christian society by referring the Danielic prophecy of the Fourth Monarchy[5] to the *imperium sine fine*[6] as the last realm before the end of the world.[7] The church as the historically concrete representation of spiritual destiny was paralleled by the Roman Empire as the historically concrete representation of human temporality. Hence, the understanding of the medieval empire as the continuation of Rome was more than a vague historical hangover; it was part of a conception of history in which the end of Rome meant the end of the world in the eschatological sense. The conception survived in the realm of ideas for centuries while its basis of sentiments and institutions was crumbling away. The history of the world was constructed in the Augustinian tradition for the last time only by Bossuet, in his *Histoire universelle,* toward the end of the seventeenth century;

5. Dan 2:44.
6. Vergil *Aeneid* i.278–79.
7. For the numerous sources, see Ernst Troeltsch, *Die Soziallehren der christlichen Kirchen und Gruppen* (Tübingen, 1912), 112.

and the first modern who dared to write a world history in direct opposition to Bossuet was Voltaire.

2

Western Christian society thus was articulated into the spiritual and temporal orders, with pope and emperor as the supreme representatives in both the existential and the transcendental sense. From this society with its established system of symbols emerge the specifically modern problems of representation, with the resurgence of the eschatology of the realm. The movement had a long social and intellectual prehistory, but the desire for a re-divinization of society produced a definite symbolism of its own only toward the end of the twelfth century. The analysis will start from the first clear and comprehensive expression of the idea in the person and work of Joachim of Fiore.

Joachim broke with the Augustinian conception of a Christian society when he applied the symbol of the Trinity to the course of history. In his speculation the history of mankind had three periods corresponding to the three persons of the Trinity. The first period of the world was the age of the Father; with the appearance of Christ began the age of the Son. But the age of the Son will not be the last one; it will be followed by a third age, of the Spirit. The three ages were characterized as intelligible increases of spiritual fulfillment. The first age unfolded the life of the layman; the second age brought the active contemplative life of the priest; the third age would bring the perfect spiritual life of the monk. Moreover, the ages had comparable internal structures and a calculable length. From the comparison of structures it appeared that each age opened with a trinity of leading figures, that is, with two precursors, followed by the leader of the age himself; and from the calculation of length it followed that the age of the Son would reach its end in 1260. The leader of the first age was Abraham; the leader of the second age was Christ; and Joachim predicted that by 1260 there would appear the *Dux e Babylone*, the leader of the third age.[8]

8. On Joachim of Fiore, see Herbert Grundmann, *Studien über Joachim von Floris* (Leipzig, 1927); Dempf, *Sacrum Imperium*, 269 ff.; Ernesto Buonaiuti, *Gioacchino da Fiore* (Rome, 1931); the same author's introduction to Joachim's *Tractatus super quatuor evangelia* (Rome, 1930); and the chapters on Joachim in Taubes, *Abendländische Eschatologie* and Karl Löwith, *Meaning in History* (Chicago, 1949).

In his trinitarian eschatology Joachim created the aggregate of symbols that govern the self-interpretation of modern political society to this day.

The first of these symbols is the conception of history as a sequence of three ages, of which the third age is intelligibly the final Third Realm. As variations of this symbol are recognizable the humanistic and encyclopedist periodization of history into ancient, medieval, and modern history; Turgot's and Comte's theory of a sequence of theological, metaphysical, and scientific phases; Hegel's dialectic of the three stages of freedom and self-reflective spiritual fulfillment; the Marxian dialectic of the three stages of primitive communism, class society, and final communism; and, finally, the national-socialist symbol of the Third Realm—though this is a special case requiring further attention.

The second symbol is that of the leader.[9] It had its immediate effectiveness in the movement of the Franciscan spirituals who saw in Saint Francis the fulfillment of Joachim's prophecy; and its effectiveness was reinforced by Dante's speculation on the *Dux* of the new spiritual age. It then can be traced in the paracletic figures, the *homines spirituales* and *homines novi*, of the late Middle Ages, the Renaissance, and Reformation; it can be discerned as a component in Machiavelli's *principe*; and in the period of secularization it appears in the supermen of Condorcet, Comte, and Marx, until it dominates the contemporary scene through the paracletic leaders of the new realms.

The third symbol, sometimes blending into the second, is that of the prophet of the new age. In order to lend validity and conviction to the idea of a final Third Realm, the course of history as an intelligible, meaningful whole must be assumed accessible to human knowledge, either through a direct revelation or through speculative Gnosis. Hence, the gnostic prophet or, in the later stages of secularization, the gnostic intellectual becomes an appurtenance of modern civilization. Joachim himself is the first instance of the species.

The fourth symbol is that of the brotherhood of autonomous persons. The third age of Joachim, by virtue of its new descent of the spirit, will transform men into members of the new realm without

9. For further transformations of Joachitism, see appendix 1, "Modern Transfigurations of Joachism," in Löwith, *Meaning in History.*

sacramental mediation of grace. In the third age the church will cease to exist because the charismatic gifts that are necessary for the perfect life will reach men without administration of sacraments. While Joachim himself conceived the new age concretely as an order of monks, the idea of a community of the spiritually perfect who can live together without institutional authority was formulated on principle. The idea was capable of infinite variations. It can be traced in various degrees of purity in medieval and Renaissance sects, as well as in the Puritan churches of the saints; in its secularized form it has become a formidable component in the contemporary democratic creed; and it is the dynamic core in the Marxian mysticism of the realm of freedom and the withering-away of the state.

The national-socialist Third Realm is a special case. To be sure, Hitler's millennial prophecy authentically derives from Joachitic speculation, mediated in Germany through the Anabaptist wing of the Reformation and through the Johannine Christianity of Fichte, Hegel, and Schelling. Nevertheless, the concrete application of the trinitarian schema to the first German Reich, which ended in 1806, the Bismarck Reich, which ended in 1918, and the *Dritte Reich* of the national-socialist movement sounds flat and provincial if compared with the world-historical speculation of the German idealists, of Comte, or of Marx. This nationalist, accidental touch is due to the fact that the symbol of the *Dritte Reich* did not stem from the speculative effort of a philosopher of rank but rather from dubious literary transfers. The national-socialist propagandists picked it up from Moeller van den Bruck's tract of that name.[10] And Moeller, who had no national-socialist intentions, had found it as a convenient symbol in the course of his work on the German edition of Dostoevski. The Russian idea of the Third Rome is characterized by the same blend of an eschatology of the spiritual realm with its realization by a political society as the national-socialist idea of the *Dritte Reich*. This other branch of political re-divinization must now be considered.

10. Moeller van den Bruck, *Das Dritte Reich* (Hamburg, 1923). See also the chapter on "Das Dritte Reich und die Jungen Völker" in Moeller van den Bruck, *Die politischen Kräfte* (Breslau, 1933). The symbol gained acceptance slowly. The second edition of the *Dritte Reich* appeared only in 1930, five years after the author's death through suicide; see the introduction by Mary Agnes Hamilton to the English edition, *Germany's Third Empire* (London, 1934).

Only in the West was the Augustinian conception of the church historically effective to the point that it resulted in the clear double representation of society through the spiritual and temporal powers. The fact that the temporal ruler was situated at a considerable geographical distance from Rome certainly facilitated this evolution. In the East developed the Byzantine form of Caesaropapism, in direct continuity with the position of the emperor in pagan Rome. Constantinople was the Second Rome, as it appeared in the declaration of Justinian concerning the *consuetudo Romae:* "By Rome, however, must be understood not only the old one but also our royal city."[11] After the fall of Constantinople to the Turks, the idea of Moscow as the successor to the Orthodox Empire gained ground in Russian clerical circles. Let me quote the famous passages from a letter of Filofei of Pskov to Ivan the Great:

> The church of the first Rome fell because of the godless heresy of Apollinaris. The gates of the second Rome at Constantinople were smashed by the Ishmaelites. Today the holy apostolic church of the third Rome in thy Empire shines in the glory of Christian faith throughout the world. Know you, O pious Tsar, that all empires of the orthodox Christians have converged into thine own. You are the sole autocrat of the universe, the only tsar of all Christians. . . . According to the prophetic books all Christian empires have an end and will converge into one empire, that of our gossudar, that is, into the Empire of Russia. Two Romes have fallen, but the third will last, and there will not be a fourth one.[12]

It took about a century to institutionalize the idea. Ivan IV was the first Rurikide to have himself crowned, in 1547, as czar of the Orthodox;[13] and in 1589 the patriarch of Constantinople was

11. *Codex Justinianus* i.xvii.1.10. We are quoting the legal formalization of the idea. On the nuances of meaning with regard to the foundation and organization of Constantinople, in 330, see Andrew Alföldi, *The Conversion of Constantine and Pagan Rome,* trans. Harold Mattingly (Oxford, 1943), chap. 9, "The Old Rome and the New." The tension between the two Romes may be gathered from Canon 3 of the Council of Constantinople in 381: "The Bishop of Constantinople to have the primacy of honor next after the Bishop of Rome, because that Constantinople is New Rome" (Henry Bettenson, *Documents of the Christian Church* [New York, 1947], 115).

12. On the Third Rome see Hildegard Schaeder, *Moskau—Das Dritte Rom: Studien zur Geschichte der politischen Theorien in der slavischen Welt* (Hamburg, 1929); Joseph Olšr, "Gli ultimi Rurikidi e le base ideologiche della sovranità dello stato Russo," *Orientalia Christiana* 12 (1946); Hugo Rahner, *Vom Ersten bis zum Dritten Rom* (Innsbruck, 1950); Paul Miliukov, *Outlines of Russian Culture,* part 1, *Religion and the Church* (Philadelphia, 1945), 15 ff.

13. George Vernadsky, *Political and Diplomatic History of Russia* (Boston, 1936), 158.

compelled to institute the first autocephalous patriarch of Moscow, now with the official recognition of Moscow as the Third Rome.[14]

The dates of rise and institutionalization of the idea are of importance. The reign of Ivan the Great coincides with the consolidation of the Western national states (England, France, and Spain), and the reigns of Ivan IV and of Theodore I coincide with the Western Reformation. Precisely at the time when the Western imperial articulation ultimately disintegrated, when Western society rearticulated itself into the nations and the plurality of churches, Russia entered on her career as the heir of Rome. From her very beginnings Russia was not a nation in the Western sense but a civilizational area, dominated ethnically by the Great Russians and formed into a political society by the symbolism of Roman continuation.

That Russian society was in a class by itself was gradually recognized by the West. In 1488 Maximilian I still tried to integrate Russia into the Western political system by offering a royal crown to Ivan the Great. The Grand Duke of Moscow refused the honor on the grounds that his authority stemmed from his ancestors, that it had the blessing of God, and, hence, that there was no need of confirmation from the Western emperor.[15] A century later, in 1576, at the time of the Western wars with the Turks, Maximilian II went a step further by offering Ivan IV recognition as the emperor of the Greek East in return for assistance.[16] Again the Russian ruler was not interested even in an imperial crown, for, at that time, Ivan was already engaged in building the Russian Empire through the liquidation of the feudal nobility and its replacement by the *oprichnina*, the new service nobility.[17] Through this bloody operation Ivan the Terrible stamped on Russia the indelible social articulation that has determined her inner political history to this day. Transcendentally Russia was distinguished from all Western nations as the imperial representative of Christian truth; and through her social rearticulation, from which the czar emerged as the existential representative, she was radically cut off from the development of representative institutions in the sense of the Western national states. Napoleon, finally, recognized the Russian problem when, in 1802, he said that there were only two nations in the world: Russia and the Occident.[18]

14. Ibid., 180.
15. Ibid., 149.
16. Rahner, *Vom Ersten bis zum Dritten Rom,* 15.
17. Vernadsky, *Political and Diplomatic History,* 169 ff.
18. Napoleon, *Vues politiques* (Rio de Janeiro, n.d.), 340.

Russia developed a type *sui generis* of representation, in both the transcendental and the existential respects. The Westernization since Peter the Great did not change the type fundamentally because it had practically no effect with regard to social articulation. One can speak, indeed, of a personal Westernization in the ranks of the high nobility, in the wake of the Napoleonic Wars, in the generation of Chaadaev, Gagarin, and Pecherin; but the individual servants of the czar did not transform themselves into an estate of the nobility, into an articulate *baronagium*. Perhaps the necessity of co-operative class action as the condition of a political Westernization of Russia was not even seen; and certainly, if the possibility for an evolution in this direction ever existed, it was finished with the Dekabrist revolt of 1825. Immediately afterward, with Khomyakov, began the Slavophilic, anti-Western philosophy of history that enhanced the apocalypse of the Third Rome, with broad effectiveness in the intelligentsia of the middle nobility, into the messianic, eschatological mission of Russia for mankind. In Dostoevski this superimposition of messianism crystallized in the curiously ambivalent vision of an autocratic, orthodox Russia that somehow would conquer the world and in this conquest blossom out into the free society of all Christians in the true faith.[19] It is the ambivalent vision that, in its secularized form, inspires a Russian dictatorship of the proletariat that in its conquest of the world will blossom out into the Marxian realm of freedom. The tentative Western articulation of Russian society under the liberal czars has become an episode of the past with the revolution of 1917. The people as a whole have become again the servants of the czar in the old Muscovite sense, with the cadres of the Communist party as its service nobility; the *oprichnina* that Ivan the Terrible had established on the basis of an agricultural economy was re-established with a vengeance on the basis of an industrial economy.[20]

3

From the exposition of Joachitic symbols, from the cursory survey of their later variants, and from their blending with the political apocalypse of the Third Rome, it will have become clear that the

19. For this view of Dostoevski see Dmitri Merezhkovski, *Die religiöse Revolution* (printed as introduction to Dostoevski's *Politische Schriften* [Munich, 1920]), and Bernhard Schultze, *Russische Denker* (Vienna, 1950), 125 ff.

20. Alexander von Schelting, *Rußland und Europa* (Bern, 1948), 123 ff., 261 ff.

new eschatology decisively affects the structure of modern politics. It has produced a well-circumscribed symbolism by means of which Western political societies interpret the meaning of their existence; and the adherents of one or the other of the variants determine the articulation of society domestically as well as on the world scene. Up to this point, however, the symbolism has been accepted on the level of self-interpretation and described as a historical phenomenon. It must now be submitted to critical analysis of its principal aspects, and the foundation for this analysis must be laid through a formulation of the theoretically relevant issue.

The Joachitic eschatology is, by its subject matter, a speculation on the meaning of history. In order to determine its specific difference, it must be set off against the Christian philosophy of history that was traditional at the time, that is, against Augustinian speculation. Into the traditional speculation had entered the Jewish-Christian idea of an end of history in the sense of an intelligible state of perfection. History no longer moved in cycles, as it did with Plato and Aristotle, but acquired direction and destination. Beyond Jewish messianism in the strict sense the specifically Christian conception of history had, then, advanced toward the understanding of the end as a transcendental fulfillment. In his elaboration of this theoretical insight Saint Augustine distinguished between a profane sphere of history in which empires rise and fall and a sacred history that culminates in the appearance of Christ and the establishment of the church. He, furthermore, imbedded sacred history in a transcendental history of the *civitas Dei* that includes the events in the angelic sphere as well as the transcendental eternal sabbath. Only transcendental history, including the earthly pilgrimage of the church, has direction toward its eschatological fulfillment. Profane history, on the other hand, has no such direction; it is a waiting for the end; its present mode of being is that of a *saeculum senescens,* of an age that grows old.[21]

By the time of Joachim, Western civilization was strongly growing; and an age that began to feel its muscles would not easily bear the Augustinian defeatism with regard to the mundane sphere of existence. The Joachitic speculation was an attempt to endow the

21. For an account of the Augustinian conception of history, see Löwith, *Meaning in History.*

immanent course of history with a meaning that was not provided in the Augustinian conception. And for this purpose Joachim used what he had at hand, that is, the meaning of transcendental history. In this first Western attempt at an immanentization of meaning the connection with Christianity was not lost. The new age of Joachim would bring an increase of fulfillment within history, but the increase would not be due to an immanent eruption; it would come through a new transcendental irruption of the spirit. The idea of a radically immanent fulfillment grew rather slowly, in a long process that roughly may be called "from humanism to enlightenment"; only in the eighteenth century, with the idea of progress, had the increase of meaning in history become a completely intramundane phenomenon, without transcendental irruptions. This second phase of immanentization shall be called "secularization."

From the Joachitic immanentization a theoretical problem arises that occurs neither in classic antiquity nor in orthodox Christianity, that is, the problem of an eidos of history.[22] In Hellenic speculation, to be sure, we also have a problem of essence in politics; the polis has an eidos both for Plato and for Aristotle. But the actualization of this essence is governed by the rhythm of growth and decay, and the rhythmical embodiment and disembodiment of essence in political reality is the mystery of existence; it is not an additional eidos. The soteriological truth of Christianity, then, breaks with the rhythm of existence; beyond temporal successes and reverses lies the supernatural destiny of man, the perfection through grace in the beyond. Man and mankind now have fulfillment, but it lies beyond nature. Again there is no eidos of history, because the eschatological supernature is not a nature in the philosophical, immanent sense. The problem of an eidos in history, hence, arises only when Christian transcendental fulfillment becomes immanentized. Such an immanentist hypostasis of the eschaton, however, is a theoretical fallacy. Things are not things, nor do they have essences, by arbitrary declaration. The course of history as a whole is no object of experience; history has no eidos, because the course of history extends into the unknown future. The meaning of history, thus, is an illusion; and this illusionary eidos is created by treating a symbol

22. On the eidos of history, see Hans Urs von Balthasar, *Theologie der Geschichte* (Einsiedeln, 1950), and Löwith, *Meaning in History*, passim.

of faith as if it were a proposition concerning an object of immanent experience.

The fallacious character of an eidos of history has been shown on principle—but the analysis can and must be carried one step further into certain details. The Christian symbolism of supernatural destination has in itself a theoretical structure, and this structure is continued into the variants of immanentization. The pilgrim's progress, the sanctification of life, is a movement toward a telos, a goal; and this goal, the beatific vision, is a state of perfection. Hence, in the Christian symbolism one can distinguish the movement as its teleological component, from a state of highest value as the axiological component.[23] The two components reappear in the variants of immanentization; and they can accordingly be classified as variants that either accentuate the teleological or the axiological component or combine them both in their symbolism. In the first case, when the accent lies strongly on movement, without clarity about final perfection, the result will be the progressivist interpretation of history. The aim need not be clarified because progressivist thinkers, men like Diderot or D'Alembert, assume a selection of desirable factors as the standard and interpret progress as qualitative and quantitative increase of the present good—the "bigger and better" of our simplifying slogan. This is a conservative attitude, and it may become reactionary unless the original standard be adjusted to the changing historical situation. In the second case, when the accent lies strongly on the state of perfection, without clarity about the means that are required for its realization, the result will be utopianism. It may assume the form of an axiological dream world, as in the utopia of More, when the thinker is still aware that and why the dream is unrealizable; or, with increasing theoretical illiteracy, it may assume the form of various social idealisms, such as the abolition of war, of unequal distribution of property, of fear and want. And, finally, immanentization may extend to the complete Christian symbol. The result will then be the active mysticism of a state of perfection, to be achieved through a revolutionary transfiguration of the nature of man, as, for instance, in Marxism.

23. For the distinction of the two components (which was introduced by Troeltsch) and the ensuing theological debate, see Hans Urs von Balthasar, *Prometheus* (Heidelberg, 1947), 12 ff.

4

The analysis can now be resumed on the level of principle. The attempt at constructing an eidos of history will lead into the fallacious immanentization of the Christian eschaton. The understanding of the attempt as fallacious, however, raises baffling questions with regard to the type of man who will indulge in it. The fallacy looks rather elemental. Can it be assumed that the thinkers who indulged in it were not intelligent enough to penetrate it? Or that they penetrated it but propagated it nevertheless for some obscure evil reason? The mere asking of such questions carries their negation. Obviously one cannot explain seven centuries of intellectual history by stupidity and dishonesty. A drive must rather be assumed in the souls of these men that blinded them to the fallacy.

The nature of this drive cannot be discovered by submitting the structure of the fallacy to an even closer analysis. The attention must rather concentrate on what the thinkers achieved by their fallacious construction. On this point there is no doubt. They achieved a certainty about the meaning of history, and about their own place in it, which otherwise they would not have had. Certainties, now, are in demand for the purpose of overcoming uncertainties with their accompaniment of anxiety; and the next question then would be: What specific uncertainty was so disturbing that it had to be overcome by the dubious means of fallacious immanentization? One does not have to look far afield for an answer. Uncertainty is the very essence of Christianity. The feeling of security in a "world full of gods" is lost with the gods themselves; when the world is de-divinized, communication with the world-transcendent God is reduced to the tenuous bond of faith, in the sense of Heb. 11:1, as the substance of things hoped for and the proof of things unseen. Ontologically, the substance of things hoped for is nowhere to be found but in faith itself; and, epistemologically, there is no proof for things unseen but again this very faith.[24] The bond is tenuous, indeed, and it may snap easily. The life of the soul in openness toward God, the waiting, the periods of aridity and dullness, guilt and despondency, contrition and repentance, forsakenness and hope

24. Our reflections on the uncertainty of faith must be understood as a psychology of experience. For the theology of the definition of faith in Heb. 11:1, which is presupposed in our analysis, see Thomas Aquinas *Summa theologica* ii-ii. Q. 4, Art. 1.

against hope, the silent stirrings of love and grace, trembling on the verge of a certainty that if gained is loss—the very lightness of this fabric may prove too heavy a burden for men who lust for massively possessive experience. The danger of a breakdown of faith to a socially relevant degree, now, will increase in the measure in which Christianity is a worldly success, that is, it will grow when Christianity penetrates a civilizational area thoroughly, supported by institutional pressure, and when, at the same time, it undergoes an internal process of spiritualization, of a more complete realization of its essence. The more people are drawn or pressured into the Christian orbit, the greater will be the number among them who do not have the spiritual stamina for the heroic adventure of the soul that is Christianity; and the likeliness of a fall from faith will increase when civilizational progress of education, literacy, and intellectual debate will bring the full seriousness of Christianity to the understanding of ever more individuals. Both of these processes characterized the high Middle Ages. The historical detail is not the present concern; it will be sufficient to refer summarily to the growing town societies with their intense spiritual culture as the primary centers from which the danger radiated into Western society at large.

If the predicament of a fall from faith in the Christian sense occurs as a mass phenomenon, the consequences will depend on the content of the civilizational environment into which the agnostics are falling. A man cannot fall back on himself in an absolute sense, because, if he tried, he would find very soon that he has fallen into the abyss of his despair and nothingness; he will have to fall back on a less differentiated culture of spiritual experience. Under the civilizational conditions of the twelfth century it was impossible to fall back into Greco-Roman polytheism, because it had disappeared as the living culture of a society; and the stunted remnants could hardly be revived, because they had lost their spell precisely for men who had tasted of Christianity. The fall could be caught only by experiential alternatives, sufficiently close to the experience of faith that only a discerning eye would see the difference, but receding far enough from it to remedy the uncertainty of faith in the strict sense. Such alternative experiences were at hand in the Gnosis that had accompanied Christianity from its very beginnings.[25]

25. The exploration of Gnosis is so rapidly advancing that only a study of the principal works of the last generation will mediate an understanding of its dimensions.

The economy of this lecture does not allow a description of the Gnosis of antiquity or of the history of its transmission into the Western Middle Ages; enough to say that at the time Gnosis was a living religious culture on which men could fall back. The attempt at immanentizing the meaning of existence is fundamentally an attempt at bringing our knowledge of transcendence into a firmer grip than the *cognitio fidei*, the cognition of faith, will afford; and gnostic experiences offer this firmer grip in so far as they are an expansion of the soul to the point where God is drawn into the existence of man. This expansion will engage the various human faculties; and, hence, it is possible to distinguish a range of gnostic varieties according to the faculty that predominates in the operation of getting this grip on God. Gnosis may be primarily intellectual and assume the form of speculative penetration of the mystery of creation and existence, as, for instance, in the contemplative Gnosis of Hegel or Schelling. Or it may be primarily emotional and assume the form of an indwelling of divine substance in the human soul, as, for instance, in paracletic sectarian leaders. Or it may be primarily volitional and assume the form of activist redemption of man and society, as in the instance of revolutionary activists like Comte, Marx, or Hitler. These gnostic experiences, in the amplitude of their variety, are the core of the re-divinization of society, for the men who fall into these experiences divinize themselves by substituting more massive modes of participation in divinity for faith in the Christian sense.[26]

A clear understanding of these experiences as the active core of immanentist eschatology is necessary, because otherwise the inner logic of the Western political development from medieval immanentism through humanism, enlightenment, progressivism, liberalism, positivism, into Marxism will be obscured. The intellectual symbols developed by the various types of immanentists will frequently be in conflict with one another, and the various types of Gnostics will oppose one another. One can easily imagine how indignant a humanistic liberal will be when he is told that his particular type of immanentism is one step on the road to Marxism.

Of special value are Eugène de Faye, *Gnostiques et gnosticisme*, 2d ed. (Paris, 1925); Hans Jonas, *Gnosis und spätantiker Geist* (Göttingen, 1934); Simone Pétrement, *Le Dualisme chez Platon, les Gnostiques et les Manichéens* (Paris, 1947); and Hans Söderberg, *La Religion des Cathares* (Uppsala, 1949).

26. For a general suggestion concerning the range of gnostic phenomena in the modern world, see Balthasar, *Prometheus*, 6.

It will not be superfluous, therefore, to recall the principle that the substance of history is to be found on the level of experiences, not on the level of ideas. Secularism could be defined as a radicalization of the earlier forms of paracletic immanentism, because the experiential divinization of man is more radical in the secularist case. Feuerbach and Marx, for instance, interpreted the transcendent God as the projection of what is best in man into a hypostatic beyond; for them the great turning point of history, therefore, would come when man draws his projection back into himself, when he becomes conscious that he himself is God, when as a consequence man is transfigured into superman.[27] This Marxian transfiguration does, indeed, carry to its extreme a less radical medieval experience that draws the spirit of God into man, while leaving God himself in his transcendence. The superman marks the end of a road on which we find such figures as the "godded man" of English Reformation mystics.[28] These considerations, moreover, will explain and justify the earlier warning against characterizing modern political movements as neopagan. Gnostic experiences determine a structure of political reality that is *sui generis.* A line of gradual transformation connects medieval with contemporary Gnosticism. And the transformation is so gradual, indeed, that it would be difficult to decide whether contemporary phenomena should be classified as Christian because they are intelligibly an outgrowth of Christian heresies of the Middle Ages or whether medieval phenomena should be classified as anti-Christian because they are intelligibly the origin of modern anti-Christianism. The best course will be to drop such questions and to recognize the essence of modernity as the growth of Gnosticism.

Gnosis was an accompaniment of Christianity from its very beginnings; its traces are to be found in Saint Paul and Saint John.[29] Gnostic heresy was the great opponent of Christianity in the early centuries; and Irenaeus surveyed and criticized the manifold of its variants in his *Adversas Haereses* (*ca.* 180)—a standard treatise on

27. On the superman of Feuerbach and Marx, see Henri de Lubac, *Le Drame de l'humanisme athée,* 3d ed. (Paris, 1945), 15 ff.; Löwith, *Meaning in History,* esp. the quotation on p. 36 concerning the "new men"; and Eric Voegelin, "The Formation of the Marxian Revolutionary Idea," *Review of Politics* 12 (1950).

28. The "godded man" is a term of Henry Nicholas (see Rufus M. Jones, *Studies in Mystical Religion* [London, 1936], 434).

29. On Gnosis in early Christianity, see Rudolf Bultmann, *Das Urchristentum im Rahmen der antiken Religionen* (Zurich, 1949).

the subject that still will be consulted with profit by the student who wants to understand modern political ideas and movements. Moreover, besides the Christian there also existed a Jewish, a pagan, and an Islamic Gnosis; and quite possibly the common origin of all these branches of Gnosis will have to be sought in the basic experiential type that prevailed in the pre-Christian area of Syriac civilization. Nowhere, however, has Gnosis assumed the form of speculation on the meaning of immanent history as it did in the high Middle Ages; Gnosis does not by inner necessity lead to the fallacious construction of history that characterizes modernity since Joachim. Hence, in the drive for certainty there must be contained a further component that bends Gnosis specifically toward historical speculation. This further component is the civilizational expansiveness of Western society in the high Middle Ages. It is a coming-of-age in search of its meaning, a conscious growth that will not put up with the interpretation as senescence. And, in fact, the self-endowment of Western civilization with meaning closely followed the actual expansion and differentiation. The spiritual growth of the West through the orders since Cluny expressed itself in Joachim's speculation in the idea of a Third Realm of the monks; the early philosophical and literary humanism expressed itself in Dante's and Petrarch's idea of an Apollinian Imperium, a Third Realm of intellectual life that succeeds the imperial spiritual and temporal orders;[30] and in the Age of Reason a Condorcet conceived the idea of a unified civilization of mankind in which everybody would be a French intellectual.[31] The social carriers of the movements, in their turn, changed with the differentiation and articulation of Western society. In the early phases of modernity they were the townspeople and peasants in opposition to feudal society; in the later phases they were the progressive bourgeoisie, the socialist workers, and the fascist lower middle class. And, finally, with the prodigious advancement of science since the seventeenth century, the new instrument of cognition would become, one is inclined to say inevitably, the symbolic vehicle of gnostic truth. In the gnostic speculation of scientism this particular variant reached its extreme

30. On the Apollinian Imperium as a Third Realm, see Karl Burdach, *Reformation, Renaissance, Humanismus,* 2d ed. (Berlin, 1926), 133 ff., and the same author's *Rienzo und die geistige Wandlung seiner Zeit* (Berlin, 1913–1928), vol. 2, pt. 1, *Vom Mittelalter zur Reformation,* 542.

31. Condorcet, *Esquisse* (1795), 310–18.

when the positivist perfector of science replaced the era of Christ with the era of Comte. Scientism has remained to this day one of the strongest gnostic movements in Western society; and the immanentist pride in science is so strong that even the special sciences have each left a distinguishable sediment in the variants of salvation through physics, economics, sociology, biology, and psychology.

5

This analysis of the components in modern gnostic speculation does not claim to be exhaustive, but it has been carried far enough for the more immediate purpose of elucidating the experiences that determine the political articulation of Western society under the symbolism of the Third Realm. There emerges the image of a society, identifiable and intelligible as a unit by its evolution as the representative of a historically unique type of gnostic truth. Following the Aristotelian procedure, the analysis started from the self-interpretation of society by means of the Joachitic symbols of the twelfth century. Now that their meaning has been clarified through theoretical understanding, a date can be assigned to the beginning of this civilizational course. A suitable date for its formal beginning would be the activation of ancient Gnosticism through Scotus Eriugena in the ninth century, because his works, as well as those of Dionysius Areopagita that he translated, were a continuous influence in the underground gnostic sects before they came to the surface in the twelfth and thirteenth centuries.

This is a long course of a thousand years, long enough to have aroused reflections on its decline and end. These reflections on Western society as a civilizational course that comes into view as a whole because it is moving intelligibly toward an end have raised one of the thorniest questions to plague the student of Western politics. On the one hand, as you know, there begins in the eighteenth century a continuous stream of literature on the decline of Western civilization; and, whatever misgivings one may entertain on this or that special argument, one cannot deny that the theorists of decline on the whole have a case. On the other hand, the same period is characterized, if by anything, by an exuberantly expansive vitality in the sciences, in technology, in the material control of environment, in the increase of population, of the standard of living, of health and comfort, of mass education, of social consciousness and responsibility; and again, whatever misgivings one may entertain with regard to this or that item on the list, one cannot deny that the progressivists have a case, too. This conflict of interpretations leaves in its wake the adumbrated thorny question, that is, the question how a civilization can advance and decline at the same time. A consideration of this question suggests itself, because it seems possible that the analysis of modern Gnosticism will furnish at least a partial solution of the problem.

Gnostic speculation overcame the uncertainty of faith by receding from transcendence and endowing man and his intramundane range of action with the meaning of eschatological fulfillment. In the measure in which this immanentization progressed experientially, civilizational activity became a mystical work of self-salvation. The spiritual strength of the soul that in Christianity was devoted to the sanctification of life could now be diverted into the more appealing, more tangible, and, above all, so much easier creation of the terrestrial paradise. Civilizational action became a *divertissement*, in the sense of Pascal, but a *divertissement* that demonically absorbed into itself the eternal destiny of man and substituted for the life of the spirit. Nietzsche most tersely expressed the nature of this demonic diversion when he raised the question why anyone should live in the embarrassing condition of a being in need of the love and grace of God. "Love yourself through grace" was his solution—"then you are no longer in need of your God, and you can act the whole drama of Fall and Redemption to its end in yourself."[32] And how can this miracle be achieved, this miracle of self-salvation, and how this redemption by extending grace to yourself? The great historical answer was given by the successive types of gnostic action that have made modern civilization what it is. The miracle was worked successively through the literary and artistic achievement that secured the immortality of fame for the humanistic intellectual, through the discipline and economic success that certified salvation to the Puritan saint, through the civilizational contributions of the liberals and Progressives, and, finally, through the revolutionary action that will establish the Communist or some other gnostic millennium. Gnosticism, thus, most effectively released human forces for the building of a civiliza-

32. Nietzsche, *Morgenröthe*, §79.

tion because on their fervent application to intramundane activity was put the premium of salvation. The historical result was stupendous. The resources of man that came to light under such pressure were in themselves a revelation, and their application to civilizational work produced the truly magnificent spectacle of Western progressive society. However fatuous the surface arguments may be, the widespread belief that modern civilization is Civilization in a pre-eminent sense is experientially justified; the endowment with the meaning of salvation has made the rise of the West, indeed, an apocalypse of civilization.

On this apocalyptic spectacle, however, falls a shadow; for the brilliant expansion is accompanied by a danger that grows apace with progress. The nature of this danger became apparent in the form that the idea of immanent salvation assumed in the Gnosticism of Comte. The founder of positivism institutionalized the premium on civilizational contributions in so far as he guaranteed immortality through preservation of the contributor and his deeds in the memory of mankind. There were provided honorific degrees of such immortality, and the highest honor would be the reception of the meritorious contributor into the calendar of positivistic saints. But what should in this order of things become of men who would rather follow God than the new Augustus Comte? Such miscreants who were not inclined to make their social contributions according to Comtean standards would simply be committed to the hell of social oblivion. The idea deserves attention. Here is a gnostic paraclete setting himself up as the world-immanent Last Judgment of mankind, deciding on immortality or annihilation for every human being. The material civilization of the West, to be sure, is still advancing; but on this rising plane of civilization the progressive symbolism of contributions, commemoration, and oblivion draws the contours of those "holes of oblivion" into which the divine redeemers of the gnostic empires drop their victims with a bullet in the neck. This end of progress was not contemplated in the halcyon days of gnostic exuberance. Milton released Adam and Eve with "a paradise within them, happier far" than the Paradise lost; when they went forth, "the world was all before them"; and they were cheered "with meditation on the happy end." But when historically man goes forth, with the gnostic "Paradise within him," and when he penetrates into the world before him, there is little cheer in meditation on the not so happy end.

The death of the spirit is the price of progress. Nietzsche revealed this mystery of the Western apocalypse when he announced that God was dead and that He had been murdered.[33] This gnostic murder is constantly committed by the men who sacrifice God to civilization. The more fervently all human energies are thrown into the great enterprise of salvation through world-immanent action, the farther the human beings who engage in this enterprise move away from the life of the spirit. And since the life of the spirit is the source of order in man and society, the very success of a gnostic civilization is the cause of its decline.

A civilization can, indeed, advance and decline at the same time —but not forever. There is a limit toward which this ambiguous process moves; the limit is reached when an activist sect that represents the gnostic truth organizes the civilization into an empire under its rule. Totalitarianism, defined as the existential rule of gnostic activists, is the end form of progressive civilization.

33. On the "murder of God" passages in Nietzsche, prehistory of the idea, and literary debate, see Lubac, *Le Drame de l'humanisme athée*, 40 ff. For the most comprehensive exposition of the idea of Nietzsche's work, see Karl Jaspers, *Nietzsche: Einführung in das Verständnis seines Philosophierens* (Berlin, 1936), under the references in the register.

5

Gnostic Revolution

The Puritan Case

I

The analysis of gnostic experiences has resulted in a concept of modernity that seems to be at variance with the conventional meaning of the term. Conventionally, Western history is divided into periods with a formal incision around 1500, the later period being the modern phase of Western society. If, however, modernity is defined as the growth of Gnosticism, beginning perhaps as early as the ninth century, it becomes a process within Western society extending deeply into its medieval period. Hence, the conception of a succession of phases would have to be replaced by that of a continuous evolution in which modern Gnosticism rises victoriously to predominance over a civilizational tradition deriving from the Mediterranean discoveries of anthropological and soteriological truth. This new conception in itself does no more than reflect the present state of empirical historiography and, therefore, is not in need of further justification. Nevertheless, there remains the question whether the conventional periodization has no bearing at all on the issue of Gnosticism; for it would be surprising, indeed, if a symbol that has gained such wide acceptance in the self-interpretation of Western society were not in some way connected with the fundamental problem of representation of truth.

In fact, such a connection exists. The conception of a modern age succeeding the Middle Ages is itself one of the symbols created by the gnostic movement. It belongs in the class of the Third Realm symbols. Ever since, in the fifteenth century, Biondo treated the millennium from the fall of Rome in 410 to the year 1410 as a closed age of the past, the symbol of a new, modern age has been used by the successive waves of humanistic, Protestant, and enlightened intellectuals for expressing their consciousness of being the representatives of a new truth. Precisely, however, because the world, under the guidance of the Gnostics, is being renewed at frequent intervals, it is impossible to arrive at a critically justified periodization while listening to their claims. By the immanent logic of its own theological symbolism each of the gnostic waves has as good a claim to consider itself the great wave of the future as any other. There is no reason why a modern period should begin with humanism rather than with the Reformation, or with Enlightenment rather than with Marxism. Hence, the problem cannot be solved on the level of gnostic symbolism. We must descend to the level of existential representation in order to find a motive for periodization. For an epoch would be marked indeed if, in the struggle for existential representation, there existed a decisive revolutionary victory of Gnosticism over the forces of Western tradition. If the question is stated in such terms, the conventional periodization becomes meaningful. While none of the movements deserves preference by the content of its truth, a clear epoch in Western history is marked by the Reformation, understood as the successful invasion of Western institutions by gnostic movements. The movements that hitherto existed in a socially marginal position—tolerated, suppressed, or underground—erupted in the Reformation with unexpected strength on a broad front, with the result of splitting the universal church and embarking on their gradual conquest of the political institutions in the national states.

The revolutionary eruption of the gnostic movements affected existential representation throughout Western society. The event is so vast in dimensions that no survey even of its general characteristics can be attempted in the present lectures. In order to convey an understanding of at least some of the more important traits of the gnostic revolution, it will be best to concentrate the analysis on a specific national area and on a specific phase within it. Certain aspects of the Puritan impact on the English public order will be the most suitable subject for a brief study. Moreover, this selection suggests itself because the English sixteenth century had the rare good fortune of a brilliant observer of the gnostic movement in the person of the "judicious Hooker." In the preface of his *Ecclesiastical Polity* Hooker gave an astute type study of the Puritan, as well as of the psychological mechanism by which gnostic mass movements operate. These pages are an invaluable asset for the student of the gnostic revolution; the present analysis will, therefore, properly begin with a summary of Hooker's portrait of the Puritan.

2

In order to start a movement moving, there must in the first place be somebody who has a "cause." From the context in Hooker it appears that the term "cause" was of recent usage in politics and that probably the Puritans had invented this formidable weapon of the gnostic revolutionaries. In order to advance his "cause," the man who has it will, "in the hearing of the multitude," indulge in severe criticisms of social evils and in particular of the conduct of the upper classes. Frequent repetition of the performance will induce the opinion among the hearers that the speakers must be men of singular integrity, zeal, and holiness, for only men who are singularly good can be so deeply offended by evil. The next step will be the concentration of popular ill-will on the established government. This task can be psychologically performed by attributing all fault and corruption, as it exists in the world because of human frailty, to the action or inaction of the government. By such imputation of evil to a specific institution the speakers prove their wisdom to the multitude of men who by themselves would never have thought of such a connection; and at the same time they show the point that must be attacked if evil shall be removed from this world. After such preparation, the time will be ripe for recommending a new form of government as the "sovereign remedy of all evils." For people who are "possessed with dislike and discontentment at things present" are crazed enough to "imagine that any thing (the virtue whereof they hear recommended) would help them; but the most, which they least have tried."

If a movement, like the Puritan, relies on the authority of a literary source, the leaders will then have to fashion "the very notions and conceits of men's minds in such a sort" that the followers will automatically associate scriptural passages and terms with their doctrine, however ill-founded the association may be, and that with equal automatism they will be blind to the content of Scripture that is incompatible with their doctrine. Next comes the decisive step in consolidating a gnostic attitude, that is, "the persuading of men credulous and overcapable of such pleasing errors, that it is the special illumination of the Holy Ghost, whereby they discern those things in the word, which others reading yet discern them not." They will experience themselves as the elect; and this experience breeds "high terms of separation between such and the rest of the world"; so that, as a consequence, mankind will be divided into the "brethren" and the "worldlings."

When gnostic experience is consolidated, the social raw material is ready for existential representation by a leader. For, Hooker continues, such people will prefer each other's company to that of the rest of the world, they will voluntarily accept counsel and direction from the indoctrinators, they will neglect their own affairs and devote excessive time to service of the cause, and they will extend generous material aid to the leaders of the movement. An especially important function in formation of such societies will have women, because they are weak in judgment, emotionally more accessible, tactically well placed to influence husbands, children, servants, and friends, more inclined than men to serve as a kind of intelligence officer concerning the state of affections in their circle, and more liberal in financial aid.

Once a social environment of this type is organized, it will be difficult, if not impossible, to break it up by persuasion. "Let any man of contrary opinion open his mouth to persuade them, they close up their ears, his reasons they weight not, all is answered with rehearsal of the words of John: 'We are of God; he that knoweth God heareth us': as for the rest ye are of the world: for this world's pomp and vanity it is that yet speak, and the world, whose ye are, heareth you." They are impermeable to argument and have their answers well drilled. Suggest to them that they are unable to judge in such matters, and they will answer, "God hath chosen the simple." Show them convincingly that they are talking nonsense, and you will hear "Christ's own apostle was accounted mad." Try the meekest warning of discipline, and they will be profuse on "the cruelty of bloodthirsty men" and cast themselves in the role of "innocency persecuted for the truth." In brief: The attitude is psychologically iron-clad and beyond shaking by argument.[1]

1. Richard Hooker, *Works*, ed. John Keble, 7th ed. (Oxford, 1888). The summary covers 1:145–55.

3

Hooker's description of the Puritan so clearly applies also to later types of gnostic revolutionaries that the point need not be labored. From his analysis, however, an issue emerges that deserves closer attention. The portrait of the Puritan resulted from a clash between Gnosticism, on the one side, and the classic and Christian tradition represented by Hooker, on the other side. It was drawn by a thinker of considerable intellectual qualities and erudition. The argument would, therefore, inevitably turn on the issue that in more recent treatments of Puritanism has been so badly neglected, that is, on the intellectual defects of the gnostic position that are apt to destroy the universe of rational discourse as well as the social function of persuasion. Hooker discerned that the Puritan position was not based on Scripture but was a "cause" of a vastly different origin. It would use Scripture when passages torn out of context would support the cause, and for the rest it would blandly ignore Scripture as well as the traditions and rules of interpretation that had been developed by fifteen centuries of Christianity. In the early phases of the gnostic revolution this camouflage was necessary—neither could an openly anti-Christian movement have been socially successful, nor had Gnosticism in fact moved so far away from Christianity that its carriers were conscious of the direction in which they were moving. Nevertheless, the distance was already large enough to make the camouflage embarrassing in the face of competent criticism. In order to ward off this embarrassment, two technical devices were developed that to this day have remained the great instruments of gnostic revolution.

In order to make the scriptural camouflage effective, the selections from Scripture, as well as the interpretation put upon them, had to be standardized. Real freedom of scriptural interpretation for everybody according to his preferences and state of education would have resulted in the chaotic conditions that characterized the early years of the Reformation; moreover, if one interpretation was admitted to be as good as another, there was no case against the tradition of the church, which, after all, was based on an interpretation of Scripture, too. From this dilemma between chaos and tradition emerged the first device, that is, the systematic formulation of the new doctrine in scriptural terms, as it was provided by Calvin's *Institutes*. A work of this type would serve the double purpose of a guide to the right reading of Scripture and of an authentic formulation of truth that would make recourse to earlier literature unnecessary. For the designation of this genus of gnostic literature a technical term is needed; since the study of gnostic phenomena is too recent to have developed one, the Arabic term *koran* will have to do for the present. The work of Calvin, thus, may be called the first deliberately created gnostic koran. A man who can write such a koran, a man who can break with the intellectual tradition of mankind because he lives in the faith that a new truth and a new world begin with him, must be in a peculiar pneumopathological state. Hooker, who was supremely conscious of tradition, had a fine sensitiveness for this twist of mind. In his cautiously subdued characterization of Calvin he opened with the sober statement: "His bringing up was in the study of civil law"; he then built up with some malice: "Divine knowledge he gathered, not by hearing or reading so much, as by teaching others"; and he concluded on the devastating sentence: "For, though thousands were debtors to him, as touching knowledge in that kind; yet he (was debtor) to none but only to God, the author of the most blessed fountain, the Book of Life, and of the admirable dexterity of wit."[2]

The work of Calvin was the first but not the last of its kind; moreover, the genus had a prehistory. In the early phases of Western gnostic sectarianism, the place of a koran was taken by the works of Scotus Eriugena and Dionysius Areopagita; and in the Joachitic movement the works of Joachim of Fiore played this role under the title of *Evangelium aeternum*. In later Western history, in the period of secularization, new korans were produced with every wave of the movement. In the eighteenth century, Diderot and D'Alembert claimed koranic function for the *Encyclopédie française* as the comprehensive presentation of all human knowledge worth preserving. According to their conception, nobody would have to use any work antedating the *Encyclopédie*, and all future sciences would assume the form of supplements to the great collection of knowledge.[3] In the nineteenth century, Auguste Comte created his own work as the koran for the positivistic future of mankind but generously supplemented it by his list of the one hundred great books—an idea that still has retained its appeal. In the Communist movement, finally,

2. Ibid., 127 ff.
3. D'Alembert, *Discours préliminaire de l'Encyclopédie*, ed. F. Picavet (Paris, 1894), 139–40.

the works of Karl Marx have become the koran of the faithful, supplemented by the patristic literature of Leninism-Stalinism.

The second device for preventing embarrassing criticism is a necessary supplement to the first one. The gnostic koran is the codification of truth and as such the spiritual and intellectual nourishment of the faithful. From contemporary experience with totalitarian movements it is well known that the device is fairly foolproof because it can reckon with the voluntary censorship of the adherents; the faithful member of a movement will not touch literature that is apt to argue against, or show disrespect for, his cherished beliefs. Nevertheless, the number of faithful may remain small, and expansion and political success will be seriously hampered, if the truth of the gnostic movement is permanently exposed to effective criticism from various quarters. This handicap can be reduced, and practically eliminated, by putting a taboo on the instruments of critique; a person who uses the tabooed instruments will be socially boycotted and, if possible, exposed to political defamation. The taboo on the instruments of critique was used, indeed, with superb effectiveness by the gnostic movements wherever they reached a measure of political success. Concretely, in the wake of the Reformation, the taboo had to fall on classic philosophy and scholastic theology; and, since under these two heads came the major and certainly the decisive part of Western intellectual culture, this culture was ruined to the extent to which the taboo became effective. In fact, the destruction went so deep that Western society has never completely recovered from the blow. An incident from Hooker's life will illustrate the situation. The anonymous *Christian Letter* of 1599, addressed to Hooker, complained bitterly: "In all your books, although we finde manie trueths and fine points bravely handled, yet in all your discourse, for the most parte, Aristotle the patriarche of philosophers (with divers other humane writers) and the ingenuous schoolemen, almost in all points have some finger: reason is highlie sett up against Holy Scripture, and reading against preaching."[4] Such complaints about violations of the taboo were not innocuous expressions of opinion. In 1585, in the affair with Travers, Hooker had been the target of similar charges; and they closed on the denunciatory tone that such "absurdities . . . have not been heard in public places within this land since Queen

4. Hooker, *Works,* 373.

Mary's day." In his answer to the Archbishop of Canterbury, Hooker very apologetically had to express his hope that he "committed no unlawful thing" when indulging in some theoretical distinctions and excursions in his sermons.[5]

Since Gnosticism lives by the theoretical fallacies that were discussed in the preceding lecture, the taboo on theory in the classic sense is the ineluctable condition of its social expansion and survival. This has a serious consequence with regard to the possibility of public debate in societies where gnostic movements have achieved social influence sufficient to control the means of communication, educational institutions, etc. To the degree to which such control is effective, theoretical debate concerning issues that involve the truth of human existence is impossible in public because the use of theoretical argument is prohibited. However well the constitutional freedoms of speech and press may be protected, however well theoretical debate may flourish in small circles, and however well it may be carried on in the practically private publications of a handful of scholars, debate in the politically relevant public sphere will be in substance the game with loaded dice that it has become in contemporary progressive societies—to say nothing of the quality of debate in totalitarian empires. Theoretical debate can be protected by constitutional guaranties, but it can be established only by the willingness to use and accept theoretical argument. When this willingness does not exist, a society cannot rely for its functioning on argument and persuasion where the truth of human existence is involved; other means will have to be considered.

This was the position of Hooker. Debate with his Puritan opponents was impossible because they would not accept argument. The ideas that he entertained in this predicament may be gathered from the notes jotted down, shortly before his death, on a copy of the previously quoted *Christian Letter.* Among the quotations from various authorities, there is a passage from Averroës:

> Discourse (*sermo*) about the knowledge which God in His glory has of Himself and the world is prohibited. And even more so is it prohibited to put it in writing. For, the understanding of the vulgar does not reach such profundities; and when it becomes the subject of their discussions, the divinity will be destroyed with them. Hence, discussion of this knowledge is prohibited to them; and it is sufficient for their felicity if they understand what they can perceive by their

5. Ibid., 3:585 ff.

intelligence. The law (that is: the *Koran*), whose primary intention it was to teach the vulgar, did not fail in intelligible communication about this subject because it is inaccessible to man; but we do not possess the human instruments that could assimilate God for intelligible communication about Him. As it is said: "His left hand founded the earth, but His right hand measured the Heaven." Hence, this question is reserved for the sage whom God dedicated to truth.[6]

In this passage Averroës expressed the solution that the problem of theoretical debate had found in Islamic civilization. The nucleus of truth is the experience of transcendence in the anthropological and soteriological sense; its theoretical explication is communicable only among the "sage." The "vulgar" have to accept, in a simple fundamentalism, the truth as it is symbolized in Scripture; they must refrain from theoretization, for which experientially and intellectually they are unfit, because they only would destroy God. Considering the "murder of God" that was committed in Western society when the progressivist "vulgar" got their fingers on the meaning of human existence in society and history, one must admit that Averroës had a point.

The structure of a civilization, however, is not at the disposition of its individual members. The Islamic solution of confining philosophical debate to esoteric circles of whose existence the people at large was hardly aware could not be transferred to Hooker's situation. Western history had taken a different course, and the debate of the "vulgar" was well under way. Hence, Hooker had to contemplate the second possibility that a debate, which could not end with agreement through persuasion, would have to be closed by governmental authority. His Puritan opponents were not partners in a theoretical debate; they were gnostic revolutionaries, engaged in a struggle for existential representation that would have resulted in the overthrow of the English social order, the control of the universities by Puritans, and the replacement of common law by scriptural law. Hence his consideration of this second solution was well in order. Hooker perfectly understood, what today is so little understood, that gnostic propaganda is political action and not perhaps a search of truth in the theoretical sense. With his unerring sensitiveness he even diagnosed the nihilistic component of Gnosticism in the Puritan belief that their discipline, being "the absolute command of Almighty God, it must be received although

6. For the Latin text of the passage see ibid., 1:cxix.

the world by receiving it should be clean turned upside down; herein lieth the greatest danger of all."[7] In the political culture of his time it was still clear beyond a doubt that the government, not the subjects, represents the order of a society. "As though when public consent of the whole hath established anything, every man's judgment being there unto compared were not private, howsoever his calling be to some public charge. So that of peace and quietness there is not any way possible, unless the probable voice of every entire society or body politic overrule all private of like nature in the same body."[8] This means concretely that a government has the duty to preserve the order as well as the truth that it represents; when a gnostic leader appears and proclaims that God or progress, race or dialectic, has ordained him to become the existential ruler, a government is not supposed to betray its trust and to abdicate. And this rule suffers no exception for governments that operate under a democratic constitution and a bill of rights. Justice Jackson in his dissent in the Terminiello case formulated the point: The Bill of Rights is not a suicide pact. A democratic government is not supposed to become an accomplice in its own overthrow by letting gnostic movements grow prodigiously in the shelter of a muddy interpretation of civil rights; and if through inadvertence such a movement has grown to the danger point of capturing existential representation by the famous "legality" of popular elections, a democratic government is not supposed to bow to the "will of the people" but to put down the danger by force and, if necessary, to break the letter of the constitution in order to save its spirit.

4

Thus far Hooker—and now the other side must be heard. The first point to be considered will be the peculiar experience of the gnostic revolutionaries. Against the usual treatment of Puritanism as a Christian movement must be held the fact that there is no passage in the New Testament from which advice for revolutionary political action could be extracted; and even the Revelation of Saint John, while burning with eschatological expectation of the realm that will deliver the saints from the oppression of this world, does not put the establishment of the realm into the hands of a Puritan

7. Ibid., 182.
8. Ibid., 171.

army. The gnostic revolutionary, however, interprets the coming of the realm as an event that requires his military co-operation. In chapter 20 of Revelation an angel comes down from heaven and throws Satan into the bottomless pit for a thousand years; in the Puritan Revolution the Gnostics arrogate this angelic function to themselves. A few passages from a pamphlet of 1641, entitled *A Glimpse of Sion's Glory*, will convey this peculiar mood of the gnostic revolution.

The author of the pamphlet is animated by eschatological expectations.[9] The fall of Babylon is at hand; the new Jerusalem will come soon. "Babylon's falling is Sion's raising. Babylon's destruction is Jerusalem's salvation." While God is the ultimate cause of the imminent happy change, men should indulge in some meritorious action, too, in order to hasten the coming. "Blessed is he that dasheth the brats of Babylon against the stones. Blessed is he that hath any hand in pulling down Babylon." And who are the men who will hasten the coming of Zion by dashing the brats of Babylon against the stones? They are "the common people." "God intends to make use of the common people in the great work of proclaiming the kingdom of his Son." The common people have a privileged status in advancing the Kingdom of Christ. For the voice of Christ "comes first from the multitude, the common people. The voice is heard from them first, before it is heard from any others. God uses the common people and the multitude to proclaim that the Lord God Omnipotent reigneth." Christ did not come to the upper classes; he came to the poor. The noble, the wise, and the rich, and especially the prelacy, are possessed by the spirit of Antichrist; and, hence, the voice of Christ "is like to begin from those that are the multitude, that are so contemptible," from "the vulgar multitude." In the past "the people of God have been, and are, a despised people." The Saints are called factious, schismatics and Puritans, seditious and disturbers of the state. This stigma, however, shall be taken from them; and the rulers will become convinced in their hearts that "the inhabitants of Jerusalem, that is, the Saints of God gathered in a church, are the best commonwealth's men." And this conviction of the rulers will be fortified by drastic changes in social relations. The author quotes Isa. 49:23: "Kings shall be thy nursing

9. *A Glimpse of Sion's Glory* (1641), attributed to Hanserd Knollys, in *Puritanism and Liberty*, ed. A. S. P. Woodhouse (London, 1938), 233–41.

fathers, and queens thy nursing mothers; they shall bow down to thee, and lick up the dust of thy feet." The Saints, on the other hand, will be glorified in the new realm; they "shall be all clothed in white linen, which is the righteousness of the Saints."

Besides the sartorial reform for the Saints and the dust-licking for the rulers, there will be incisive changes in the structure of legal and economic institutions. With regard to legal institutions, the beauty and glory of the realm will quite probably make legal compulsion unnecessary. "It is questionable whether there shall be need of ordinances, at least in that way that now there is. . . . The presence of Christ shall be there and supply all kind of ordinances." With regard to economic conditions there shall be abundance and prosperity. The whole world is purchased by Christ for the Saints; and it will be delivered. "All is yours, says the Apostle, the whole world"; and most candidly the author supplies the motive for his conviction: "You see that the Saints have little now in this world; now they are the poorest and meanest of all;, but then . . . the world shall be theirs. . . . Not only heaven shall be your kingdom, but this world bodily."

All this has nothing to do with Christianity. The scriptural camouflage cannot veil the drawing of God into man. The Saint is a gnostic who will not leave the transfiguration of the world to the grace of God beyond history but will do the work of God himself, right here and now, in history. To be sure, the author of the pamphlet knows that not ordinary human powers will establish the realm but that human efforts will be subsidiary to the action of God. The Omnipotent God will come to the aid of the Saints and "shall do these things, by that power, whereby he is able to subdue all things unto himself. Mountains shall be made plain, and he shall come skipping over mountains and over difficulties. Nothing shall hinder him." But in this God who comes skipping over the mountains we recognize the dialectics of history that comes skipping over thesis and antithesis, until it lands its believers in the plain of the Communist synthesis.

The second point to be considered will be the program of the revolutionaries for the organization of society after the old world has been made new by their efforts. As a rule, Gnostics are not very explicit on this point. The new, transfigured world is supposed to be free of the evils of the old world; and the description will, therefore, ordinarily indulge in negations of the present grievances.

The "glimpse" of Zion's glory is a category of gnostic description rather than the title of a random pamphlet. The "glimpse" will typically reveal a state of prosperity and abundance, a minimum of work, and the abolition of governmental compulsion; and as an entertainment of rather common appeal there may be thrown in some maltreatment of members of the former upper class. Beyond such glimpses the description usually peters out; and the better thinkers among gnostic revolutionaries, as, for instance, Marx and Engels, justify their reticence with the argument that one cannot say much about institutions of a transfigured society because we have no present experience of social relations under the condition of a transfigured nature of man. Fortunately, there is extant a Puritan document concerning the organization of the new world, in the form of the *Queries* directed by a group of Fifth Monarchy men to Lord Fairfax.[10]

At the time of the *Queries*, in 1649, the revolution was well under way; it had reached a stage corresponding to the stage of the Russian Revolution at which Lenin wrote about the "next tasks." In a similar manner one of the queries is phrased: "What then is the present interest of the Saints and people of God?" The reply advises that the Saints should associate in church societies and corporations according to the Congregational way; when enough such congregations have grown, they should combine into general assemblies or church parliaments according to the Presbyterian way; "and then shall God give them authority and rule over the nations and kingdoms of the world." Since this will be a spiritual kingdom, it cannot be established "by human power and authority." The Spirit itself will call and gather a people "and form them into several less families, churches and corporations"; and only when these spiritual nucleuses have sufficiently multiplied shall they "rule the world" through assemblies "of such officers of Christ, and representatives of the churches, as they shall choose and delegate." It all sounds comparatively harmless and harmonious; the worst that can happen will be some disillusionment when the Spirit takes its time in animating the new world.

As a matter of fact the affair is not quite so harmless. The Saints present their *Queries* to the Lord General of the Army and to the General Council of War. Under these conditions the formula that

10. *Certain Queries Presented by Many Christian People* (1649), 241–47.

God will give the Saints "authority and rule over the nations and kingdoms of the world" sounds a disturbing note. One may ask: Who are these nations and kingdoms of the world over whom the Saints will rule? Are they the nations and kingdoms of the old world? But in that case we would not yet be in the new world. And when we are in the new world—over whom could the Saints rule except themselves? Or will there be some miscreant old-world nations left whom the Saints can bully at their ease in order to add flavor to their new ruling position? In brief: The shape of things to come looks very much like what later Gnostics call the dictatorship of the proletariat.

The suspicion is confirmed by further details. The *Queries* distinguish between "officers of Christ" and "Christian magistrates." The rule of the spirit will put down all worldly rule, including the rule of the Christian magistrates of England. The distinction is the best evidence that in revolutions of the Puritan variety, indeed, two types of truth are struggling for existential representation. The *Queries* accord the name of Christianity to both types of truth, but the types are so radically different that they represent the worlds of darkness and light, respectively. The Puritan victory may preserve the structure of the world, including the parliamentary institutions of England, but the animating spirit will have radically changed. And this radical change will express itself politically in the radical change of the ruling personnel. The petitioners ask persuasively: "Consider whether it be not a far greater honour for parliaments, magistrates, etc., to rule as Christ's officers and the churches' representatives than as officers of a worldly kingdom and representatives of a mere natural and worldly people?" It is not enough to be a Christian representative of the English people in Parliament, for the people as such belong in the natural order of the old world; the member of Parliament must represent the Saints and the communities of the new kingdom that are informed by the Spirit itself. Hence, the old political ruling group must be eliminated for "what right or claim have mere natural and worldly men to rule and government, that want a sanctified claim to the least outward blessings?" And even more pointedly: "How can the kingdom be the Saints' when the ungodly are electors, and elected to govern?" The attitude is uncompromising. If we expect new heavens and a new earth, "how then can it be lawful to patch up the old worldly government?" The only righteous course will be the one that results in "suppressing the enemies of godliness for ever."

No elaborate interpretation is necessary. A few modernizations of language are sufficient to bring out the meaning of these suggestions. The historical order of the people is broken by the rise of a movement that does not belong to "this world." Social evils cannot be reformed by legislation; defects of governmental machinery cannot be repaired by changes in the constitution; differences of opinion cannot be settled by compromise. "This world" is darkness that must give way to the new light. Hence, coalition governments are impossible. The political figures of the old order cannot be re-elected in the new world; and the men who are not members of the movement will be deprived of their right to vote in the new order. All these changes will arrive substantially through the "Spirit" or, as Gnostics would say today, through the dialectics of history; but in political procedure the saintly comrades will take a hand, and the hand will be well armed. If the personnel of the old order should not disappear with a smile, the enemies of godliness will be suppressed or, in contemporary language, will be purged. In the *Queries* the realization of the new world has reached the stage at which, in the Russian Revolution, Lenin wrote his reflections under the coquettish title, "Will the Bolsheviks Retain State Power?" They will, indeed; and nobody will share it with them.

The new kingdom will be universal in substance as well as universal in its claim to dominion; it will extend "to all persons and things universally." The revolution of the Gnostics has for its aim the monopoly of existential representation. The Saints can foresee that the universalism of their claim will not be accepted without a struggle by the world of darkness but that it will produce an equally universal alliance of the world against them. The Saints, therefore, will have to combine "against the Antichristian powers of the world"; and the Antichristian powers in their turn will "combine against them universally." The two worlds that are supposed to follow each other chronologically will, thus, become in historical reality two universal armed camps engaged in a death struggle against each other. From the gnostic mysticism of the two worlds emerges the pattern of the universal wars that has come to dominate the twentieth century. The universalism of the gnostic revolutionary produces the universal alliance against him. The real danger of contemporary wars does not lie in the technologically determined global extent of the theater of war; their true fatality stems from their character as gnostic wars, that is, of wars between worlds that are bent on mutual destruction.

The selection of materials that are meant to illustrate the nature and direction of the gnostic revolution may seem unfair. A critic might object that Puritanism as a whole cannot be identified with its left wing. Such criticism would be justified if it had been the intention to give a historical account of Puritanism. The present analysis, however, is concerned with the structure of gnostic experiences and ideas; and this structure is also to be found where the consequences are toned down to the respectability of Calvin's *Institutes* or of Presbyterian covenantism. The amplitude from right to left within every wave of the movement, the struggle between the two wings on occasion of the acute outbreaks in the several national areas, as well as the temporary stabilizations of a viable order, are phenomena within the gnostic revolution that will receive further attention in the last of these lectures. These phenomena, the dynamics of the revolution, however, do not affect its nature; and the nature can, indeed, be studied best in its radical expressions where it is not obscured by compromises with the exigencies of political success. Moreover, this is not a mere matter of convenience but a methodological necessity. The gnostic revolution has for its purpose a change in the nature of man and the establishment of a transfigured society. Since this program cannot be carried out in historical reality, gnostic revolutionaries must inevitably institutionalize their partial or total success in the existential struggle by a compromise with reality; and whatever emerges from this compromise—it will not be the transfigured world envisaged by gnostic symbolism. If, therefore, the theorist would study the gnostic revolution at the level of its temporary stabilizations, of its political tactics, or of the moderate programs that already envisage the compromise, the nature of Gnosticism, the driving force of Western revolution, could never come into view. The compromise would be taken for the essence, and the essential unity of the variegated gnostic phenomena would disappear.

5

The English Revolution made it clear that the struggle of gnostic revolutionaries for existential representation could destroy the public order of a great nation—if such proof was needed after the eight civil wars in France and the Thirty Years' War in Germany. The problem of public order was overdue for theoretical restatement, and in Thomas Hobbes this task found a thinker who was equal to it. The new theory of representation that Hobbes developed in the *Leviathan,* to be sure, purchased its impressive consistency at the price of a simplification that itself belongs in the class of gnostic misdeeds; but when a fierce and relentless thinker simplifies, he will nevertheless bring a new clarity to the issue. The simplification can be repaired, while the new clarity will be a permanent gain.

The Hobbesian theory of representation cuts straight to the core of the predicament. On the one hand, there is a political society that wants to maintain its established order in historical existence; on the other hand, there are private individuals within the society who want to change the public order, if necessary by force, in the name of a new truth. Hobbes solved the conflict by deciding that there was no public truth except the law of peace and concord in a society; any opinion or doctrine conducive to discord was thereby proved untrue.[11] In order to support his decision, Hobbes used the following argument:

(1) There is conscious to man a dictate of reason that disposes him to peace and obedience under a civil order. Reason makes him, first, understand that he can live out his natural life in pursuit of his worldly happiness only under the condition that he lives in peace with his fellow-men; and it makes him, second, understand that he can live in peace, without distrust of the other man's intentions, only under the condition that every man's passions are curbed to mutual forbearance by the overwhelming force of a civil government.[12]

(2) This dictate of reason, however, would be no more than a theorem without obligatory force unless it were understood as the hearing of the word of God, as His command promulgated in the soul of man; only in so far as the dictate of reason is believed to be a divine command is it a law of nature.[13]

(3) This law of nature, finally, is not a law actually governing human existence before the men, in whom it lives as a disposition

---

11. Thomas Hobbes, *Leviathan,* ed. Michael Oakeshott (Oxford: Blackwell, 1946), chap. 18, p. 116.

12. Ibid., chap. 14.

13. Ibid., chap. 15, pp. 104 ff., chap. 31, p. 233.

toward peace, have followed its precept by combining in a civil society under a public representative, the sovereign. Only when they have covenanted to submit to a common sovereign, has the law of nature actually become the law of a society in historical existence.[14] "The law of nature, and the civil law, therefore, contain each other, and are of equal extent."[15]

Existential and transcendental representation, thus, meet in the articulation of a society into ordered existence. By combining into a political society under a representative, the covenanting members actualize the divine order of being in the human sphere.[16]

Into this somewhat empty vessel of a political society, now, Hobbes pours the Western-Christian civilizational content by letting it pass through the bottleneck of sanction by the sovereign representative. The society may well be a Christian commonwealth because the Word of God revealed in Scripture is not at variance with natural law.[17] Nevertheless, the canon of Scripture to be received,[18] the doctrinal and ritual interpretations put on it,[19] as well as the form of clerical organization,[20] will derive their authority not from revelation but from the enactment by the sovereign as the law of the land. There will be no freedom of debate concerning the truth of human existence in society; public expression of opinion and doctrine must be under regulation and permanent supervision of the government. "For the actions of men proceed from their opinions; and in the well-governing of opinions, consisteth the well-governing of men's actions, in order to their peace, and concord." Hence, the sovereign has to decide who will be allowed to speak in public to an audience, on what subject and in what tendency; there will be necessary, furthermore, a preventive censorship of books.[21] For the rest, there will be freedom for the peaceable, civilizational pursuits of the citizens, since this is the purpose for which men combine in a civil society.[22]

In judging the Hobbesian theory of representation, one must avoid the ready pitfalls of current political jargon. Nothing can

14. Ibid., chap. 15, p. 94.
15. Ibid., chap. 26, p. 174.
16. Ibid., chap. 31, p. 233.
17. Ibid., chap. 32, p. 242.
18. Ibid., chap. 33, pp. 246 ff.
19. Ibid., 254 ff.
20. Ibid., chap. 42, pp. 355–56.
21. Ibid., chap. 18, pp. 116 ff.
22. Ibid., chap. 21, pp. 138 ff.

be gained from weighing the theory on the scales of liberty and authority; nothing from classifying Hobbes as an absolutist or fascist. A critical interpretation must follow the theoretical intentions indicated by Hobbes himself in his work. These intentions can be gathered from the following passage:

> For it is evident to the meanest capacity, that men's actions are derived from their opinions they have of the good or evil, which from those actions redound unto themselves; and consequently, men that are once possessed of an opinion, that their obedience to the sovereign power will be more hurtful to them than their disobedience, will disobey the laws, and thereby overthrow the commonwealth, and introduce confusion and civil war; for the avoiding whereof all civil government was ordained. And therefore in all commonwealths of the heathen, the sovereigns have had the name of pastors of the people, because there was no subject that could lawfully teach the people, but by their permission and authority.

And it cannot be the purpose of Christianity, Hobbes continues, to deprive the sovereigns "of the power necessary for the conservation of peace amongst their subjects, and for their defence against foreign enemies."[23]

From the passage emerges Hobbes's intention of establishing Christianity (understood as identical in substance with the law of nature) as an English *theologia civilis* in the Varronic sense. At the first hearing such an intention may sound self-contradictory. How can the Christian *theologia supranaturalis* be established as a *theologia civilis*? In making this curious attempt, Hobbes brought into the open a problem that was left in suspense in our own earlier analysis of the *genera theologiae* and their conflict in the Roman Empire. You will remember that Saint Ambrose and Saint Augustine were oddly insensitive to the fact that a Christian on the throne would, under their guidance, treat pagans in the same manner in which pagan emperors had formerly treated Christians. They understood Christianity as a truth of the soul superior to polytheism but did not recognize that the Roman gods symbolized the truth of Roman society; that with the cult a culture was destroyed, as Celsus had discerned; that an existential victory of Christianity was not a conversion of individual human beings to a higher truth but the forceful imposition of a new *theologia civilis* on a society. In the case of Hobbes the situation is reversed. When he

23. Ibid., chap. 42, p. 355.

treats Christianity under the aspect of its substantial identity with the dictate of reason and derives its authority from governmental sanction, he shows himself as oddly insensitive to its meaning as a truth of the soul as were the Patres to the meaning of the Roman gods as a truth of society. In order to reach the root of these oddities, it will be necessary to reconsider the epochal event of the opening of the soul and to add a theoretical distinction.

The opening of the soul was an epochal event in the history of mankind because, with the differentiation of the soul as the sensorium of transcendence, the critical, theoretical standards for the interpretation of human existence in society, as well as the source of their authority, came into view. When the soul opened toward transcendent reality, it found a source of order superior in rank to the established order of society as well as a truth in critical opposition to the truth at which society had arrived through the symbolism of its self-interpretation. Moreover, the idea of a universal God as the measure of the open soul had as its logical correlate the idea of a universal community of mankind, beyond civil society, through the participation of all men in the common measure, be it understood as the Aristotelian nous, the Stoic or the Christian logos. The impact of such discoveries might well obscure the fact that the new clarity about the structure of reality had not changed this structure itself. The opening of the soul, indeed, marked an epoch through its advancement from compactness to differentiation of experience, from dimness to clarity of insight; but the tension between a truth of society and a truth of the soul had existed before this epoch, and the new understanding of transcendence could sharpen the consciousness of the tension but not remove it from the constitution of being. The idea of a universal God, for instance, achieved its specific purity through the mystic philosophers, but its existence, imbedded in a compact cosmological myth, is attested by Egyptian inscriptions for about 3000 B.C.; and since, even at this early date, the idea appeared in the course of a polemical, critical speculation on hierarchy and function of gods, there must have existed the tension between a truth as understood by the speculating thinker and the truth of the received myth.[24] The Stoic understanding of the cosmopolis to which men belong

24. William F. Albright, *From the Stone Age to Christianity: Monotheism and the Historical Process* (Baltimore, 1946), 132 ff.; Hermann Junker, *Pyramidenzeit: Das Wesen der altägyptischen Religion* (Zurich, 1949), 18 ff.

by virtue of their participation in the Logos, on the other hand, did not abolish the existence of man in finite historical societies. Hence, we must distinguish between the opening of the soul as an epoch in experiential differentiation and the structure of reality, which remains unchanged.

From the distinction it follows for the present problem that the tension between a differentiated truth of the soul and the truth of society cannot be eliminated from historical reality by throwing out the one or the other. Human existence in natural societies remains what it was before its orientation toward a destiny beyond nature. Faith is the anticipation of a supernatural perfection of man; it is not this perfection itself. The realm of God is not of this world; and the representative of the *civitas Dei* in history, the church, is not a substitute for civil society. The result of the epochal differentiation is not the replacement of the closed society by an open society—if we may use the Bergsonian terms—but a complication of symbolism that corresponds to the differentiation of experiences. Both types of truth will from now on exist together; and the tension between the two, in various degrees of consciousness, will be a permanent structure of civilization. This insight had been gained already by Plato; in his work it is reflected in the evolution from the *Republic* to the *Laws*. In the *Republic* he constructed a polis that would incarnate the truth of the soul under the immediate rule of mystic philosophers; it was an attempt to dissolve the tension by making the order of the soul the order of society. In the *Laws* he removed the truth of the soul into the distance of its revelation in the *Republic*; the polis of the *Laws* relied on institutions that mirrored the order of the cosmos, while the truth of the soul was mediated by administrators who received it as dogma. Plato himself, the potential philosopher-king of the Republic, became the Athenian Stranger of the Laws who assisted in devising institutions that embodied as much of the spirit as was compatible with the continued natural existence of society.

The Christian Patres did not display the perspicacity of Plato when the same problem was forced upon them by historical circumstance. Apparently they did not understand that Christianity could supersede polytheism but not abolish the need of a civil theology. When the truth of the soul had prevailed, the vacuum was left that Plato had tried to fill with his construction of the polis as a cosmic analogue. The filling of this vacuum became a major problem wherever Christianity dissolved the pre-Christian truth of the closed society as a living force; wherever, as a consequence, the church achieved existential representation by the side of the civil ruler and now had to provide transcendental legitimation for the order of society, in addition to its representation of the supranatural destiny of man. The one great solution was Byzantine Caesaropapism, with its tendency toward transforming the church into a civil institution. Against this tendency, at the end of the fifth century, Gelasius wrote his letters and tracts that formulated the other great solution, that of the two balancing powers. This balance functioned in the West as long as the work of civilizational expansion and consolidation provided parallel interests for ecclesiastic and civil organizations. But the tension between the two types of truth became noticeable as soon as a certain degree of civilizational saturation was reached. When the church, in the wake of the Cluniac reform, reasserted its spiritual substance and tried to disengage itself from its civil entanglements, the investiture struggle was the consequence. On the other hand, when the gnostic sectarian movements gained momentum in the twelfth century, the church co-operated, through the Inquisition, with the civil power in the persecution of heretics; it leaned strongly toward its function as the agent of the *theologia civilis* and thereby became untrue to its essence as the representative of the *civitas Dei* in history. The tension, finally, reached the breaking point when a plurality of schismatic churches and gnostic movements entered into violent competition for existential representation. The vacuum now became manifest in the religious civil wars.

Hobbes saw that public order was impossible without a civil theology beyond debate; it is the great and permanent achievement of the *Leviathan* to have clarified this point. Less fortunate was his hand when he tried to fill the vacuum by establishing Christianity as the English civil theology. He could entertain this idea because he assumed Christianity, if properly interpreted, to be identical with the truth of society that he had developed in the first two parts of the *Leviathan*. He denied the existence of a tension between the truth of the soul and the truth of society; the content of Scripture, in his opinion, coincided in substance with the truth of Hobbes. On the basis of this assumption, he could indulge in the idea of solving a crisis of world-historical proportions by tendering his expert advice to any sovereign who was willing to take it. "I recover some hope," he said, "that one time or other, this writing of mine may fall into the hands of a sovereign, who will consider it himself, (for it is short, and I think clear), without the help of any interested, or envious interpreter; and by the exercise of entire sovereignty, in protecting the public teaching of it, convert this truth of speculation, into the utility of practice."[25] He saw himself in the role of a Plato, in quest of a king who would adopt the new truth and indoctrinate the people with it. The education of the people was an essential part of his program. Hobbes did not rely on governmental force for suppressing religious movements; he knew that public order was genuine only if the people accepted it freely and that free acceptance was possible only if the people understood obedience to the public representative as their duty under eternal law. If the people were ignorant of this law, they would consider punishment for rebellion an "act of hostility; which when they think they have strength enough, they will endeavour by acts of hostility, to avoid." He, therefore, declared it the duty of the sovereign to repair the ignorance of the people by appropriate information. If that were done, there might be hope that his principles would "make their constitution, excepting by external violence, everlasting."[26] With this idea, however, of abolishing the tensions of history by the spreading of a new truth, Hobbes reveals his own gnostic intentions; the attempt at freezing history into an everlasting constitution is an instance of the general class of gnostic attempts at freezing history into an everlasting final realm on this earth.

The idea of solving the troubles of history through the invention of the everlasting constitution made sense only under the condition that the source of these troubles, that is, the truth of the soul, would cease to agitate man. Hobbes, indeed, simplified the structure of politics by throwing out anthropological and soteriological truth. This is an understandable desire in a man who wants his peace; things, to be sure, would be so much simpler without philosophy and Christianity. But how can one dispose of them without abolishing the experiences of transcendence that belong to the nature of

25. Hobbes, *Leviathan*, chap. 31, p. 241.
26. Ibid., chap. 30, pp. 220 ff.

man? Hobbes was quite able to solve this problem, too; he improved on the man of God's creation by creating a man without such experiences. At this point, however, we are entering the higher regions of the gnostic dream world. This further Hobbesian enterprise must be placed in the larger context of the Western crisis; and that will be a task for the last of these lectures.

6

The End of Modernity

I

Hobbes had discerned the lack of a *theologia civilis* as the source of difficulties that plagued the state of England in the Puritan crisis. The various groups engaged in the civil war were so heaven-bent on having the public order represent the right variety of transcendent truth that the existential order of society was in danger of floundering in the melee. It certainly was an occasion to rediscover the discovery of Plato that a society must exist as an ordered cosmion, as a representative of cosmic order, before it can indulge in the luxury of also representing a truth of the soul. To represent the truth of the soul in the Christian sense is the function of the church, not of civil society. If a plurality of churches and sects starts fighting for control of the public order, and none of them is strong enough to gain an unequivocal victory, the logical result can only be that, by the existential authority of the public representative, the whole lot will be relegated to the position of private associations within the society. This problem of existence was touched on several occasions in these lectures; it now requires a summary elucidation before the Hobbesian idea of man can be presented and evaluated. The analysis will suitably start from the points that have already been secured.

Christianity had left in its wake the vacuum of a de-divinized natural sphere of political existence. In the concrete situation of the late Roman Empire and the early Western political foundations, this vacuum did not become a major source of troubles as long as the myth of the empire was not seriously disturbed by the consolidation of national realms and as long as the church was the predominant civilizing factor in the evolution of Western society, so that Christianity in fact could function as a civil theology. As soon, however, as a certain point of civilizational saturation was reached, when centers of lay culture formed at the courts and in the cities, when competent lay personnel increased in royal administrations and city governments, it became abundantly clear that the problems of a society in historical existence were not exhausted by waiting for the end of the world. The rise of Gnosticism at this critical juncture now appears in a new light as the incipient formation of a Western civil theology. The immanentization of the Christian eschaton made it possible to endow society in its natural existence with a meaning that Christianity denied to it. And the totalitarianism of our time must be understood as journey's end of the gnostic search for a civil theology.

The gnostic experiment in civil theology, however, was fraught with dangers, flowing from its hybrid character as a Christian derivative. The first of these dangers has been discussed already. It was the tendency of Gnosticism not to supplement but to supplant the truth of the soul. Gnostic movements were not satisfied with filling the vacuum of civil theology; they tended to abolish Christianity. In the earlier phases of the movement the attack was still disguised as Christian "spiritualization" or "reform"; in the later phases, with the more radical immanentization of the eschaton, it became openly anti-Christian. As a consequence, wherever gnostic movements spread they destroyed the truth of the open soul; a whole area of differentiated reality that had been gained by philosophy, and Christianity was ruined. And again it is necessary to remember that the advance of Gnosticism is not a return to paganism. In the pre-Christian civilizations the truth that differentiated with the opening of the soul was present in the form of compact experiences; in gnostic civilizations the truth of the soul does not return to compactness but is repressed altogether. This repression of the authoritative source of order in the soul is the cause of the bleak atrocity of totalitarian governments in their dealings with individual human beings.

The peculiar, repressive result of the growth of Gnosticism in Western society suggests the conception of a civilizational cycle of world-historic proportions. There emerge the contours of a giant cycle, transcending the cycles of the single civilizations. The acme of this cycle would be marked by the appearance of Christ; the pre-Christian high civilizations would form its ascending branch; modern, gnostic civilization would form its descending branch. The pre-Christian high civilizations advanced from the compactness of experience to the differentiation of the soul as the sensorium of transcendence; and, in the Mediterranean civilizational area, this evolution culminated in the maximum of differentiation, through the revelation of the Logos in history. In so far as the pre-Christian civilizations advance toward this maximum of the advent, their dynamics may be called "adventitious." Modern gnostic civilization reverses the tendency toward differentiation, and, in so far as it recedes from the maximum, its dynamics may be called "recessive." While Western society has its own cycle of growth, flowering, and decline, it must be considered—because of the growth of Gnosticism in its course—as the declining branch of the larger advent-recession cycle.

These reflections open a perspective on the future dynamics of civilization. Modern Gnosticism has by far not spent its drive. On the contrary, in the variant of Marxism it is expanding its area of influence prodigiously in Asia, while other variants of Gnosticism, such as progressivism, positivism, and scientism, are penetrating into other areas under the title of "Westernization" and development of backward countries. And one may say that in Western society itself the drive is not spent but that our own "Westernization" is still on the increase. In the face of this worldwide expansion it is necessary to state the obvious: that human nature does not change. The closure of the soul in modern Gnosticism can repress the truth of the soul, as well as the experiences that manifest themselves in philosophy and Christianity, but it cannot remove the soul and its transcendence from the structure of reality. Hence the question imposes itself: How long can such a repression last? And what will happen when prolonged and severe repression will lead to an explosion? It is legitimate to ask such questions concerning the dynamics of the future because they spring from a methodically correct application of theory to an empirically observed component of contemporary civilization. It would not be legitimate, however, to indulge in speculations about the form that the explosion will assume, beyond the reasonable assumption that the reaction against Gnosticism will be as worldwide as its expansion. The number of complicating factors is so large that predictions seem futile. Even for our own Western society one can hardly do more than point to the fact that Gnosticism, in spite of its noisy ascendancy, does by far not have the field for itself; that the classic and Christian tradition of Western society is rather alive; that the building-up of spiritual and intellectual resistance against Gnosticism in all its variants is a notable factor in our society; that the reconstruction of a science of man and society is one of the remarkable events of the last half-century and, in retrospect from a future vantage point, will perhaps appear as the most important event in our time. Still less can be said, for obvious reasons, about the probable reaction of a living Christian tradition against Gnosticism in the Soviet empire, and nothing at all about the manner in which Chinese, Hindu, Islamic, and primitive civilizations will react to a prolonged exposure to gnostic devastation and repression. Only on one point at least a reasonable surmise is possible, that is, on the date of the explosion. The date in objective time, of course, is quite unpredictable; but Gnosticism contains a self-defeating factor, and this factor makes it at least probable that the date is less distant than one would assume under the impression of gnostic power of the moment. This self-defeating factor is the second danger of Gnosticism as a civil theology.

2

The first danger was the destruction of the truth of the soul. The second danger is intimately connected with the first one. The truth of Gnosticism is vitiated, as you will remember, by the fallacious immanentization of the Christian eschaton. This fallacy is not simply a theoretical mistake concerning the meaning of the eschaton, committed by this or that thinker, perhaps an affair of the schools. On the basis of this fallacy, gnostic thinkers, leaders, and their followers interpret a concrete society and its order as an eschaton; and, in so far as they apply their fallacious construction to concrete social problems, they misrepresent the structure of immanent reality. The eschatological interpretation of history results in a false picture of reality; and errors with regard to the structure of reality have practical consequences when the false conception is made the basis of political action. Specifically, the gnostic fallacy destroys the oldest wisdom of mankind concerning the rhythm of growth and decay that is the fate of all things under the sun. The Kohelet says:

> To every thing there is a season,
> And a time to every purpose under heaven:
> A time to be born and a time to die.

And then, reflecting on the finiteness of human knowledge, the Kohelet continues to say that the mind of man cannot fathom "the work that God maketh from the beginning to the end."[1] What comes into being will have an end, and the mystery of this stream of being is impenetrable. These are the two great principles governing existence. The gnostic speculation on the eidos of history, however, not only ignores these principles but perverts them into their opposite. The idea of the final realm assumes a society that will come into being but have no end, and the mystery of the stream is solved through the speculative knowledge of its goal. Gnosticism, thus, has produced something like the counterprinciples to the principles of existence; and, in so far as these principles determine an image of reality for the masses of the faithful, it has created a dream world that itself is a social force of the first importance in motivating attitudes and actions of gnostic masses and their representatives.

The phenomenon of a dream world, based on definite principles, requires some explanation. It could hardly be possible as a historical mass phenomenon unless it were rooted in a fundamental experiential drive. Gnosticism as a counterexistential dream world can perhaps be made intelligible as the extreme expression of an experience that is universally human, that is, of a horror of existence and a desire to escape from it. Specifically, the problem can be stated in the following terms: A society, when it exists, will interpret its order as part of the transcendent order of being. This self-interpretation of society as a mirror of cosmic order, however, is part of social reality itself. The ordered society, together with its self-understanding, remains a wave in the stream of being; the Aeschylean polis with its ordering Dike is an island in a sea of demonic disorder, precariously maintaining itself in existence. Only the order of an existing society is intelligible; its existence itself is unintelligible. The successful articulation of a society is a fact that has become possible under favorable circumstances; and this fact may be annulled by unfavorable circumstances, as, for instance, by the appearance of a stronger, conquering power. The *fortuna secunda et adversa* is the smiling and terrible goddess who rules over this realm of existence. This

1. Eccles. 3:1–2 and 3:11.

hazard of existence without right or reason is a demonic horror; it is hard to bear even for the stronghearted; and it is hardly bearable for tender souls who cannot live without believing they deserve to live. It is a reasonable assumption, therefore, that in every society there is present, in varying degrees of intenseness, the inclination to extend the meaning of its order to the fact of its existence. Especially when a society has a long and glorious history, its existence will be taken for granted as part of the order of things. It has become unimaginable that the society could simply cease to exist; and when a great symbolic blow falls, as, for instance, when Rome was conquered in 410, a groan went through the *orbis terrarum* that now the end of the world had come.

In every society, thus, is present an inclination to extend the meaning of order to the fact of existence, but in predominantly gnostic societies this extension is erected into a principle of self-interpretation. This shift from a mood, from a lassitude to take existence for granted, to a principle determines a new pattern of conduct. In the first case, one can speak of an inclination to disregard the structure of reality, of relaxing into the sweetness of existence, of a decline of civic morality, of a blindness to obvious dangers, and a reluctance to meet them with all seriousness. It is the mood of late, disintegrating societies that no longer are willing to fight for their existence. In the second, the gnostic case, the psychological situation is entirely different. In Gnosticism the nonrecognition of reality is a matter of principle; in this case, one would have rather to speak of an inclination to remain aware of the hazard of existence in spite of the fact that it is not admitted as a problem in the gnostic dream world; nor does the dream impair civic responsibility or the readiness to fight valiantly in case of an emergency. The attitude toward reality remains energetic and active, but neither reality nor action in reality can be brought into focus; the vision is blurred by the gnostic dream. The result is a very complex pneumopathological state of mind, as it was adumbrated by Hooker's portrait of the Puritan.

The study of the phenomenon in its contemporary varieties, however, has become more difficult than it was at Hooker's time. In the sixteenth century the dream world and the real world were still held apart terminologically through the Christian symbolism of the two worlds. The disease, and its special variety, could be diagnosed easily because the patient himself was supremely conscious that the new world was not the world in which he lived in reality. With radical immanentization the dream world has blended into the real world terminologically; the obsession of replacing the world of reality with the transfigured dream world has become the obsession of the one world in which the dreamers adopt the vocabulary of reality, while changing its meaning, as if the dream were reality.

An example will best show the nature of the difficulty for the student. In classic and Christian ethics the first of the moral virtues is *sophia* or *prudentia*, because without adequate understanding of the structure of reality, including the *conditio humana*, moral action with rational co-ordination of means and ends is hardly possible. In the gnostic dream world, on the other hand, nonrecognition of reality is the first principle. As a consequence, types of action that in the real world would be considered as morally insane because of the real effects that they have will be considered moral in the dream world because they intended an entirely different effect. The gap between intended and real effect will be imputed not to the gnostic immorality of ignoring the structure of reality but to the immorality of some other person or society that does not behave as it should behave according to the dream conception of cause and effect. The interpretation of moral insanity as morality, and of the virtues of *sophia* and *prudentia* as immorality, is a confusion difficult to unravel. And the task is not facilitated by the readiness of the dreamers to stigmatize the attempt at critical clarification as an immoral enterprise. As a matter of fact, practically every great political thinker who recognized the structure of reality, from Machiavelli to the present, has been branded as an immoralist by gnostic intellectuals—to say nothing of the parlor game, so much beloved among liberals, of panning Plato and Aristotle as fascists. The theoretical difficulty, therefore, is aggravated by personal problems. And there can be no doubt that the continuous gnostic barrage of vituperation against political science in the critical sense has seriously affected the quality of public debate on contemporary political issues.

The identification of dream and reality as a matter of principle has practical results that may appear strange but can hardly be considered surprising. The critical exploration of cause and effect in history is prohibited; and consequently the rational co-ordination of means and ends in politics is impossible. Gnostic societies and their leaders will recognize dangers to their existence when they develop, but such dangers will not be met by appropriate actions in the world of reality. They will rather be met by magic operations in the dream world, such as disapproval, moral condemnation, declarations of intention, resolutions, appeals to the opinion of mankind, branding of enemies as aggressors, outlawing of war, propaganda for world peace and world government, etc. The intellectual and moral corruption that expresses itself in the aggregate of such magic operations may pervade a society with the weird, ghostly atmosphere of a lunatic asylum, as we experience it in our time in the Western crisis.

A complete study of the manifestations of gnostic insanity in the practice of contemporary politics would go far beyond the framework of this lecture. The analysis must concentrate on the symptom that will best illustrate the self-defeating character of gnostic politics, that is, the oddity of continuous warfare in a time when every political society, through its representatives, professes its ardent desire for peace. In an age when war is peace, and peace is war, a few definitions will be in order to assure the meaning of the terms. Peace shall mean a temporary order of social relations that adequately expresses a balance of existential forces. The balance may be disturbed by various causes, such as population increases in one area or decreases in another one, technological developments that favor areas rich in the necessary raw materials, changes of trade routes, etc. War shall mean the use of violence for the purpose of restoring a balanced order by either repressing the disturbing increase of existential force or by reordering social relations so that they will adequately express the new relative strength of existential forces. Politics shall mean the attempt to restore the balance of forces or to readjust the order, by various diplomatic means, or by building up discouraging counterforces short of war. These definitions should not be taken for the last word of wisdom in such formidable matters as war, peace, and politics but merely as a declaration of the rules that will govern the formulation of the present problem.

Gnostic politics is self-defeating in the sense that measures that are intended to establish peace increase the disturbances that will lead to war. The mechanics of this self-defeat has just been set forth in the description of magic operations in the dream world. If an incipient disturbance of the balance is not met by appropriate political action in the world of reality, if instead it is met with magic incantations, it may grow to such proportions that war becomes inevitable. The model case is the rise of the National Socialist movement to power, first in Germany, then on the continental scale, with the gnostic chorus wailing its moral indignation at such barbarian and reactionary doings in a progressive world— without however raising a finger to repress the rising force by a minor political effort in proper time. The prehistory of the second World War raises the serious question whether the gnostic dream has not corroded Western society so deeply that rational politics has become impossible, and war is the only instrument left for adjusting disturbances in the balance of existential forces.

The conduct of the war and its aftermath unfortunately are apt to confirm this fear rather than to assuage it. If a war has a purpose at all, it is the restoration of a balance of forces and not the aggravation of disturbance; it is the reduction of the unbalancing excess of force, not the destruction of force to the point of creating a new unbalancing power vacuum. Instead the gnostic politicians have put the Soviet army on the Elbe, surrendered China to the Communists, at the same time demilitarized Germany and Japan, and in addition demobilized our own army. The facts are trite, and yet it is perhaps not sufficiently realized that never before in the history of mankind has a world power used a victory deliberately for the purpose of creating a power vacuum to its own disadvantage. And again, as in previous contexts, it is necessary to warn that phenomena of this magnitude cannot be explained by ignorance and stupidity. These policies were pursued as a matter of principle, on the basis of gnostic dream assumptions about the nature of man, about a mysterious evolution of mankind toward peace and world order, about the possibility of establishing an international order in the abstract without relation to the structure of the field of existential forces, about armies being the cause of war and not the forces and constellations that build them and set them into motion, etc. The enumerated series of actions, as well as the dream assumptions on which they are based, seem to show that the contact with reality is at least badly damaged and that the pathological substitution of the dream world is fairly effective.

Moreover, it should be noted that the unique phenomenon of a great power creating a power vacuum to its own disadvantage was accompanied by the equally unique phenomenon of military conclusion of a war without conclusion of peace treaties. This rather disturbing further phenomenon again cannot be explained by the baffling complexity of the problems that require settlement. It is again the dream obsession that makes it impossible for the representatives of gnostic societies to formulate policies that take into account the structure of reality. There can be no peace, because the dream cannot be translated into reality and reality has not yet broken the dream. No one, of course, can predict what nightmares of violence it will take to break the dream, and still less so what Western society will look like *au bout de la nuit.*

Gnostic politics, thus, is self-defeating in so far as its disregard for the structure of reality leads to continuous warfare. This system of chain wars can end only in one of two ways. Either it will result in horrible physical destructions and concomitant revolutionary changes of social order beyond reasonable guesses; or, with the natural change of generations, it will lead to the abandoning of gnostic dreaming before the worst has happened. In this sense should be understood the earlier suggestion that the end of the gnostic dream is perhaps closer at hand than one ordinarily would assume.

3

This exposition of the dangers of Gnosticism as a civil theology of Western society will probably have aroused some misgivings. The analysis did fully pertain only to the progressive and idealistic varieties that prevail in Western democracies; it would not equally well apply to the activist varieties that prevail in totalitarian empires. Whatever share of responsibility for the present plight may be laid on the doorsteps of progressivists and idealists, the most formidable source of imminent danger seems to be the activists. The intimate connection between the two dangers, therefore, requires clarification—all the more so because the representatives of the two gnostic varieties are antagonists in battle on the world scene. The analysis of this further question can appropriately use as a preface the pronouncements of a famous liberal intellectual on the problem of communism:

> Lenin was surely right when the end he sought for was to build his heaven on earth and write the precepts of his faith into the inner fabric of a universal humanity. He was surely right, too, when he recognized

that the prelude to peace is a war, and that it is futile to suppose that the tradition of countless generations can be changed, as it were, overnight.[2]

The power of any supernatural religion to build that tradition has gone; the deposit of scientific inquiry since Descartes has been fatal to its authority. It is therefore difficult to see upon what basis the civilized tradition can be rebuilt save that upon which the idea of the Russian Revolution is founded. It corresponds, its supernatural basis apart, pretty exactly to the mental climate in which Christianity became the official religion of the West.[3]

It is, indeed, true in a sense to argue that the Russian principle cuts deeper than the Christian since it seeks salvation for the masses by fulfilment in this life, and, thereby, orders anew the actual world we know.[4]

Few passages could be more revealing for the plight of the liberal intellectual in our time. Philosophy and Christianity are beyond his range of experience. Science, besides being an instrument for power over nature, is something that makes you sophisticated enough not to believe in God. Heaven will be built on earth. Self-salvation, the tragedy of Gnosticism that Nietzsche experienced to the full until it broke his soul, is a fulfilment of life that will come to every man with the feeling that he is making his contribution to society according to his ability, compensated by a weekly paycheck. There are no problems of human existence in society except the immanent satisfaction of the masses. Political analysis tells you who will be the winner, so that the intellectual can advance in proper time to the position of a court theologian of the Communist empire. And, if you are bright, you will follow him in his expert surf-riding on the wave of the future. The case is too well known today to need further comment. It is the case of the petty paracletes in whom the spirit is stirring, who feel the duty to play a public role and be teachers of mankind, who with good faith substitute their convictions for critical knowledge, and with a perfectly good conscience express their opinions on problems beyond their reach. Moreover, one should not deny the immanent consistency and honesty of this transition from liberalism to communism; if liberalism is understood as the immanent salvation of man and society, communism certainly is its most radical expression; it is an evolution that was already

2. Harold J. Laski, *Faith, Reason and Civilization: An Essay in Historical Analysis* (New York: Viking Press, 1944), 184.
3. Ibid., 51.
4. Ibid., 143.

anticipated by John Stuart Mill's faith in the ultimate advent of communism for mankind.

In more technical language one can formulate the problem in the following manner. The three possible varieties of immanentization —teleological, axiological, and activist—are not merely three co-ordinated types but are related to one another dynamically. In every wave of the gnostic movement the progressivist and utopian varieties will tend to form a political right wing, leaving a good deal of the ultimate perfection to gradual evolution and compromising on a tension between achievement and ideal, while the activist variety will tend to form a political left wing, taking violent action toward the complete realization of the perfect realm. The distribution of the faithful from right to left will in part be determined by such personal equations as enthusiasm, temperament, and consistency; to another, and perhaps the more important part, however, it will be determined by their relation to the civilizational environment in which the gnostic revolution takes place. For it must never be forgotten that Western society is not all modern but that modernity is a growth within it, in opposition to the classic and Christian tradition. If there were nothing in Western society but Gnosticism, the movement toward the left would be irresistible because it lies in the logic of immanentization, and it would have been consummated long ago. In fact, however, the great Western revolutions of the past, after their logical swing to the left, settled down to a public order that reflected the balance of the social forces of the moment, together with their economic interests and civilizational traditions. The apprehension or hope, as the case may be, that the "partial" revolutions of the past will be followed by the "radical" revolution and the establishment of the final realm rests on the assumption that the traditions of Western society are now sufficiently ruined and that the famous masses are ready for the kill.[5]

The dynamics of Gnosticism, thus, moves along two lines. In the dimension of historical depth, Gnosticism moves from the partial immanentization of the high Middle Ages to the radical immanentization of the present. And with every wave and revolutionary outburst it moves in the amplitude of right and left. The thesis, however, that these two lines of dynamics must now meet

5. The concepts of "partial" and "radical" revolution were developed by Karl Marx in "Kritik der Hegelschen Rechtsphilosophie: Einleitung" (1843), *Gesamtausgabe*, 1:617.

according to their inner logic, that Western society is ripe to fall for communism, that the course of Western history is determined by the logic of its modernity and nothing else, is an impertinent piece of gnostic propaganda at both its silliest and most vicious and certainly has nothing to do with a critical study of politics. Against this thesis must be held a number of facts that today are obscured because the public debate is dominated by the liberal clichés. In the first place, the Communist movement in Western society itself, wherever it had to rely on its own mass appeal without aid from the Soviet government, has got exactly nowhere at all. The only gnostic activist movement that achieved a noteworthy measure of success was the National Socialist movement on a limited national basis; and the suicidal nature of such an activist success is amply testified by the atrocious internal corruption of the regime while it lasted as well as by the ruins of the German cities. Second, the present Western plight in the face of the Soviet danger, in so far as it is due to the creation of the previously described power vacuum, is not of Communist making. The power vacuum was created by the Western democratic governments freely, on the height of a military victory, without pressure from anybody. Third, that the Soviet Union is an expanding great power on the Continent has nothing to do with communism. The present extension of the Soviet empire over the satellite nations corresponds substantially to the program of a Slavic empire under Russian hegemony as it was submitted, for instance, by Bakunin to Nicolai I. It is quite conceivable that a non-Communist Russian hegemonic empire would today have the same expanse as the Soviet empire and be a greater danger because it might be better consolidated. Fourth, the Soviet empire, while it is a formidable power, is no danger to Western Europe on the level of material force. Elementary statistics shows that Western manpower, natural resources, and industrial potential are a match to any strength the Soviet empire can muster—not counting our own power in the background. The danger strictly arises from national particularism and the paralyzing intellectual and moral confusion.

The problem of Communist danger, thus, is thrown back on the problem of Western paralysis and self-destructive politics through the gnostic dream. The previously quoted passages show the source of the trouble. The danger of a sliding from right to left is inherent in the nature of the dream; in so far as communism is a more radical and consistent type of immanentization than progressivism or social utopianism, it has the *logique du coeur* on its side. The Western gnostic societies are in a state of intellectual and emotional paralysis because no fundamental critique of left-wing Gnosticism is possible without blowing up right-wing Gnosticism in its course. Such major experiential and intellectual revolutions, however, take their time and the change of at least one generation. One can do no more than formulate the conditions of the problem. There will be a latent Communist danger under the most favorable external circumstances as long as the public debate in Western societies is dominated by the gnostic clichés. That is to say: as long as the recognition of the structure of reality, the cultivation of the virtues of *sophia* and *prudentia,* the discipline of the intellect, and the development of theoretical culture and the life of the spirit are stigmatized in public as "reactionary," while disregard for the structure of reality, ignorance of facts, fallacious misconstruction and falsification of history, irresponsible opining on the basis of sincere conviction, philosophical illiteracy, spiritual dullness, and agnostic sophistication are considered the virtues of man and their possession opens the road to public success. In brief: as long as civilization is reaction, and moral insanity is progress.

4

The function of Gnosticism as the civil theology of Western society, its destruction of the truth of the soul, and its disregard for the problem of existence have been set forth in sufficient detail to make the fatal importance of the problem clear. The inquiry can now return to the great thinker who discovered its nature and tried to solve it by his theory of representation. In the seventeenth century the existence of the English national society seemed in danger of being destroyed by gnostic revolutionaries, as today on a larger scale the same danger seems to threaten the existence of Western society as a whole. Hobbes tried to meet the danger by devising a civil theology that made the order of a society in existence the truth that it represented—and by the side of this truth no other should be held. This was an eminently sensible idea in so far as it put the whole weight on existence that had been so badly neglected by the Gnostics. The practical value of the idea, however, rested on the assumption that the transcendent truth that men tried to represent in their societies, after mankind had gone through the experiences of philosophy and Christianity, could be neglected in its turn. Against the Gnostics who did not want society to exist unless its order represented a specific type of truth, Hobbes insisted that any order would do if it secured the existence of society. In order to make this conception valid, he had to create his new idea of man. Human nature would have to find fulfilment in existence itself—a purpose of man beyond existence would have to be denied. Hobbes countered the gnostic immanentization of the eschaton which endangered existence by a radical immanence of existence which denied the eschaton.

The result of this effort was ambivalent. In order to maintain his position against the fighting churches and sects, Hobbes had to deny that their zeal was inspired, however misguided, by a search for truth. Their struggle had to be interpreted, in terms of immanent existence, as an unfettered expression of their lust for power; and their professed religious concern had to be revealed as a mask for their existential lust. In carrying out this analysis, Hobbes proved to be one of the greatest psychologists of all times; his achievements in unmasking the *libido dominandi* behind the pretense of religious zeal and reforming idealism are as solid today as they were at the time when he wrote. This magnificent psychological achievement, however, was purchased at a heavy price. Hobbes rightly diagnosed the corruptive element of passion in the religiousness of the Puritan Gnostics. He did not, however, interpret passion as the source of corruption in the life of the spirit, but rather the life of the spirit as the extreme of existential passion. Hence, he could not interpret the nature of man from the vantage point of the maximum of differentiation through the experiences of transcendence so that passion, and especially the fundamental passion, *superbia*, could be discerned as the permanently present danger of the fall from true nature; but he had, on the contrary, to interpret the life of passion as the nature of man so that the phenomena of spiritual life appeared as extremes of *superbia*.

According to this conception, the generic nature of man must be studied in terms of human passions; the objects of the passions are no legitimate object of inquiry.[6] This is the fundamental counterposition to classic and Christian moral philosophy. Aristotelian ethics starts from the purposes of action and explores the order

6. Introduction to Hobbes, *Leviathan*, 6.

of human life in terms of the ordination of all actions toward a highest purpose, the *summum bonum*; Hobbes, on the contrary, insists that there is no *summum bonum*, "as is spoken of in the books of the old moral philosophers."[7] With the *summum bonum*, however, disappears the source of order from human life; and not only from the life of individual man but also from life in society; for, as you will remember, the order of the life in community depends on *homonoia*, in the Aristotelian and Christian sense, that is, on the participation in the common nous. Hobbes, therefore, is faced with the problem of constructing an order of society out of isolated individuals who are not oriented toward a common purpose but only motivated by their individual passions.

The details of the construction are well known. It will be sufficient to recall the main points. Human happiness is for Hobbes a continuous progress of desire from one object to another. The object of man's desire "is not to enjoy once only, and for one instant of time; but to assure for ever, the way of his future desire."[8] "So that in the first place, I put for a general inclination of all mankind, a perpetual and restless desire of power after power, that ceaseth only in death."[9] A multitude of men is not a community but an open field of power drives in competition with each other. The original drive for power, therefore, is aggravated by diffidence of the competitor and by the lust of glorying in successfully outstripping the other man.[10] "This race we must suppose to have no other goal, no other garland, but being foremost." And in this race "continually to be outgone is misery. Continually to outgo the next is felicity. And to forsake the course, is to die."[11] Passion aggravated by comparison is pride.[12] And this pride may assume various forms, of which the most important for the analysis of politics was to Hobbes the pride in having divine inspirations, or generally to be in possession of undoubted truth. Such pride in excess is madness.[13] "If some man in Bedlam should entertain you with sober discourse; and you desire in taking leave, to know what he were, that you might another time

7. Ibid., chap. 11, p. 63.
8. Ibid.
9. Ibid., 64.
10. Ibid., chap. 13, p. 81.
11. Thomas Hobbes, *The Elements of Law, Natural and Politic*, ed. Ferdinand Tönnies (Cambridge, 1928), part 1, chap. 9, sec. 21.
12. Hobbes, *Leviathan*, chap. 8, p. 46.
13. Ibid., 46–47.

requite his civility; and he should tell you, he were God the Father; I think you need expect no extravagant action for argument of his madness."[14] If this madness becomes violent and the possessors of the inspiration try to impose it on others, the result in society will be "the seditious roaring of a troubled nation."[15]

Since Hobbes does not recognize sources of order in the soul, inspiration can be exorcised only by a passion that is even stronger than the pride to be a paraclete, and that is the fear of death. Death is the greatest evil; and if life cannot be ordered through orientation of the soul toward a *summum bonum*, order will have to be motivated by fear of the *summum malum*.[16] Out of mutual fear is born the willingness to submit to government by contract. When the contracting parties agree to have a government, they "confer all their power and strength upon one man, or assembly of men, that may reduce all their wills, by plurality of voices, unto one will."[17]

The acumen of Hobbes shows itself at its best in his understanding that the contractual symbolism that he uses, in accordance with the conventions of the seventeenth century, is not the essence of the matter. The combining into a commonwealth under a sovereign may express itself in legal form, but essentially it is a psychological transformation of the combining persons. The Hobbesian conception of the process in which a political society comes into existence is rather close to Fortescue's conception of the creation of a new *corpus mysticum* through the eruption of a people. The covenanters do not create a government that would represent them as single individuals; in the contracting act they cease to be self-governing persons and merge their power drives into a new person, the commonwealth, and the carrier of this new person, its representative, is the sovereign.

This construction required a few distinctions concerning the meaning of the term "person." "A person, is he, whose words or actions are considered, either as his own, or as representing the words and actions of another man, or of any other thing." When he represents himself, he is a natural person; when he represents another, he is called an artificial person. The meaning of person is

---

14. Ibid., 47–48.
15. Ibid., 47.
16. Thomas Hobbes, *De homine*, chap. 11, art. 6; *De cive*, chap. 1, art. 7. On the problem of fear of death as the *summum malum*, see Leo Strauss, *The Political Philosophy of Hobbes* (Oxford, 1934).
17. Hobbes, *Leviathan*, chap. 17, p. 112.

referred back to the Latin *persona,* and the Greek *prosopon,* as the face, the outward appearance, or the mask of the actor on the stage. "So that a person, is the same that an actor is, both on the stage and in common conversation; and to personate, is to act, or represent himself, or another."[18]

This concept of a person allows Hobbes to separate the visible realm of representative words and deeds from the unseen realm of processes in the soul, with the consequence that the visible words and actions, which always must be those of a definite, physical human being, may represent a unit of psychic processes that arises from the interaction of individual human souls. In the natural condition every man has his own person in the sense that his words and actions represent the power drive of his passions. In the civil condition the human units of passion are broken and fused into a new unit, called the commonwealth. The actions of the single human individuals whose souls have coalesced cannot represent the new person; its bearer is the sovereign. The creation of this person of the commonwealth, Hobbes insists, is "more than consent, or concord," as the language of contract would suggest. The single human persons cease to exist and merge into the one person represented by the sovereign. "This is the generation of that great Leviathan, or rather, to speak more reverently, of that *mortal god,* to which we owe under the *immortal God,* our peace and defence." The covenanting men agree "to submit their wills, every one to his will, and their judgments to his judgment." The fusion of wills is "a real unity of them all"; for the mortal god "hath the use of so much power and strength conferred upon him, that by terror thereof, he is enabled to form the wills of them all, to peace at home, and mutual aid against their enemies abroad."[19]

The style of the construction is magnificent. If human nature is assumed to be nothing but passionate existence, devoid of ordering resources of the soul, the horror of annihilation will, indeed, be the overriding passion that compels submission to order. If pride cannot bow to Dike, or be redeemed through grace, it must be broken by the Leviathan who "is king of all the children of pride."[20] If the souls cannot participate in the Logos, then the sovereign who strikes terror into the souls will be "the essence of the commonwealth."[21]

18. Ibid., chap. 16, pp. 105 ff.
19. Ibid., chap. 17, p. 112.
20. Ibid., chap. 28, p. 209.
21. Ibid., chap. 17, p. 112.

The "King of the Proud" must break the *amor sui* that cannot be relieved by the *amor Dei*.[22]

5

Joachim of Fiore had created an aggregate of symbols that dominated the self-interpretation of modern political movements in general; Hobbes created a comparable aggregate that expressed the component of radical immanence in modern politics.

The first of these symbols may be called the new psychology. Its nature can be defined best by relating it to the Augustinian psychology from which it derives. Saint Augustine distinguished between the *amor sui* and the *amor Dei* as the organizing volitional centers of the soul. Hobbes threw out the *amor Dei* and relied for his psychology on the *amor sui*, in his language the self-conceit or pride of the individual, alone. In this elimination of the *amor Dei* from the interpretation of the psyche a development was consummated that can be traced back at least to the twelfth century. With the appearance of the self-reliant individual on the social scene, the new type and its striving for public success beyond its status attracted attention. In fact, John of Salisbury described it in his *Policraticus* in terms closely resembling those of Hobbes.[23] In the wake of the institutional upheavals of the late Middle Ages and the Reformation, then, the type became so common that it appeared as the "normal" type of man and became a matter of general concern. The psychological work of Hobbes was paralleled in his own time by the psychology of Pascal, though Pascal preserved the Christian

22. Ibid., chap. 18, p. 209.
23. John of Salisbury, *Policraticus: Sive De nugis curialium, et vestigiis philosophorum libri octo*, ed. Clement C. J. Webb (Oxford, 1909). The following passages are quoted in the translation of *The Statesman's Book of John of Salisbury*, translated into English with an introduction by John Dickinson (New York, 1927). Man, ignorant of his true status and the obedience which he owes to God, "aspires to a kind of fictitious liberty, vainly imagining that he can live without fear and can do with impunity whatsoever pleases him, and somehow be straightway like unto God" (viii.17). "Though it is not given to all men to seize princely or royal power, yet the man who is wholly untainted by tyranny is rare or non-existent. In common speech the tyrant is one who oppresses a whole people by rulership based on force; and yet it is not over a people as a whole that a man can play the tyrant, but he can do so if he will even in the meanest station. For if not over the whole body of the people, still each man will lord it as far as his power extends" (vii.17). Even the Hobbesian metaphor of the race can be found in John: "And so all contend in the race, and when the goal is reached, that one among them receives the prize who emerges swifter than the rest in the race of ambition, and outruns Peter or any of the disciples of Christ" (vii.19).

tradition and described the man who was guided by his passions alone as the man who had fallen a prey to one or the other type of *libido*. And also contemporaneously, with La Rochefoucauld, began the psychology of the man of the "world" who was motivated by his *amour-propre* (the Augustinian *amor sui*). The national ramifications into the French psychology of the *moralistes* and novelists, the English psychology of pleasure-pain, associationism and self-interest, the German enrichments through the psychology of the unconscious of the Romantics and the psychology of Nietzsche, may be recalled in order to suggest the pervasiveness of the phenomenon. A specifically "modern" psychology developed as the empirical psychology of "modern" man, that is, of the man who was intellectually and spiritually disoriented and hence motivated primarily by his passions. It will be useful to introduce the terms of psychology of orientation and psychology of motivation in order to distinguish a science of the healthy psyche, in the Platonic sense, in which the order of the soul is created by transcendental orientation, from the science of the disoriented psyche that must be ordered by a balance of motivations. "Modern" psychology, in this sense, is an incomplete psychology in so far as it deals only with a certain pneumopathological type of man.

The second symbol concerns the idea of man itself. Since the disoriented type, because of its empirical frequency, was understood as the "normal" type, a philosophical anthropology developed in which the disease was interpreted as the "nature of man." Time does not permit us to enter more deeply into this problem. It must be sufficient to suggest the line that connects contemporary existentialists with the first philosophers of existence in the seventeenth century. What has to be said in criticism of this philosophy of immanent existence was said, on principle, by Plato in his *Gorgias*.

The third symbol, finally, is the specifically Hobbesian creation of the Leviathan. Its significance is hardly understood today because the symbol is smothered under the jargon of absolutism. The preceding account should have made it clear that the Leviathan is the correlate of order to the disorder of gnostic activists who indulge their *superbia* to the extreme of civil war. The Leviathan cannot be identified with the historical form of absolute monarchy; the royalist contemporaries understood that quite well, and their distrust of Hobbes was amply justified. Nor can the symbol be identified with totalitarianism on its own symbolic level of the final realm of perfection. It rather adumbrates a component in totalitarianism that comes to the fore when a group of gnostic activists actually achieves the monopoly of existential representation in a historical society. The victorious Gnostics can neither transfigure the nature of man nor establish a terrestrial paradise; what they actually do establish is an omnipotent state that ruthlessly eliminates all sources of resistance and, first of all, the troublesome Gnostics themselves. As far as our experience with totalitarian empires goes, their characteristic feature is the elimination of debate concerning the gnostic truth that they themselves profess to represent. The National Socialists suppressed the debate of the race question, once they had come to power; the Soviet government prohibits the debate and development of Marxism. The Hobbesian principle that the validity of Scripture derives from governmental sanction and that its public teaching should be supervised by the sovereign is carried out by the Soviet government in the reduction of communism to the "party line." The party line may change, but the change of interpretation is determined by the government. Intellectuals who still insist on having opinions of their own concerning the meaning of the koranic writings are purged. The gnostic truth that was produced freely by the original gnostic thinkers is now channeled into the truth of public order in immanent existence. Hence, the Leviathan is the symbol of the fate that actually will befall the gnostic activists when in their dream they believe they realize the realm of freedom.

6

The symbol of the Leviathan was developed by an English thinker in response to the Puritan danger. Of the major European political societies, however, England has proved herself most resistant against gnostic totalitarianism; and the same must be said for the America that was founded by the very Puritans who aroused the fears of Hobbes. A word on this question will be in order in conclusion.

The explanation must be sought in the dynamics of Gnosticism. You will remember the frequent reminders that modernity is a growth within Western society, in competition with the Mediterranean tradition; and you will, furthermore, remember that Gnosticism itself underwent a process of radicalization, from the medieval immanentization of the Spirit that left God in his transcendence to the later radical immanentization of the eschaton as it was to be found in Feuerbach and Marx. The corrosion of Western civilization through Gnosticism is a slow process extending over a thousand years. The several Western political societies, now, have a different relation to this slow process according to the time at which their national revolutions occurred. When the revolution occurred early, a less radical wave of Gnosticism was its carrier, and the resistance of the forces of tradition was, at the same time, more effective. When the revolution occurred at a later date, a more radical wave was its carrier, and the environment of tradition was already corroded more deeply by the general advance of modernity. The English Revolution, in the seventeenth century, occurred at a time when Gnosticism had not yet undergone its radical secularization. You have seen that the left-wing Puritans were eager to present themselves as Christians, though of an especially pure sort. When the adjustments of 1690 were reached, England had preserved the institutional culture of aristocratic parliamentism as well as the mores of a Christian commonwealth, now sanctioned as national institutions. The American Revolution, though its debate was already strongly affected by the psychology of enlightenment, also had the good fortune of coming to its close within the institutional and Christian climate of the *ancien régime.* In the French Revolution, then, the radical wave of Gnosticism was so strong that it permanently split the nation into the laicist half that based itself on the revolution and the conservative half that tried, and tries, to salvage the Christian tradition. The German Revolution, finally, in an environment without strong institutional traditions, brought for the first time into full play economic materialism, racist biology, corrupt psychology, scientism, and technological ruthlessness—in brief, modernity without restraint. Western society as a whole, thus, is a deeply stratified civilization in which the American and English democracies represent the oldest, most firmly consolidated stratum of civilizational tradition, while the German area represents its most progressively modern stratum.

In this situation there is a glimmer of hope, for the American and English democracies, which most solidly in their institutions represent the truth of the soul, are, at the same time, existentially the strongest powers. But it will require all our efforts to kindle this glimmer into a flame by repressing gnostic corruption and restoring the forces of civilization. At present the fate is in the balance.

Science,
Politics, and
Gnosticism

Two Essays

CONTENTS

Preface to the American Edition

The more we come to know about the Gnosis of antiquity, the more it becomes certain that modern movements of thought, such as progressivism, positivism, Hegelianism, and Marxism, are variants of Gnosticism. The continuous interest in this problem goes back to the 1930s, when Hans Jonas published his first volume of *Gnosis und spätantiker Geist* on ancient Gnosis and Hans Urs von Balthasar his *Prometheus* on modern Gnosticism. Their work was followed by more comprehensive studies of eighteenth- and nineteenth-century movements, such as Henri de Lubac's *Drame de l'humanisme athée* and Albert Camus's *L'Homme révolté*. The lecture "Science, Politics and Gnosticism," delivered in 1958 at the University of Munich, was an attempt to apply to the Gnosticism of Hegel, Marx, Nietzsche, and Heidegger the insights gained by these predecessors, as well as by my own *New Science of Politics*, and to draw more clearly the lines that separate political Gnosticism from a philosophy of politics. For the publication of this lecture the introduction on the nature of Gnosis and the section "The Murder of God" were added. The essay "Ersatz Religion" was first published in *Wort und Wahrheit* (Vienna, 1960) in the interest of presenting to the general public a further elucidation of the symbolism and psychology of the mass movements of our time.

In America, the gnostic nature of the movements mentioned had been recognized early in the twentieth century by William James. He knew Hegel's speculation to be the culmination of modern Gnosticism. The philosopher's critical opposition, however, had little effect; today, various intellectual movements of the gnostic type dominate the public scene in America no less than in Europe.

A representative case of the resultant intellectual confusion may be found in the "God is dead" movement. The death of God is the cardinal issue of Gnosis, both ancient and modern. From Hegel to Nietzsche it is the great theme of gnostic speculation, and Protestant theology has been plagued by it ever since Hegel's time. In recent years, it has been taken up by American theologians who are faced with the pressing phenomena of urbanization and alienation. The attempt to come to grips with the problems of personal and social order when it is disrupted by Gnosticisms, however, has not been very successful, because the philosophical knowledge that would be required for the purpose has itself been destroyed by the prevailing intellectual climate. The struggle against the consequences of Gnosticism is being conducted in the very language of Gnosticism. In this confused situation, the present essays will perhaps help us understand more clearly certain points currently under debate.

In the present state of science, a study of modern Gnosticism is inevitably work in progress. Still, I find nothing to retract or correct, though a good deal would have to be added after the lapse of a decade, especially with regard to the problem of alienation. The reader who is interested in the subject of alienation might refer to my recent article "Immortality: Experience and Symbol" in the *Harvard Theological Review* 60 (July 1967): 235–79.

There remains the pleasant obligation to thank William J. Fitzpatrick for translating the first lecture and Gregor Sebba for his kind assistance.

ERIC VOEGELIN
Ann Arbor, Michigan

PART I
SCIENCE, POLITICS, AND GNOSTICISM
Translated by
William J. Fitzpatrick

1

·❦·

Introduction

The reader will be surprised to see modern political thinkers and movements treated under the heading of "gnosticism." Since the state of science in this area is as yet largely unknown to the general public, an introductory explanation will not be unwelcome.

The idea that one of the main currents of European, especially of German, thought is essentially gnostic sounds strange today, but this is not a recent discovery. Until about a hundred years ago the facts of the matter were well known. In 1835 appeared Ferdinand Christian Baur's monumental work *Die christliche Gnosis, oder die Religionsphilosophie in ihrer geschichtlichen Entwicklung.* Under the heading "Ancient Gnosticism and Modern Philosophy of Religion," the last part of this work discusses: (1) Böhme's theosophy, (2) Schelling's philosophy of nature, (3) Schleiermacher's doctrine of faith, and (4) Hegel's philosophy of religion. The speculation of German idealism is correctly placed in its context in the gnostic movement since antiquity. Moreover, Baur's work was not an isolated event: It concluded a hundred years of preoccupation with the history of heresy—a branch of scholarship that not without reason developed during the Enlightenment. I shall mention only Johann Lorenz von Mosheim's encyclopedic *Versuch einer unparteiischen und gründlichen Ketzergeschichte* (2d edition, 1748) and two works on ancient Gnosticism from Baur's own day, Johann August Neander's *Genetische Entwicklung der vornehmsten gnostischen Systeme* (1818) and Jacques Matter's *Histoire critique du Gnosticisme et de son influence sur les sectes religieuses et philosophiques des six premiers siècles de l'ère chrétienne* (1828). It was well understood that with the Enlightenment and German idealism the gnostic movement had acquired great social significance.

On this issue as on many others, the learning and self-understanding of Western civilization were not submerged until the liberal era, the latter half of the nineteenth century, during the reign of positivism in the sciences of man and society. The submergence was so profound that when the gnostic movement reached its revolutionary phase its nature could no longer be recognized. The movements deriving from Marx and Bakunin, the early activities of Lenin, Sorel's myth of violence, the intellectual movement of neopositivism, the communist, fascist, and national-socialist revolutions—all fell in a period, now fortunately part of the past, when science was at a low point. Europe had no conceptual tools with which to grasp the horror that was upon her. There was a scholarly study of the Christian churches and sects; there was a science of government, cast in the categories of the sovereign nation-state and its institutions; there were the beginnings of a sociology of power and political authority; but there was no science of the non-Christian, non-national intellectual and mass movements into which the Europe of Christian nation-states was in the process of breaking up. Since in its massiveness this new political phenomenon could not be disregarded, a number of stopgap notions were coined to cope with it. There was talk of neopagan movements, of new social and political myths, or of *mystiques politiques.* I, too, tried one of these ad hoc explanations in a little book on "political religions."

The confused state of science and the consequent impossibility of adequately understanding political phenomena lasted until well into the period of World War II. And for the general public this unfortunate situation still continues—otherwise, this preface would not be necessary. However, science has been undergoing a transformation, the beginnings of which go back some two generations. The recent catastrophes, which were centuries in the making, have not retarded, but accelerated it. And considering the extent of this change and the results already achieved, one can say that we are living in one of the great epochs of Western science. To be sure, the corruption persists; but if it does not lead to further catastrophes that put an end to the free existence of Western society, future historians may well date the spiritual and intellectual regeneration of the West from this flowering of science.

This is not the place, however, to go into the background and ramifications of this fascinating development. I can give only the briefest suggestion of recent scholarly work on ancient Gnosticism and on the political expression of modern Gnosticism.

The research on ancient Gnosticism has a complex history of more than two hundred years. For this development one should consult the historical surveys in Wilhelm Bousset's *Die Hauptprobleme der Gnosis* (1907) and Hans Jonas's *Gnosis und spätantiker Geist* (1934; 1954). For the problems of Gnosticism itself, see both these works and *Die Gnosis* (1924; 4th edition, 1955) by Hans Leisegang. Gilles Quispel's *Gnosis als Weltreligion* (1951) is a concise introduction by one of the foremost authorities.[1]

Under the influence of a deepened understanding of Gnosticism and its connections with Judaism and Christianity, a new interpretation of European intellectual history and of modern politics has been developing. For example, Hans Urs von Balthasar's *Apokalypse der deutschen Seele* (1937), the first volume of which was reissued in 1947 under the title *Prometheus*, helps to clarify German history since the eighteenth century. The parallel work on French history is *L'Homme révolté* (1951) by Albert Camus. And the interpretation of intellectual history that forms the basis for my present essay has moreover been strongly influenced by Henri de Lubac's *Drame de l'humanisme athée* (2d edition, 1945) [*The Drama of Atheist Humanism*, trans. Edith M. Riley (1950)]. Jacob Taubes's *Abendländische Eschatologie* (1947) is important for reestablishing the historical continuity of Gnosticism from antiquity through the Middle Ages down to the political movements of modern times. Indispensable to any attempt to understand political sectarianism from the eleventh century to the sixteenth century is the extensive presentation of material in Norman Cohn's *The Pursuit of the Millennium* (1957; 2d edition, 1961). Finally, my own studies on modern political Gnosticism may be found in *The New Science of Politics* (1952).

And now a word on Gnosticism itself—its origins and some of its essential characteristics.

For the cosmological civilizations of Mesopotamia, Syria, and Egypt, as well as for the peoples of the Mediterranean, the seventh century before Christ inaugurates the age of ecumenical empires.

---

1. Since the original German presentation of this essay, there has appeared a valuable comprehensive introduction to the whole subject by Hans Jonas, *The Gnostic Religion* (Boston, 1958), 2d ed. (Boston, 1963).

The Persian Empire is followed by the conquests of Alexander, the Diadochian empires, the expansion of the Roman Empire, and the creation of the Parthian and Sassanian empires. The collapse of the ancient empires of the East, the loss of independence for Israel and the Hellenic and Phoenician city-states, the population shifts, the deportations and enslavements, and the interpenetration of cultures reduce men who exercise no control over the proceedings of history to an extreme state of forlornness in the turmoil of the world, of intellectual disorientation, of material and spiritual insecurity. The loss of meaning that results from the breakdown of institutions, civilizations, and ethnic cohesion evokes attempts to regain an understanding of the meaning of human existence in the given conditions of the world. Among these efforts, which vary widely in depth of insight and substantive truth, are to be found: the Stoic reinterpretation of man (to whom the polis had become meaningless) as the *polites* (citizen) of the cosmos; the Polybian vision of a pragmatic ecumene destined to be created by Rome; the mystery religions; the Heliopolitan slave cults; the Hebrew apocalyptic; Christianity; and Manichaeism. And in this sequence, as one of the most grandiose of the new formulations of the meaning of existence, belongs Gnosticism.

Of the profusion of gnostic experiences and symbolic expressions, one feature may be singled out as the central element in this varied and extensive creation of meaning: the experience of the world as an alien place into which man has strayed and from which he must find his way back home to the other world of his origin. "Who has cast me into the suffering of this world?" asks the "Great Life" of the gnostic texts, which is also the "first, alien Life from the worlds of light."[2] It is an alien in this world and this world is alien to it.

"This world was not made according to the desire of the Life." "Not by the will of the Great Life art thou come hither." Therefore the question, "Who conveyed me into the evil darkness?" and the entreaty, "Deliver us from the darkness of this world into which we are flung." The world is no longer the well-ordered, the cosmos, in which Hellenic man felt at home; nor is it the Judaeo-Christian world that God created and found good. Gnostic man no longer wishes to perceive in admiration the intrinsic order of the cosmos.

---

2. Discussions of these and the following texts can be found in Hans Jonas, *The Gnostic Religion.*

For him the world has become a prison from which he wants to escape: "The wretched soul has strayed into a labyrinth of torment and wanders around without a way out. . . . It seeks to escape from the bitter chaos, but knows not how to get out." Therefore the confused, plaintive question asked of the Great Life, "Why didst thou create this world, why didst thou order the tribes here from thy midst?" From this attitude springs the programmatic formula of Gnosticism, which Clement of Alexandria recorded: Gnosis is "the knowledge of who we were and what we became, of where we were and whereinto we have been flung, of whereto we are hastening and wherefrom we are redeemed, of what birth is and what rebirth." The great speculative mythopoems of Gnosticism revolve around the questions of origin, the condition of having-been-flung, escape from the world, and the means of deliverance.

In the quoted texts the reader will have recognized Hegel's alienated spirit and Heidegger's flungness (*Geworfenheit*) of human existence. This similarity in symbolic expression results from a homogeneity in experience of the world. And the homogeneity goes beyond the experience of the world to the image of man and salvation with which both the modern and the ancient Gnostics respond to the condition of "flungness" in the alien world.

If man is to be delivered from the world, the possibility of deliverance must first be established in the order of being. In the ontology of ancient Gnosticism this is accomplished through faith in the "alien," "hidden" God who comes to man's aid, sends him his messengers, and shows him the way out of the prison of the evil God of this world (be he Zeus or Yahweh or one of the other ancient father-gods). In modern Gnosticism it is accomplished through the assumption of an absolute spirit that in the dialectical unfolding of consciousness proceeds from alienation to consciousness of itself; or through the assumption of a dialectical-material process of nature that in its course leads from the alienation resulting from private property and belief in God to the freedom of a fully human existence; or through the assumption of a will of nature that transforms man into superman.

Within the ontic possibility, however, gnostic man must carry on the work of salvation himself. Now, through his psyche ("soul") he belongs to the order, the *nomos*, of the world; what impels him toward deliverance is the *pneuma* ("spirit"). The labor of salvation, therefore, entails the dissolution of the worldly constitution of the psyche and at the same time the gathering and freeing of the powers of the *pneuma*. However the phases of salvation are represented in the different sects and systems—and they vary from magic practices to mystic ecstasies, from libertinism through indifferentism to the world to the strictest asceticism—the aim always is destruction of the old world and passage to the new. The instrument of salvation is Gnosis itself—knowledge. Since according to the gnostic ontology entanglement with the world is brought about by *agnoia*, ignorance, the soul will be able to disentangle itself through knowledge of its true life and its condition of alienness in this world. As the knowledge of falling captive to the world, Gnosis is at the same time the means of escaping it. Thus, Irenaeus recounts this meaning that Gnosis had for the Valentinians:

> Perfect salvation consists in the cognition, as such, of the Ineffable Greatness. For since sin and affliction resulted from ignorance (*agnoia*), this whole system originating in ignorance is dissolved through knowledge (*gnosis*). Hence, gnosis is the salvation of the inner man. . . . Gnosis redeems the inner, pneumatic man; he finds his satisfaction in the knowledge of the Whole. And this is the true salvation.

This will have to suffice by way of clarification, save for one word of caution. Self-salvation through knowledge has its own magic, and this magic is not harmless. The structure of the order of being will not change because one finds it defective and runs away from it. The attempt at world destruction will not destroy the world, but will only increase the disorder in society. The Gnostic's flight from a truly dreadful, confusing, and oppressive state of the world is understandable. But the order of the ancient world was renewed by that movement that strove through loving action to revive the practice of the "serious play" (to use Plato's expression)—that is, by Christianity.

2

Science, Politics, and Gnosticism

I

Political science, *politike episteme,* was founded by Plato and Aristotle.

At stake in the spiritual confusion of the time was whether there could be fashioned an image of the right order of the soul and society—a paradigm, a model, an ideal—that could function for the citizens of the polis as had the paraenetic myth for the Homeric heroes. To be sure, fourth-century Athens afforded plenty of opinions about the right manner of living and the right order of society. But was it possible to show that one of the multitude of sceptic, hedonist, utilitarian, power-oriented, and partisan *doxai* was the true one? Or, if none of them could stand up to critical examination, could a new image of order be formed that would not also bear the marks of nonbinding, subjective opinion (*doxa*)? The science of political philosophy resulted from the efforts to find an answer to this question.

In its essentials the classical foundation of political science is still valid today. We shall outline briefly its subject matter, analytical method, and anthropological presuppositions.

As for the subject matter, it is nothing esoteric; rather, it lies not far from the questions of the day and is concerned with the truth of things that everyone talks about. What is happiness? How should a man live in order to be happy? What is virtue? What, especially, is the virtue of justice? How large a territory and a population are best for a society? What kind of education is best? What professions, and what form of government? All of these questions arise from the conditions of the existence of man in society. And the philosopher is a man like any other: As far as the order of society is concerned, he has no other questions to ask than those of his fellow citizens.

However, his questioning leads to a conflict with opinion. This is quite another kind of conflict than that between differing opinions; for although the philosopher's questions are concerned with the same subjects as those of the philodoxer (these are the terms Plato adopted to describe the adversaries), the nature of his inquiry is radically different. The philosopher's question represents an attempt to advance beyond opinion to truth through the use of scientific analysis as developed by Aristotle in the *Analytica Posteriora*. With the instrument of analysis current statements about political matters are broken down into pre-analytic opinions and scientific propositions in the strict sense; and the verbal symbols, into pre-analytic or insufficiently analyzed expressions and the analytic concepts of political science. In this way, advocates of opinions who attack one another in daily politics are grouped together over against their common adversary, the philosopher.

When we speak of scientific analysis, we wish to emphasize the contrast with formal analysis. An analysis by means of formal logic can lead to no more than a demonstration that an opinion suffers from an inherent contradiction, or that different opinions contradict one another, or that conclusions have been invalidly drawn. A scientific analysis, on the other hand, makes it possible to judge of the truth of the premises implied by an opinion. It can do this, however, only on the assumption that truth about the order of being—to which, of course, opinions also refer—is objectively ascertainable. And Platonic-Aristotelian analysis does in fact operate on the assumption that there is an order of being accessible to a science beyond opinion. Its aim is knowledge of the order of being, of the levels of the hierarchy of being and their interrelationships, of the essential structure of the realms of being, and especially of human nature and its place in the totality of being. Analysis, therefore, is scientific and leads to a science of order through the fact that, and in so far as, it is ontologically oriented.

The assumption alone, however—that the order of being is accessible to knowledge, that ontology is possible—is still not enough to carry out an analysis; for the assumption might be unfounded. Therefore, an insight concerning being must always be really present—not only so that the first steps of the analysis can be taken, but so that the very idea of the analysis can be conceived and developed at all. And indeed, Platonic-Aristotelian analysis did not in the least begin with speculations about its own possibility, but with the actual insight into being that motivated the analytical process. The decisive event in the establishment of *politike episteme* was the specifically philosophical realization that the levels of being discernible within the world are surmounted by a transcendent source of being and its order. And this insight was itself rooted in the real movements of the human spiritual soul toward divine being experienced as transcendent. In the experiences of love for the world-transcendent origin of being, in *philia* toward the *sophon* (the wise), in *eros* toward the *agathon* (the good) and the *kalon* (the beautiful), man became philosopher. From these experiences arose the image of the order of being. At the opening of the soul—that is the metaphor Bergson uses to describe the event—the order of being becomes visible even to its ground and origin in the beyond, in the Platonic *epekeina*, in which the soul participates as it suffers and achieves its opening.

Only when the order of being as a whole, unto its origin in transcendent being, comes into view, can the analysis be undertaken with any hope of success; for only then can current opinions about right order be examined as to their agreement with the order of being. When the strong and successful are highly rated, they can then be contrasted with those who possess the virtue of *phronesis*, wisdom, who live *sub specie mortis* and act with the Last Judgment in mind. When statesmen are praised for having made their people great and powerful, as Themistocles and Pericles had made Athens, Plato can confront them with the moral decline that was the result of their policies. (One thinks here not only of classical examples, but perhaps also of what Gladstone said of Bismarck: He made Germany great and the Germans small.) Again: When impetuous young men are repelled by the vulgarity of democracy, Plato can point out to them that energy, pride, and will to rule can indeed establish the despotism of a spiritually corrupt elite, but not a just government; and when democrats rave about freedom and equality and forget that government requires spiritual training and intellectual discipline, he can warn them that they are on the way to tyranny.

These examples will suffice to indicate that political science goes beyond the validity of propositions to the truth of existence. The opinions for the clarification of which the analysis is undertaken are not merely false: They are symptoms of spiritual disorder in the men who hold them. And the purpose of the analysis is to persuade—to have its own insights, if possible, supplant the opinions in social reality. Analysis is concerned with the therapy of order.[3]

Society resists the therapeutic activity of science. Because not only the validity of the opinions is called into question but also the truth of the human attitudes expressed in the opinions, because the effort in behalf of truth is directed at the untruth of existence in particular men, the intellectual debate is intensified beyond the point of analysis and argument to that of existential struggle for and against truth—struggle that can be waged on every level of human existence, from spiritual persuasion, *peitho* in the Platonic sense, to psychological propaganda, to even physical attack and destruction. Today, under the pressure of totalitarian terror, we are perhaps inclined to think primarily of the physical forms of opposition. But they are not the most successful. The opposition becomes truly radical and dangerous only when philosophical questioning is itself called into question, when *doxa* takes on the appearance of philosophy, when it arrogates to itself the name of science and prohibits science as nonscience. Only if this prohibition can be made socially effective will the point have been reached where *ratio* can no longer operate as a remedy for spiritual disorder. Hellenic civilization never came to this: Philosophizing could be mortally dangerous, but philosophy, especially political science, flourished. Never did it occur to a Greek to prohibit analytical inquiry as such.

The frame of reference of political science has changed considerably in the more than two thousand years since its founding. The broadening of temporal and spatial horizons has yielded to comparative analysis enormous amounts of material that were unknown in antiquity. And the appearance of Christianity in history, with the resulting tension between reason and revelation, has profoundly affected the difficulties of philosophizing. The Platonic-Aristotelian paradigm of the best polis cannot provide an answer for the great questions of our time—either for the organizational problems of industrial society or for the spiritual problems of the struggle between Christianity and ideology. But the basic situation of political science, which I have briefly outlined here, has, except

3. On the problem of rational debate in a heavily ideologized society, see Eric Voegelin, "On Debate and Existence," *The Intercollegiate Review* 3 (1967): 143–52.

in one respect, not changed at all. Today, just as two thousand years ago, *politike episteme* deals with questions that concern everyone and that everyone asks. Although different opinions are current in society today, its subject matter has not changed. Its method is still scientific analysis. And the prerequisite of analysis is still the perception of the order of being unto its origin in transcendent being, in particular, the loving openness of the soul to its transcendent ground of order.

Only in one respect has the situation of political science changed. As indicated, there has emerged a phenomenon unknown to antiquity that permeates our modern societies so completely that its ubiquity scarcely leaves us any room to see it at all: the prohibition of questioning. This is not a matter of resistance to analysis—that existed in antiquity as well. It does not involve those who cling to opinions by reason of tradition or emotion, or those who engage in debate in a naïve confidence in the rightness of their opinions and who take the offensive only when analysis unnerves them. Rather, we are confronted here with persons who know that, and why, their opinions cannot stand up under critical analysis and who therefore make the prohibition of the examination of their premises part of their dogma. This position of a conscious, deliberate, and painstakingly elaborated obstruction of *ratio* constitutes the new phenomenon.

II

We shall now try to present the phenomenon of the prohibition of questions through an analysis of representative opinions. Thus, this effort will present not only the phenomenon, but the exercise of analysis as well. It should show that the spiritual disorder of our time, the civilizational crisis of which everyone so readily speaks, does not by any means have to be borne as an inevitable fate; that, on the contrary, everyone possesses the means of overcoming it in his own life. And our effort should not only indicate the means, but also show how to employ them. No one is obliged to take part in the spiritual crisis of a society; on the contrary, everyone is obliged to avoid this folly and live his life in order. Our presentation of the phenomenon, therefore, will at the same time furnish the remedy for it through therapeutic analysis.

I

The prohibition of questions as it appears in some of the early writings of Karl Marx—the "Economic and Philosophical Manuscripts" of 1844—can serve as the point of departure.

Marx is a speculative Gnostic. He construes the order of being as a process of nature complete in itself. Nature is in a state of becoming, and in the course of its development it has brought forth man: "Man is directly a *being of nature.*"[4] Now, in the development of nature a special role has devolved upon man. This being, which is itself nature, also stands over against nature and assists it in its development by human labor—which in its highest form is technology and industry based on the natural sciences: "Nature as it develops in human history . . . as it develops through industry . . . is true *anthropological* nature."[5] In the process of creating nature, however, man at the same time also creates himself to the fullness of his being; therefore, "*all of so-called world history* is nothing but the production of man by human labor."[6] The purpose of this speculation is to shut off the process of being from transcendent being and have man create himself. This is accomplished by playing with equivocations in which "nature" is now all-inclusive being, now nature as opposed to man, and now the nature of man in the sense of *essentia.* This equivocal wordplay reaches its climax in a sentence that can easily be overlooked: "A being that does not have its nature outside of itself is not a *natural* being; it does not participate in the being of nature."[7]

In connection with this speculation Marx himself now brings up the question of what objection the "particular individual" would probably have to the idea of the spontaneous generation (*"generatio aequivoca"*) of nature and man: "The being-of-itself (*Durchsichselbstsein*) of nature and man is *inconceivable* to him, because it contradicts all the *tangible aspects* of practical life." The individual man will, going back from generation to generation in search of his origin, raise the question of the creation of the first man. He will introduce the argument of infinite regress, which in Ionian

---

4. Karl Marx, "Nationalökonomie und Philosophie," in Karl Marx, *Der Historische Materialismus: Die Frühschriften,* ed. Landshut and Meyer (Leipzig, 1932), 333 ["Economic and Philosophical Manuscripts," in *Early Writings,* ed. and trans. T. B. Bottomore (New York, 1964), 206].
    5. Ibid., 304 [Bottomore, 164].
    6. Ibid., 307 [Bottomore, 166].
    7. Ibid., 333 [Bottomore, 207].

philosophy led to the problem of the *arche* (origin). To such questions, prompted by the "tangible" experience that man does not exist of himself, Marx chooses to reply that they are "a product of abstraction." "When you inquire about the creation of nature and man, you abstract from nature and man." Nature and man are real only as Marx construes them in his speculation. Should his questioner pose the possibility of their non-existence, then Marx could not prove that they exist.[8]

In reality, his construct would collapse with this question. And how does Marx get out of the predicament? He instructs his questioner, "Give up your abstraction and you will give up your question along with it." If the questioner were consistent, says Marx, he would have to think of himself as not existing—even while, in the very act of questioning, he *is*. Hence, again the instruction: "Do not think, do not question me."[9] The "individual man," however, is not obliged to be taken in by Marx's syllogism and think of himself as not existing because he is aware of the fact that he does not exist of himself. Indeed, Marx concedes this very point—without, however, choosing to go into it. Instead, he breaks off the debate by declaring that "for socialist man"—that is, for the man who has accepted Marx's construct of the process of being and history—such a question "becomes a practical impossibility." The questions of the "individual man" are cut off by the ukase of the speculator who will not permit his construct to be disturbed. When "socialist man" speaks, man has to be silent.[10]

This, then, is the evidence from which we have to proceed. But before we take up the analysis itself, let us first establish that the Marxian prohibition of questions is neither isolated nor harmless. It was not isolated in its own time, for we find the same prohibition in Comte, in the first lecture of his *Cours de Philosophie Positive*. Comte also anticipates objections to his construct, and he bluntly dismisses them as idle questions. For the present he is interested only in the laws of social phenomena. Whoever asks questions about the nature, calling, and destiny of man may be temporarily ignored; later, after the system of positivism has prevailed in society, such persons will have to be silenced by appropriate measures.[11]

8. Ibid., 306–7 [Bottomore, 165–66].
9. Ibid., 307 [Bottomore, 166].
10. Ibid. [Bottomore, pp. 166–67].
11. Auguste Comte, *Cours de Philosophie Positive* (Paris, 1830), vol. 1.

And the prohibition of questions is not harmless, for it has attained great social effectiveness among men who forbid themselves to ask questions in critical situations. One thinks of the observation of Rudolf Höss, the commandant of the extermination camp in Auschwitz. When asked why he did not refuse to obey the order to organize the mass executions, he replied: "At that time I did not indulge in deliberation: I had received the order, and I had to carry it out. . . . I do not believe that even one of the thousands of SS leaders could have permitted such a thought to occur to him. Something like that was just completely impossible."[12] This is very close to the wording of Marx's declaration that for "socialist man" such a question "becomes a practical impossibility." Thus, we see delineated three major types for whom a human inquiry has become a practical impossibility: socialist man (in the Marxian sense), positivist man (in the Comtean sense), and national-socialist man.

And now for the Marxian suppression of questions. It represents, as we shall see, a very complicated psychological phenomenon, and we must isolate each of its components in turn. First, the most "tangible": Here is a thinker who knows that his construct will collapse as soon as the basic philosophical question is asked. Does this knowledge induce him to abandon his untenable construct? Not in the least: it merely induces him to prohibit such questions. But his prohibition now induces us to ask, Was Marx an intellectual swindler? Such a question will perhaps give rise to objections. Can one seriously entertain the idea that the lifework of a thinker of considerable rank is based on an intellectual swindle? Could it have attracted a mass following and become a political world power if it rested on a swindle? But we today are inured to such scruples: We have seen too many improbable and incredible things that were nonetheless real. Therefore, we hesitate neither to ask the question that the evidence presses upon us, nor to answer, Yes, Marx *was* an intellectual swindler. This is certainly not the last word on Marx. We have already referred to the complexity of the psychological phenomenon behind the passages quoted. But it must unrelentingly be the first word if we do not want to obstruct our understanding of the prohibition of questions.

When we establish that Marx was an intellectual swindler, the

12. Rudolf Höss, *Kommandant in Auschwitz*, as quoted in *Süddeutsche Zeitung*, 1, October 1958.

further question of why immediately arises. What can prompt a man to commit such a swindle? Is there not something pathological about this act? For an answer to this question let us turn to Nietzsche, who was also a speculative Gnostic, but a more sensitive psychologist than Marx.

2

Nietzsche introduces the will to power, the will to dominion, the *libido dominandi,* as the passion that accounts for the will to intellectual deception. Let us examine the *via dolorosa* along which this passion drives the gnostic thinker from one station to the next.

In *Jenseits von Gut und Böse,* aphorism 230, Nietzsche speaks of a "fundamental will of the spirit" that wants to feel itself master. The spirit's will to mastery is served in the first place by "a suddenly emptying resolve for ignorance, for arbitrary occlusion . . . a kind of defensive stand against much that is knowable." Moreover, the spirit *wills* to let itself be deceived on occasion, "perhaps with a mischievous suspicion that things are *not* thus and so, but rather only allowed to pass as such . . . a satisfaction in the arbitrariness of all these manifestations of power." Finally, there belongs here "that not unscrupulous readiness of the spirit to deceive other spirits and to dissemble before them," the enjoyment of "cunning and a variety of masks."[13]

The *libido dominandi,* however, has a violence and cruelty that go beyond the delight in masquerade and in the deception of others. It turns on the thinker himself and unmasks his thought as a cunning will to power. "A kind of cruelty of the intellectual conscience," "an extravagant honesty," clears up the deception; however—and this is the decisive point—not in order to advance to the truth beyond the deception, but only to set up a new one in place of the old. The game of masks continues; and those who allow themselves to be deceived remain deceived. In this "cruelty of the intellectual conscience" can be seen the movement of the spirit that in Nietzsche's Gnosis corresponds functionally to the Platonic *periagoge,* the turning-around and opening of the soul. But in the gnostic movement man remains shut off from transcendent being. The will to power strikes against the wall of being, which has

13. Nietzsche, No. 230, *Jenseits von Gut und Böse,* in *Werke,* 8 (Leipzig, 1903), 187–88 [*Beyond Good and Evil,* trans. Marianne Cowan (Chicago, 1955), 158–59].

become a prison. It forces the spirit into the rhythm of deception and self-laceration.[14]

The compulsion to deceive must now be examined further. Does the spirit really strike against the wall of being? Or does it not perhaps *will* to stop there? The remoter depths of the will to power are revealed through the following aphorism: "To rule, and to be no longer a servant of a god: this means was left behind to ennoble man." To rule means to be God; in order to be God gnostic man takes upon himself the torments of deception and self-laceration.[15]

But the spirit's action is not yet at an end. The question of whether the thinker really wants to be God takes us still further; perhaps the affirmation of this desire is just another deception. In the "Night Song" in *Zarathustra* this question is answered in a revealing confession:

> It is night: only now awaken all the songs of the lovers. . . . A craving for love is in me. . . . [But] light am I: oh, that I were night! . . . This is my loneliness, that I am begirt with light. . . . I do not know the happiness of those who receive. . . . This is my poverty, that my hand never rests from giving. . . . You only, you dark ones, you of the night, extract your warmth from what shines. . . . Ice is around me; my hand is burnt up with iciness. . . . It is night: alas, that I must be light.

In this confession the voice of a spiritually sensitive man seems to be speaking, who is suffering in the consciousness of his demonic occlusion. Mystic night is denied him. He is imprisoned in the icy light of his existence. And from this prison rises the protestation— half lament, half prayer, and still not free of the defiance of the rebel—"And my soul, too, is the song of a lover."[16]

No one will hear this lament of a man to whom humility before God was not given without being moved. Beyond the psychology of the will to power, we are confronted with the inscrutable fact that grace is granted or denied.

Yet emotion should not prevent our seeing the dubiousness of this confession. We introduced it by asking whether the gnostic thinker really wants to be God, or whether the affirmation of his will is

14. Ibid., 189 [Cowan, 160].
15. Nietzsche, No. 250, *Sprüche und Sentenzen* (1882–1884), in *Werke*, 12 (Leipzig, 1901), 282.
16. Nietzsche, "Night Song," *Also sprach Zarathustra*, in *Werke*, 6 (Leipzig, 1904), 153–55 [*Thus Spoke Zarathustra*, trans. Marianne Cowan (Chicago, 1957), 106–8].

not just another deception. The "Night Song" appears to admit the deception: It is not that he *wants* to be God; he *has* to be God—for inscrutable reasons. But this latter conclusion, which nullifies the former one, immediately prompts us to ask if we have to accept it. Must we now consider the game of deceptions ended? I do not think so. Let us continue with the game and ask if the "Night Song" is not yet another mask. Bearing in mind that Nietzsche confesses that he knows his occlusion and suffers in it, let us turn his confession against him and ask, Does a man really have to make a virtue out of the misery of his condition, which he perceives to be the graceless disorder of the soul, and set it up as a superhuman ideal? Does his deficiency entitle him to perform Dionysian dances with masks? Let us, with the brutality that the times compel if we are not to fall victim to them, ask if he is not rather obliged to be silent. And if his lament were more than a mask, if it were genuine, if he suffered from his condition, would he not then be speechless? But Nietzsche is not in the least speechless; and his eloquence is convincing proof that the lament is only an act of sympathetic understanding, that it has not been allowed to touch the core of his existence in rebellion against God, and therefore that it is not genuine, but a mask. Just as Marx will not permit his game of equivocations to be disturbed, so Nietzsche refuses to break off his game of masks.

The phenomenon of the prohibition of questions is becoming clearer in its outlines. The gnostic thinker really does commit an intellectual swindle, and he knows it. One can distinguish three stages in the action of his spirit. On the surface lies the deception itself. It could be self-deception; and very often it is, when the speculation of a creative thinker has culturally degenerated and become the dogma of a mass movement. But when the phenomenon is apprehended at its point of origin, as in Marx or Nietzsche, deeper than the deception itself will be found the awareness of it. The thinker does not lose control of himself: The *libido dominandi* turns on its own work and wishes to master the deception as well. This gnostic turning back on itself corresponds spiritually, as we have said, to the philosophic conversion, the *periagoge* in the Platonic sense. However, the gnostic movement of the spirit does not lead to the erotic opening of the soul, but rather to the deepest reach of persistence in the deception, where revolt against God is revealed to be its motive and purpose.

With the three stages in the spirit's action it is now possible also to differentiate more precisely the corresponding levels of deception:

(1) For the surface act it will be convenient to retain the term Nietzsche used, "deception." But in content this action does not necessarily differ from a wrong judgment arising from another motive than the Gnostic. It could also be an "error." It becomes a deception only because of the psychological context.

(2) In the second stage the thinker becomes aware of the untruth of his assertion or speculation, but persists in it in spite of this knowledge. Only because of his awareness of the untruth does the action become a deception. And because of the persistence in the communication of what are recognized to be false arguments, it also becomes an "intellectual swindle."

(3) In the third stage the revolt against God is revealed and recognized to be the motive of the swindle. With the continuation of the intellectual swindle in full knowledge of the motive of revolt the deception further becomes "demonic mendacity."

3

The first and second of the three stages Nietzsche described can be seen in the texts that we have quoted from Marx. How does Marx stand with respect to the third stage in this movement of the spirit, where rebellion against God is revealed to be the motive for the deception? This is exactly what is revealed in the context of the quoted passages:

> A *being* regards itself as independent only when it stands on its own feet; and it stands on its feet only when it owes its *existence* to itself alone. A man who lives by the grace of another considers himself a dependent being. But I live by the grace of another completely if I owe him not only the maintenance of my life but also *its creation*: if he is the *source* of my life; and my life necessarily has such a cause outside itself if it is not my own creation.[17]

Marx does not deny that "tangible experience" argues for the dependence of man. But reality must be destroyed—this is the great concern of Gnosis. In its place steps the Gnostic who produces the independence of his existence by speculation. It would indeed be

17. Marx, "Nationalökonomie und Philosophie," 305–6 [Bottomore, 165].

difficult to find another passage in gnostic literature that so clearly exposes this speculation as an attempt to replace the reality of being with a "second reality" (as Robert Musil called this undertaking).

A passage from Marx's doctoral dissertation of 1840–1841 takes us still further into the problem of revolt:

> Philosophy makes no secret of it. The confession of Prometheus, "In a word, I hate all the gods," is its own confession, its own verdict against all gods heavenly and earthly who do not acknowledge human self-consciousness as the supreme deity. There shall be none beside it.[18]

In this confession, in which the young Marx presents his own attitude under the symbol of Prometheus, the vast history of the revolt against God is illuminated as far back as the Hellenic creation of the symbol.

Let us first clarify the relationship between Marx's comments and the verse he quotes from Aeschylus.

Prometheus is riveted to a rock by the sea. Below on the strip of beach stands Hermes looking up at him. The fettered Prometheus gives his bitterness free reign. Hermes tries to calm him and urges moderation. Then, Prometheus crams his impotence and rebellion into the line quoted by Marx: "In a word, I hate all the gods."[19] But the line is not part of a monologue. At this outbreak of hatred the messenger of the gods replies admonishingly: "It appears you have been stricken with no small madness."[20] The word translated here as "madness" is the Greek *nosos*, which Aeschylus employed as a synonym for *nosema*.[21] It means bodily or mental sickness. In the sense of a disease of the spirit it can mean hatred of the gods or simply being dominated by one's passions. For example, Plato speaks of the *nosema tes adikias*, the sickness of injustice.[22] Here we touch on the diseased—the pneumopathological—nature of the revolt that was pointed out earlier. And what does Marx say to this

---

18. Marx, *Differenz der demokritischen und epikureischen Naturphilosophie nebst einem Anhang*, in Karl Marx and Friedrich Engels, *Historisch-Kritische Gesamtausgabe*, part 1, I/1 (Frankfurt, 1927), 10. The dissertation was written in 1839–1841; the preface was dated: Berlin, March 1841 ["Foreword to Thesis: The Difference Between the Natural Philosophy of Democritus and the Natural Philosophy of Epicurus," in Karl Marx and Friedrich Engels, *On Religion* (New York, 1964), p. 15].

19. Aeschylus *Prometheus Bound* 975.

20. Ibid., 977.

21. Ibid., 978.

22. Plato *Gorgias* 480b.

observation of the messenger of the gods? He says nothing. Anyone who does not know *Prometheus Bound* must conclude that the quoted "confession" sums up the meaning of the tragedy, not that Aeschylus wished to represent hatred of the gods as madness. In the distortion of the intended meaning into its opposite the suppression of questions can be seen again on all its levels: the deception of the reader by isolating the text (the confession appears in the preface to a doctoral dissertation), the awareness of the swindle (for we assume that Marx had read the tragedy), and the demonic persistence in the revolt against better judgment.

The soul's rebellion against the order of the cosmos, hatred of the gods, and the revolt of the Titans are not, to be sure, unheard of in Hellenic myth. But the Titanomachia ends with the victory of Jovian justice (*dike*), and Prometheus is fettered. The revolutionary reversal of the symbol—the dethronement of the gods, the victory of Prometheus—lies beyond classical culture; it is the work of Gnosticism. Not until the gnostic revolt of the Roman era do Prometheus, Cain, Eve, and the serpent become symbols of man's deliverance from the power of the tyrannical god of this world. Marx's confession iterates the reinterpretation of the Prometheus symbol that can be found in an alchemist text of the third century, the treatise of Zosimos *On the Letter Omega:*

> Hermes and Zoroaster have said that the tribe of philosophers is above fate (*heimarmene*): they do not rejoice in the good fortune it brings, for they master their desires; nor are they affected by the bad fortune it sends—if it is true that they look ahead to the end of all their misfortune; nor do they accept the fine gifts that come from it, for they pass their lives in immateriality. This is the point of Prometheus' advice to Epimetheus in Hesiod:
> [PROMETHEUS.] What in the eyes of men is the greatest good fortune?
> [EPIMETHEUS.] A beautiful woman and lots of money.
> [PROMETHEUS.] Beware of accepting gifts from Olympian Zeus; put them far from you.
> In this way, he teaches his brother to reject the gifts of Zeus, i.e., of heimarmene, through the power of philosophy.[23]

This text has a special significance for us, because it confirms the connection between the revolt against the gods and the proclama-

---

23. *Collection des Anciens Alchemistes Grecs,* ed. Berthelot (Paris, 1888), 3:228 f. (Greek text), 221 ff. (translation). Our translation follows that of Festugière, together with his emendations: A. J. Festugière, *La Révelation d'Hermès Trismégiste,* vol. 1, *L'Astrologie et les Sciences Occultes,* 2d ed. (Paris, 1950), 266. For Prometheus' answer in Hesiod, see *Works and Days,* 85–87.

tion of "philosophy" as the new source of order and authority. Not only does Prometheus become the hero of revolution; the symbol of philosophy undergoes a similar perversion of its meaning. The "philosophy" of Zosimos is not the philosophy that Plato founded. His "philosophers" are not, as in the Platonic myth, the Sons of Zeus who follow his lead in this world and the next; nor are they the priests and helpers of the gods, as in Marcus Aurelius; their efforts are not concerned with forming men for the order of Zeus and *dike.* And "philosophizing" is not the Socratic practice of dying so that a man may measure up at the Last Judgment. The "philosophy" of Zosimos is concerned with something else, although the text, to the extent quoted, does not sufficiently make clear with what. Certainly, it is concerned with a new asceticism, with the attempt to remove oneself from the world and its entanglements— the gnostic motive of doing away with reality. (The transformation of Pandora and her gifts into "a beautiful woman and lots of money" carries overtones of antibourgeois criticism.) Certainly, it has to do with a revolt against the father-gods of classical myth, for the identification of the gifts of Zeus with the dispensations of what by Zosimos's time was a thoroughly discredited *heimarmene* is doubtless intended disparagingly. Certainly, it is involved in an opus of delivering man from the evil of the world. And finally, it is certain that "philosophy" is, in some way or other, intended as an instrument of salvation available for man's use.[24]

Whether Marx knew this text either directly or indirectly, we cannot say. Probably he did not. All the more, then, would the parallel in symbolic expression corroborate the essential sameness of attitudes and motives in ancient and modern Gnosticism.[25]

4

Now just what is this new "philosophy"? What is its connection with the Promethean revolt and with the suppression of questions?

24. For the Prometheus symbolism in Zosimos, see Hans Jonas, *Gnosis und spätantiker Geist,* vol. 1, *Die mythologische Gnosis* (Göttingen, 1954), 218–20; for the revolutionary element in Gnosticism, see the entire section 214–51. There is also a brief discussion in Jonas, *The Gnostic Religion,* 91–97.

25. The Prometheus complex in Marx can be fully understood only when seen in the context of German idealism. For the relevant historical background, see Hans Urs von Balthasar's masterly work *Prometheus: Studien zur Geschichte des deutschen Idealismus,* 2d ed. (Heidelberg, 1947). Unfortunately the book contains no study of Marx. See also Eric Voegelin, "The Formation of the Marxian Revolutionary Idea," *Review of Politics* 12 (1950): 275–302.

Marx modeled his idea of science and philosophy on Hegel. Let us turn, therefore, to the greatest of speculative Gnostics for the answer to these questions.

It is to be found in a fundamental statement in the preface to the *Phänomenologie* of 1807:

> The true form in which truth exists can only be the scientific system of it. To contribute to bringing philosophy closer to the form of science— the goal of being able to cast off the name love of *knowledge (Liebe zum Wissen)* and become *actual knowledge (wirkliches Wissen)*—is the task I have set for myself.[26]

The expressions "love of knowledge" and "actual knowledge" are italicized by Hegel himself. If we translate them back into the Greek, into *philosophia* and *gnosis*, we then have before us the program of advancing from philosophy to Gnosis. Thus, Hegel's programmatic formula implies the perversion of the symbols science and philosophy.

By philosophy Hegel means an undertaking of thought that approaches and can finally attain actual knowledge. Philosophy is subsumed under the idea of progress in the eighteenth-century sense of the term. As opposed to this progressivist idea of philosophy let us recall Plato's efforts to clarify its nature. In the *Phaedrus* Plato has Socrates describe the characteristics of the true thinker. When Phaedrus asks what one should call such a man, Socrates, following Heraclitus, replies that the term *sophos*, one who knows, would be excessive: This attribute may be applied to God alone; but one might well call him *philosophos*.[27] Thus, "actual knowledge" is reserved to God; finite man can only be the "lover of knowledge," not himself the one who knows. In the meaning of the passage, the lover of the knowledge that belongs only to the knowing God, the *philosophos*, becomes the *theophilos*, the lover of God. If we now place Hegel's idea of philosophizing alongside Plato's, we shall have to conclude that while there is indeed a progress in clarity and precision of knowledge of the order of being, the leap over the bounds of the finite into the perfection of actual knowledge is impossible. If a thinker attempts it, he is not advancing philosophy, but abandoning it to become a Gnostic. Hegel conceals the leap by

---

26. Hegel, *Phänomenologie des Geistes*, ed. Johannes Hoffmeister (Hamburg, 1952), 12 [*The Phenomenology of Mind*, trans. J. B. Baillie, 2d ed., rev. (London, 1949), 70].
27. Plato *Phaedrus* 278d.

translating *philosophia* and *gnosis* into German so that he can shift from one to the other by playing on the word "knowledge." This wordplay is structurally analogous to Plato's in the *Phaedrus*. But the philosophic wordplay serves to illuminate the thought, while the gnostic wordplay is designed to conceal the non-thought. This point is worth noting because the German Gnostics, especially, like to play with language and hide their non-thought in wordplay.

The result of such transitions—which are in fact leaps—is that the meanings of words are changed. The gnostic program that Hegel successfully carries out retains for itself the name "philosophy," and the speculative system in which the Gnostic unfolds his will to make himself master of being insists on calling itself "science."

Philosophy springs from the love of being; it is man's loving endeavor to perceive the order of being and attune himself to it. Gnosis desires dominion over being; in order to seize control of being the Gnostic constructs his system. The building of systems is a gnostic form of reasoning, not a philosophical one.

But the thinker can seize control of being with his system only if being really lies within his grasp. As long as the origin of being lies beyond the being of this world; as long as eternal being cannot be completely penetrated with the instrument of world-immanent, finite cognition; as long as divine being can be conceived of only in the form of the *analogia entis*, the construction of a system will be impossible. If this venture is to be seriously launched at all, the thinker must first eliminate these inconveniences: He must so interpret being that on principle it lies within the grasp of his construct. Here is Hegel addressing himself to this problem:

> According to my view, which will have to be justified only through the presentation of the system itself, everything depends on comprehending and expressing the true as *subject* no less than as *substance*.[28]

The conditions required for the solution are formulated just as for a mathematical problem: If being is at one and the same time substance and subject, then, of course, truth lies within the grasp of the apprehending subject. But, we must ask, are substance and subject really identical? Hegel dispenses with this question by declaring that the truth of his "view" is proven if he can justify it "through the presentation of the system." If, therefore, I can build a system, the truth of its premise is thereby established; that I can build a

28. Hegel, *Phänomenologie*, 19 [Baillie, 80].

system on a false premise is not even considered. The system is justified by the fact of its construction; the possibility of calling into question the construction of systems, as such, is not acknowledged. That the form of science is the system must be assumed as beyond all question. We are confronted here with the same phenomenon of the suppression of questions that we met in Marx. But we now see more clearly that an essential connection exists between the suppression of questions and the construction of a system. Whoever reduces being to a system cannot permit questions that invalidate systems as a form of reasoning.[29]

5

The essential connection between the *libido dominandi,* the system, and the prohibition of questions, although by no means completely worked out, has been made clear by the testimony of the Gnostics themselves. Let us return now for the last time to Marx's prohibition against questions.

We recall that Marx un-Socratically breaks off the dialogue with his philosophical interrogator with a ukase. But though he refuses to go any further into the arguments, he is still very careful to base his refusal on the logic of his system. He does not simply dismiss the questioner; he directs him to the path of reason. When the man brings up the problem of the *arche,* Marx admonishes: "Ask yourself whether that progression exists as such for rational thought."[30] Let this person become reasonable; then he will stop his questioning. For Marx, however, reason is not the reason of man but in the perversion of symbols, the standpoint of his system. His questioner is supposed to cease to be man: He is to become socialist man. Marx thus posits that his construct of the process of being (which comprises the historical process) represents reality. He takes the historical evolution of man into socialist man—which is part of his conceptual construct—and inserts it into his encounters with others; he calls upon the man who questions the assumptions of his system to enter into the system and undergo the evolution it prescribes. In the clash between system and reality, reality must give way. The intellectual swindle is justified by referring to the

29. An analysis of Hegel's "philosophy of history" will reveal the same gnostic program that we have seen in the *Phänomenologie.* See the Note on Hegel's "Philosophy of World History" (below).

30. Marx, "Nationalökonomie und Philosophie," 306 (Bottomore, 166].

demands of the historical future, which the gnostic thinker has speculatively projected in his system.

The position of the gnostic thinker derives its authority from the power of being. He is the herald of being, which he interprets as approaching us from the future. This interpretation of being is no doubt active in the speculation of Marx and Nietzsche, but it is not yet worked out in all its consequences. It remained for that ingenious Gnostic of our own time, Martin Heidegger, to think the problem through, under the heading of "fundamental ontology." The following examples of speculation on being are taken from his *Einführung in die Metaphysik.*

In Heidegger's speculation being is interpreted on the basis of the original Greek meaning of *parousia* as presence (*An-wesen*).[31] Being is not to be understood statically, as substance, but actively, as presence, in the sense of a coming into presence, as an emerging or appearing—somewhat in the way a ruler makes an appearance or is present. The essence of being as *actio* is a dominating power wherein being creates for itself a world; and it creates this world through man.[32] Man is to be understood historically as an existence that can either open or shut itself to the domination of being. In the historical process, therefore, there can be times of falling away from essential being into the nonessential, whence human existence can find its way back only by opening itself again to the parousia of being. Applying these possibilities to contemporary history, Heidegger decides—as did Marx and Nietzsche in their cruder fashion—that today we in the Western world live in a period of nonessential existence. Hence, the future of the West depends on our opening ourselves again to the essential power of being. Heavy with fate fall the formulas: "This means leading man's historical existence (*Dasein*) . . . in the totality of the history allotted us, back to the power of being which originally was to have been opened up"; or: That which is referred to by the word "being" holds "the spiritual fate of the West."[33]

Heidegger's speculation occupies a significant place in the history of Western Gnosticism. The construct of the closed process

31. Martin Heidegger, *Einführung in die Metaphysik,* 2d ed. (Tübingen, 1958), 46 [*An Introduction to Metaphysics,* trans. Ralph Manheim (New Haven, 1950); Anchor Books edition (Garden City, New York, 1961), 50].

32. Ibid., 47 [Manheim, 511].

33. Ibid., 32 [Manheim, 34–35].

of being, the shutting off of immanent from world-transcendent being, the refusal to acknowledge the experiences of *philia, eros, pistis* (faith), and *elpis* (hope)—which were described and named by the Hellenic philosophers—as the ontic events wherein the soul participates in transcendent being and allows itself to be ordered by it; the refusal, thus, to acknowledge them as the events in which philosophy, especially Platonic philosophy, has its origin; and finally, the refusal to permit the very idea of a construct of a closed process of being to be called into question in the light of these events—all of this was, in varying degrees of clarity, doubtless to be found in the speculative Gnostics of the nineteenth century. But Heidegger has reduced this complex to its essential structure and purged it of period-bound visions of the future. Gone are the ludicrous images of positivist, socialist, and super man. In their place Heidegger puts being itself, emptied of all content, to whose approaching power we must submit. As a result of this refining process, the nature of gnostic speculation can now be understood as the symbolic expression of an anticipation of salvation in which the power of being replaces the power of God and the parousia of being, the Parousia of Christ.

6

This completes the analysis. There remains only the task of defining the results conceptually and terminologically.

For this purpose we shall take over from Heidegger's interpretation of being the term "parousia," and speak of parousiasm as the mentality that expects deliverance from the evils of the time through the advent, the coming in all its fullness, of being construed as immanent. We can then speak of the men who express their parousiasm in speculative systems as parousiastic thinkers, of their structures of thought as parousiastic speculations, of the movements connected with some of these thinkers as parousiastic mass movements, and of the age in which these movements are socially and politically dominant as the age of parousiasm. We thus acquire a concept and a terminology for designating a phase of Western Gnosticism that have hitherto been lacking. Moreover, by conceiving of it as parousiastic we can distinguish this phase more adequately than heretofore from the preceding chiliastic phase of the Middle Ages and the Renaissance, when the gnostic movements expressed themselves in terms of the Judaeo-Christian apocalypse.[34] The long history of post-classical Western Gnosticism thus appears in its continuity as the history of Western sectarianism.

In the Middle Ages this movement could still be kept below the threshold of revolution. Today it has become, not, to be sure, the power of being, but world power. To break the spell of this world and its power—each of us in himself—is the great task at which we all must work. Political science can assist in exorcising the demons in the modest measure of effectiveness that our society grants to *episteme* and its therapy.

34. For the history of the chiliastic phase, see Norman Cohn, *The Pursuit of the Millennium*, 2d ed. (New York, 1961).

3

The Murder of God

Our analysis of parousiastic *doxa* began with the Marxian texts that have to do with the prohibition of questions. The examination was based on these passages because in them the motives, symbols, and patterns of thought of the gnostic mass movements of our time can be seen in rare concentration. It would be difficult to find another document of modern Gnosticism that in power and clarity of expression, in intellectual vigor and ingenious determination, would compare with the manuscript of the young Marx. Nevertheless, the selection has a disadvantage in that one of the most powerful motives of the speculation does not stand out with a distinctness in keeping with its actual importance. This is the motive of the murder of God.

The aim of parousiastic Gnosticism is to destroy the order of being, which is experienced as defective and unjust, and through man's creative power to replace it with a perfect and just order. Now, however the order of being may be understood—as a world dominated by cosmic-divine powers in the civilizations of the Near and Far East, or as the creation of a world-transcendent God in Judaeo-Christian symbolism, or as an essential order of being in philosophical contemplation—it remains something that is given, that is not under man's control. In order, therefore, that the attempt to create a new world may seem to make sense, the givenness of the order of being must be obliterated; the order of being must be interpreted, rather, as essentially under man's control. And taking control of being further requires that the transcendent origin of being be obliterated: It requires the decapitation of being—the murder of God.

The murder of God is committed speculatively by explaining divine being as the work of man. Let us consider what Nietzsche's

Zarathustra has to say on this point: "Alas, my brothers, that God whom I created was human work and human madness, like all gods."[35] Man should stop creating gods because this sets absurd limits to his will and action; and he should realize that the gods he has already created have in fact been created by him. "Let will to truth mean this to you: that everything be changed into the humanly conceivable, the humanly visible, the humanly sensible." This demand also extends to the world, which of old was understood to have been created by God: "What you called 'the world' shall be created only by you: it shall be your reason, your image, your will, your love."[36] "God is a conjecture"—but man's conjectures should not go beyond his creative will,[37] and they should be limited "to the conceivable." There may be no being or image of being that might make human will and thought appear finite: "Neither into the incomprehensible could you have been born, nor into the irrational." In order to appear the unlimited master of being, man must so delimit being that limitations are no longer evident. And why must this magic act be performed? The answer is: "*If* there were gods, how could I endure not being a god! *Therefore,* there are no gods."[38]

It does not suffice, therefore, to replace the old world of God with a new world of man: the world of God itself must have been a world of man, and God a work of man that can therefore be destroyed if it prevents man from reigning over the order of being. The murder of God must be made retroactive speculatively. This is the reason man's "being-of-himself" (*Durchsichselbstsein*) is the principal point in Marx's Gnosis. And he gets his speculative support from the explanation of nature and history as a process in which man creates himself to his full stature. The murder of God, then, is of the very essence of the gnostic re-creation of the order of being.

Like the Promethean hatred of the gods, the murder of God is a general possibility in human response to God. It is not confined to parousiastic speculation. In order to clarify the phenomenon we shall first describe it in the relatively simple form in which it appears in the golem legends of the Cabbala of the twelfth and early thirteenth centuries. The legends have been made available

35. Nietzsche, *Also sprach Zarathustra,* in *Werke,* 6:42 [Cowan, 271].
36. Ibid., 124 [Cowan, 84].
37. Ibid., 124 [Cowan, 84].
38. Ibid., 124 [Cowan, 85].

by Gerschom Scholem in his article "Die Vorstellung vom Golem in ihren tellurischen und magischen Beziehungen."[39]

The late twelfth-century commentary of Pseudo-Saadia on the book Yezirah includes the golem legend in the following form:

> Thus is it said in the Midrash, that Jeremiah and Ben Sira made a man by means of the book Yezirah; and on his brow was the word *emeth*, the name that He had uttered over the creature that was the perfection of all his work. But that man erased the *aleph* so as to say that God alone is truth and he had to die.[40]

The Hebrew word *emeth* means "truth." If the first of its three consonants is crossed out (in Hebrew the initial sound of the word *emeth* is represented by a consonant), *meth* is left. Meth means "dead." The adepts made the man "by means of the book Yezirah"—that is, by means of a magic operation with the letters of the Hebrew alphabet. This is essentially the same kind of operation as Marx's creation of "socialist man" by means of gnostic speculation. The golem legend now sheds additional light on its nature. In view of the reality of the order of being in which we live, Marx's prohibition of questions had to be characterized as an attempt to protect the "intellectual swindle" of his speculation from exposure by reason; but from the standpoint of the adept Marx the swindle was the "truth" that he had created through his speculation, and the prohibition of questions was designed to defend the truth of the system against the unreason of men. The curious tension between first and second reality, first and second truth, on the pneumopathological nature of which we have remarked, is now revealed to be the tension between the order of God and magic. But this tension, which results from magic's will to power, can be eliminated. For what does the golem do, bearing, like Adam, the man whom God created, the seal of truth on its forehead? It erases the letter *aleph* in order to warn the adepts that the truth is God's; the second truth is death: The golem dies.

The implications of the tension, as well as the means of its resolution, are set forth in greater detail in another version of the golem legend, which is to be found in an early thirteenth-century

---

39. *Eranos Jahrbuch 1953*, 22 (Zurich, 1954), 235–89 ["The Idea of the Golem," in *On the Kabbalah and Its Symbolism*, trans. Ralph Manheim (New York, 1965), 158–204].

40. Ibid., 259–60 [*On the Kabbalah*, 178–79].

Cabbalistic text attributed to Juda ben Bathyra. The first part of the legend reads as follows:

> The prophet Jeremiah was alone, working with the book Yezirah. There came a voice from heaven saying, "Obtain for yourself a companion." He went to his son Sira, and they studied the book for three years. Then they set to work on the alphabets, according to the Cabbalistic principles of combination, compilation, and word formation; and there was created unto them a man on whose brow were the words: YHWH Elohim Emeth. But there was a knife in the hand of that newly created man with which he scratched out the *aleph* from *emeth;* this left *meth*. Thereupon, Jeremiah rent his garments and said: "Why do you scratch out the *aleph* from *emeth?*"[41]

Important aspects of magic creation that were only implied in the first legend are now clarified. The second golem carries on its forehead the seal "God is truth." With the effacing of the letter *aleph* it becomes the proclamation "God is dead." After this deed, however, the second golem does not die, as did its predecessor. It remains standing there, the knife it used for the murder in its hand. It goes on living and bears the new seal on its brow.

Jeremiah rends his clothing—in the ritual gesture of horror before an act of blasphemy. He asks his creature the meaning of its action, and receives this answer:

> I will tell you a parable. There was an architect who built many houses, towns, and squares. But no one could imitate his art and match his knowledge and skill, until two persons prevailed upon him. He then taught them the secret of his art, and they now knew all the proper techniques. When they had acquired his secret and his abilities, they began to badger him until they broke with him and became architects like him; only, things for which he took a thaler they made for six groschen. When people noticed this, they ceased to honor the artist, but honored them instead and gave them the commission when they needed a building. Similarly, God has created you in his image, likeness, and form. But now that you have created a man as He did, it will be said, There is no God in the world other than these two![42]

Gerschom Scholem interprets the legend to mean that a successful creation of a golem would be the prelude to the "death of God"; the hubris of the creator would turn against God. The adept Jeremiah is of the same opinion, and he therefore asks the golem

41. Ibid., 261 [On the Kabbalah, 180].
42. Ibid., 261 [On the Kabbalah, 180].

for the way out of this dreadful situation. He then receives from it the formula for the destruction of the magic creature, uses it, "and before their eyes that man became dust and ashes." Jeremiah asks the relevant question; and when he gets an answer that should induce him to destroy his work, he does not suppress the question, but goes ahead and destroys his work.

The legend concludes with Jeremiah saying:

> Truly, these things should only be studied in order to recognize the might and omnipotence of the creator of this world and not with the intention of bringing them to pass.[43]

The murder of God in parousiastic Gnosticism is a well-known and thoroughly explored phenomenon. But many things generally understood under the headings "dialectics of consciousness," "point of view of immanence," "will to pure immanence," and the like sound different with the golem legend in mind. Again, within the scope of this essay, only an illustrative analysis can be attempted. Nietzsche's famous aphorism 125 from *Die fröhliche Wissenschaft* can serve as doxic material. It bears the title "The Madman."[44] Nietzsche carefully constructed the aphorism to set forth the spiritual action that constitutes the murder of God. We shall go through the various phases of this movement of the spirit.

In the bright morning the madman runs out into the marketplace with a lantern crying, "I seek God! I seek God!" Nietzsche thus begins by changing Diogenes' symbolism: The philosopher in search of man has become the madman in search of God. The meaning of the change is not immediately clear. The philosophical seeker might well find men in the marketplace; but is that the place to look for God? If we assume that Nietzsche has made an intelligible construct, then we are forced to ask whether the madman is really seeking God; and we thus anticipate the underlying significance of the change in the symbol, which becomes apparent as the aphorism progresses.

The seeker finds in the marketplace just what one would expect to find in a marketplace—men. But these men are of a special breed: "They do not believe in God." They greet his search with laughter and ridicule: "Did he get lost?" they ask; "or is he in hiding? Is

---

43. Ibid., 261 [*On the Kabbalah*, 180].
44. Nietzsche, No. 125, *Die fröhliche Wissenschaft*, in *Werke*, 5 (Leipzig, 1900), 163–64 [*The Gay Science*, in *The Portable Nietzsche*, ed. Kauffmann, 95–96].

he afraid of us? Has he taken a ship? emigrated?" The madman exclaims to the unbelievers:

Whither has he gone? I will tell you. *We have killed him*— you and I! We are all his murderers.

And how was such a deed possible?

How were we able to drink up the sea? . . . What did we do when we unchained this earth from its sun? Whither is it moving now? Whither are we moving? Away from all suns? . . . Are we not wandering as through an infinite nothingness?

But the deed is done. The murder of God cannot be undone:

God is dead! God will stay dead!

With this outcry the aphorism moves beyond the golem legend. The murder of God is seen for what it is, but the murderer stands by his action. The new creature who committed the murder does not recognize his own death in what happened. The golem lives. "The holiest and mightiest thing the world has yet possessed has bled to death under our knives." The golem stands there, the knife in his hand, ready for other feats.

And what is he seeking with his knife? The God who has already bled to death? No, he seeks "consolation":

How are we to find consolation, we, the murderers of all murderers? . . . With what water could we cleanse ourselves? . . . Is not the greatness of this deed too great for us?

Nietzsche's questioning recalls the situation in the golem legend, but the golem's instructions to undo the magic murder of God have already been rejected. The madman does not go backward, but forward: If the deed is too great for man, then man must rise up above himself to the greatness of the deed:

Must we not ourselves become gods just to seem worthy of it? There has never been a greater deed; and whoever is born after us will, because of this act, belong to a higher history than all previous history!

Who murders God will himself become God—the warning of the parable in the second golem legend.

The parable is a warning (and is so understood by the adepts in the legend) because man cannot become God. If he tries, in the process of self-idolization he will become a demon willfully shutting himself off from God. But Nietzsche wishes to continue on just this path. When the madman finishes his speech, his listeners, the unbelievers, are silent and look at him strangely. Then he throws his lantern on the ground and says:

> I have come too soon; my time has not yet come. This stupendous event is still wandering on its way. . . . Deeds need time—even after they have been done—to be seen and heard. This deed is still farther from them than the remotest stars—*and yet they have done it themselves!*

The underlying significance of the Diogenes symbolism is now clear. The new Diogenes does seek God, but not the God who is dead: He seeks the new god in the men who have murdered the old one—he seeks the superman. The madman is therefore looking for man, but not the man of the philosopher: He is looking for the being that springs from the magic of the murder of God. It is necessary to elucidate this symbolism, for, in the conscientious efforts in behalf of Nietzsche's "philosophical" intentions, it is all too often forgotten that the interpreter of a magic *opus* need not, to put it bluntly, be taken in by the magic. It is not enough to examine the symbol of the superman on the basis of the texts and determine the meaning Nietzsche intended; for the symbol occurs in a context of magic. What really takes place in the order of being when this magic is practiced must also be determined. The nature of a thing cannot be changed; whoever tries to "alter" its nature destroys the thing. Man cannot transform himself into a superman; the attempt to create a superman is an attempt to murder man. Historically, the murder of God is not followed by the superman, but by the murder of man: the deicide of the gnostic theoreticians is followed by the homicide of the revolutionary practitioners.

The transition to revolutionary practice is evidenced in the propositions with which Marx opens his *Kritik der Hegelschen Rechtsphilosophie* (1843). The argument is set down so clearly that it scarcely requires commentary.

As in Nietzsche, the magic *opus* presupposes the murder of God: "The critique of religion is the pre-supposition of all critique." God was never anything but a human product. The critique of religion yields this revelation and thereby restores man to the fullness of his nature:

The foundation of irreligious critique is this: *Man makes religion;* religion does not make man. Indeed, religion is man's self-consciousness and self-awareness insofar as he has either not yet found himself or has lost himself again.[45]

Once this relationship has been grasped, the reality of man will manifest itself again:

Man, who sought a superman in the imaginary reality of heaven and found only a *reflection* of himself, will no longer be inclined to find just a *semblance* of himself, just a non-man, where he seeks and must seek his true reality.[46]

Marx is a great deal closer to Nietzsche in these remarks than the use of the symbol "superman" for God might at first reading lead one to suppose. For God, of course, does not exist. "God" is, as in Feuerbach's psychology of religion, the projection of the best in man into a supernatural world. But though the projection in the supernatural is illusionary, this does not mean that the content of the projection is also an illusion. The best in man is real; it must—and here Marx goes beyond the psychology of projection, which exposes religion as an illusion—be drawn back into man. The Marxian *homo novus* is not a man without religious illusions, but one who has taken God back into his being. The "non-man," who has illusions, becomes fully human by absorbing the "superman." In reality, therefore, the new man is, like Nietzsche's superman, the man who has made himself God.

When through the critique of religion man has taken God back himself and has thereby come into full possession of his powers, the critique of politics begins:

The summons to abandon illusions about his condition is a *summons to abandon a condition that requires illusions.* The critique of religion is therefore *in embryo the critique of the vale of tears* of which religion is the *halo.*[47]

The struggle against religion is therefore indirectly a struggle against *that world* of which religion is the spiritual *aroma.*[48]

45. Marx, "Zur Kritik der Hegelschen Rechtsphilosophie: Einleitung," in Karl Marx, *Der Historische Materialismus: Die Frühschriften,* 263 ["Contribution to the Critique of Hegel's Philosophy of Right: Introduction," in Bottomore, 431].
46. Ibid.
47. Ibid., 264 [Bottomore, 44].
48. Ibid., 263 [Bottomore, 43].

Real man "is the *world of man*—the state, society."[49] Only when this world is perverted does it produce the perverted world consciousness of religion:

> Religion is the groan of the oppressed creature, the heart of a heartless world, the spirit of a spiritless condition. It is the *opium* of the people.[50]

It is therefore the task of history,

> ... once the *world beyond truth* has disappeared, to establish the truth of this *world*.[51]
>
> Thus, the critique of heaven is transformed into the critique of earth; *the critique of religion*, into the *critique of law*, the *critique of theology*, into the *critique of politics*.[52]

The transformed critique is no longer theory, but practice:

> Its subject is its *enemy*, which it seeks not to refute, but to *annihilate*. . . . It no longer acts as an *end in itself*, but only as a *means*. Its essential emotion is *indignation*; its essential task is *denunciation*.[53]

Here speaks the will to murder of the gnostic magician. The bonds of reality have been broken. One's fellowman is no longer a partner in being; critique is no longer rational debate. Sentence has been passed; the execution follows.

Marx's critical proclamations refer back to Hegel. Let us turn again to the *Phänomenologie*, that *magnum opus* of the murder of God.

We can only offer some reflections on it. A thorough consideration and analysis is impossible in the present context, for it is a rigorously constructed system of more than five hundred pages. The first sentence states the subject of speculation and its limits:

> The knowledge that is first or immediately our object can be nothing else but that which is itself immediate knowledge—*knowledge* of the *immediate* or *existent*.[54]

The restriction of the order of being is made even more explicit:

> I, *this particular person*, am *certain* of *this* thing, not because *I* have developed as consciousness herewith and in various ways prompted

---

49. Ibid., 263 [Bottomore, 43].
50. Ibid., 264 [Bottomore, 43–44].
51. Ibid. [Bottomore, 44].
52. Ibid., 265 [Bottomore, 44].
53. Ibid., 266 [Bottomore, 46].
54. Hegel, *Phänomenologie*, 79 [Baillie, 149].

thought; nor because *the thing* of which I am certain was, because of a number of distinct qualities, a complex of relations within itself or a manifold of relations with other things. Neither has anything to do with the truth of sensible certitude.[55]

The nature of the order of being as it is given, together with man's place in it, is obliterated: the being of world and ego is restricted to the knowledge of the immediate or existent; questions about the context of the order of being in which this knowledge occurs are declared irrelevant; the prohibition of questions is solemnly made a principle of the speculation. From this beginning the substance of the order of being—which, for the philosopher, is something given—is systematically construed as a succession of phases of consciousness that proceed in dialectical development from the initial consciousness of sensible certitude. In its language the *Phänomenologie* is philosophical; in its substance and intention it is radically anti-philosophical. It must be recognized as a work of magic—indeed, it is one of the great magic performances.

Nothing can be plucked out of this masterpiece of rigorous magical speculation without destroying the meaning of the whole. Therefore, we can only advert to a few passages where the theme of the murder of God—the object of the whole enterprise—appears. The most prominent text takes up the death of Christ:

> The death of the Mediator is not just the death of his *natural* aspect . . . ; what dies is not merely the dead husk that has been stripped from the essence, but the *abstraction* of divine being as well. . . . The death of this mental image (*Vorstellung*), therefore, comprises at the same time the death of the *abstraction of divine being*, which is not established as self. This death is the unhappy consciousness' painful feeling that *God himself has died.*[56]

What seems here to be a simple statement—the mere observation of a fact—is actually something more. For God has died because he was no more than a phase of consciousness that is now outmoded. And it is outmoded because consciousness in its dialectical progress has gone beyond it. The death of God is not an event, but the feat of a dialectician. The "harsh utterance" that God has died marks

> the return of consciousness to the depth of the night where the ego=ego, where the night no longer distinguishes or knows anything

55. Ibid., 79–80 [Baillie, 149–50].
56. Ibid., 546 [Baillie, 781–82].

outside of itself. . . . This knowledge is thus the *spiritualization* whereby substance, its abstraction and lifelessness having died, has become subject, whereby it has therefore *actually* become simple and universal self-consciousness.[57]

What at the stage of "religion" was still a mental image of an other has here become the inherent "action of the self." This last form of the spirit is absolute knowledge.[58] To be sure, religion expresses what spirit is earlier in time than does science; "but science alone is the spirit's true knowledge of itself."[59] When the spirit appears to consciousness in the medium of the concept, or rather is generated by consciousness in this medium, it has become "science."[60] The spirit as knowing what it is does not exist until it has completed the task

> of providing for its consciousness the form of its essence and in this manner of putting its *self-consciousness* on a level with its consciousness.[61]

Or, to put it all more simply and directly, the spirit as system requires the murder of God; and, conversely, in order to commit the murder of God the system is fashioned.

The *Phänomenologie* ends with a meditation on history as the spirit attaining its self-consciousness in time:

> This process of becoming presents a slow movement and succession of spirits, a gallery of images, each endowed with the entire wealth of the spirit and moving so slowly just because the self must penetrate and digest all this wealth of its substance.[62]

A realm of spirits unfolds in the temporal existence of history, in which each spirit takes over the realm of the world from the preceding one, until, in the final phase of self-consciousness, the completely unfolded history has become "internalizing recollection" (*Er-Innerung*). The goal—absolute knowledge—is attained through

> the recollection of the spirits as they are in themselves and as they accomplish the organization of their realm.[63]

57. Ibid., 556 [Baillie, 797].
58. Ibid., 559 [Baillie, 801].
59. Ibid., 556 [Baillie, 798].
60. Ibid., 557 [Baillie, 799].
61. Ibid., 557 [Baillie, 799].
62. Ibid., 564 [Baillie, 807].
63. Ibid., 557 [Baillie, 799].

The preservation of this succession of spirits according to the temporality of their existence is history; their preservation as a comprehended organization is the science of emergent knowledge. Both together, as history comprehended,

> form the recollection and the golgotha of the absolute spirit, the actuality, truth, and certainty of its throne, without which it would be a lifeless solitary thing; only—
> from the chalice of this realm of spirits
> its infinity foams out to it.[64]

When we were analyzing Nietzsche's aphorism we had occasion to remark that the interpreter of a magic *opus* need not himself be taken in by the magic. Let us therefore step out of the magic circle of the *opus* back onto the solid ground of reality. Let us consider what is taking place in the order of being as Hegel concludes his work at the golgotha of the spirit. If we attempt to summarize his summary for this purpose, we shall have to say: On the grave of the murdered God the golem is celebrating a ghastly ritual—a kind of triumphal dance accompanied with chant. The goal has been attained. The "revelation of the depth" has been successfully carried out. But the depth is nothing but the "absolute concept," and "this revelation" is therefore the "cancellation" (*Aufheben*) of the depth. And there is no other revelation. Then sounds the chant:

> from the chalice of this realm of spirits
> its infinity foams out to it.

These last two lines of the work, which are printed as if they were poetry, alter the conclusion of Schiller's poem "Friendship":

> Though the Supreme Being found no equal,
> From the chalice of the whole realm of souls
> There foams *to him*—infinity.[65]

This is the closing act of the gnostic destruction of reality. For the fate of the order of being when gnostic magicians lay hands on it Hegel has found a fitting symbol: the mutilation of a poem.[66]

64. "aus dem Kelche dieses Geisterreiches
schäumt ihm seine Unendlichkeit." Ibid.
65. "Fand das höchste Wesen schon kein Gleiches,
aus dem Kelch des ganzen Seelenreiches
Schäumt ihm—die Unendlichkeit."
66. For a more extensive analysis of this mutilation, see Alexandre Kojève, *Introduction à la lecture de Hegel* (Paris, 1947), 442.

4

Note on Hegel's "Philosophy of World History"

In the foregoing analysis I have illustrated Hegel's program of advancing from philosophy to Gnosis, as well as the conditions required for building his system, with passages from the *Phänomenologie* only—that is, on the level of "philosophy itself." Hegel reiterates essentially the same formulas on the level of the "philosophy of world history." I shall now give the parallel passages from the "Second Draft" of the *Philosophische Weltgeschichte* of 1830 (in *Die Vernunft in der Geschichte*, ed. Johannes Hoffmeister [Hamburg, 1955]).

(1) Hegel distinguishes between "philosophy itself" and the "philosophy of world history." The philosopher approaches the interpretation of world history with the "presupposition" that "reason governs the world and that, therefore, in world history things have come to pass rationally."

> In philosophy itself this is not a presupposition; there, it is *demonstrated* by speculative cognition that reason—we can accept this term without going into the question of the relationship to God—which is substance as well as infinite *power*, is itself the *infinite matter* of all natural and spiritual life and is *infinite form* as well, the actualization of this matter which is its content. (28)

The relationship of reason to God, which in this sentence remains undefined, becomes apparent as the "Second Draft" progresses. Under the denomination "idea," reason is the absolute revealing itself:

> Now, that this same idea is the true, the eternal, the absolutely powerful, that it reveals itself in the world, and that nothing is manifested

in the world but it, its majesty and glory—this, as has been said, is proved in philosophy and is presupposed here as proved. (29)

That the attributes are intended as divine and that God is identified with reason that unfolds itself in speculation and history is made clear in the following passage:

> The *world spirit* is the spirit of the world as it explains itself in human consciousness; men are related to this spirit as individual parts to the whole that is their substance. And this world spirit conforms to the divine spirit, which is absolute spirit. Insofar as God is omnipresent, he is in every man, he appears in everyone's consciousness; and this is the world spirit. (60)

(2) Since the idea is identical with the self-revealing deity, the design of progressing from philosophy to Gnosis is carried over from the sphere of "philosophy itself" to the "philosophy of world history." It is the philosopher's task to advance from the partial revelation of God through Christ to the complete comprehension of God. He is committed to this task by "Holy Scripture," according to which "it is the spirit that leads to truth, that it may know all things, even the depths of the godhead" (40–41). The task itself is formulated in the following passage:

> In the Christian religion God has revealed himself—that is, he has made known to men what he is, so that he is no longer something concealed and secret. With the possibility of knowing God it becomes incumbent upon us to do so; and the development of thinking spirit, which has proceeded from this foundation, from the revelation of the divine being, must ultimately mature to the point where what was in the first instance presented to feeling and imagining spirit is grasped in thought. Whether the time has come for such knowledge necessarily depends on whether the ultimate goal of the world has finally made its appearance in actuality in a universally valid and conscious way. (45)

(3) The program of exhaustively penetrating the depths of the godhead through its unfolding in world history is tied to the condition that the ultimate goal of the world has indeed fully unfolded in world history and become comprehensible. Just as on the level of "philosophy itself" the truth of Hegel's "view" is justified by "the presentation of the system," so on the level of the "philosophy of world history" the validity of his thesis about complete revelation is proved by the execution of the program:

Thus, the result of the study of world history itself has been and is that things have come to pass rationally, that world history has been the rational, necessary course of the world spirit. (30) [Note the perfect tense.]

That a last end is the governing principle in the events of peoples, that reason is in world history—not the reason of a particular subject, but the divine, absolute reason—is a truth that we presuppose; its proof is the treatise on world history itself the image and the work of reason (29).

PART II
ERSATZ RELIGION
The Gnostic Mass Movements of Our Time

Ersatz Religion

The term "gnostic mass movement" is not in common use. There-fore, when one encounters it one expects it first to be defined. This, however, is not possible, since for methodological reasons definitions come at the end of the analytical process and not at the beginning. And if the analysis has been carefully carried out, definitions are no longer of any great importance, for they can provide no more than a summary of the results of the analysis. We shall follow the Aristotelian method and speak first illustratively of the subject to be examined, and then, when it is secured at the common-sense level of our experience, proceed with the analysis.

I

By gnostic movements we mean such movements as progressivism, positivism, Marxism, psychoanalysis, communism, fascism, and national socialism. We are not dealing, therefore, in all of these cases with political mass movements. Some of them would more accurately be characterized as intellectual movements—for exam-ple, positivism, neo-positivism, and the variants of psychoanal-ysis. This draws attention to the fact that mass movements do not represent an autonomous phenomenon and that the difference between masses and intellectual elites is perhaps not so great as is conventionally assumed, if indeed it exists at all. At any rate, in social reality the two types merge. None of the movements cited began as a mass movement; all derived from intellectuals and small groups. Some of them, according to the intentions of their founders, should have grown into political mass movements, but did not. Others, such as neo-positivism or psychoanalysis, were meant to be intellectual movements; but they have had, if not the form, at least the success of political mass movements, in that their theories and jargons have shaped the thinking of millions of people in the Western world, very often without their being aware of it.

A brief outline of Comteian positivism may serve as a representative example of how mass and intellectual movements are connected. Positivism was an intellectual movement that began with Saint-Simon, with Comte and his friends, and was intended by its founders to become a mass movement of worldwide extent. All mankind was expected to compose the fellowship of the positivist congregation under the spiritual leadership of the *"fondateur de la religion de l'humanité."* Comte tried to enter into diplomatic correspondence with Nicholas I, with the Jesuit General, and with the Grand Vizier, in order to incorporate into positivism Russian Orthodoxy, the Catholic Church, and Islam. Even though these grandiose plans fell through, something significant was achieved. There have been strong positivist movements, especially in South America; and to this day the Republic of Brazil has on its flag the Comteian motto "Order and Progress." Comteian positivism engaged the best minds of the time in Europe. It decidedly influenced John Stuart Mill; and the echo of the Comteian view of history can still be heard in the philosophy of Max Weber, Ernst Cassirer, and Edmund Husserl. Finally, the entire Western world can thank Comte for the word "altruism"—the secular-immanent substitute for "love," which is associated with Christianity: Altruism is the basis of the conception of a brotherhood of man without a father. In the case of positivism one can see perhaps most clearly how problems concerning intellectual and mass movements converge.

II

We have located the subject of our inquiry at the level of common sense, and must now proceed to clarify further the degree to which the movements cited can be characterized as gnostic.

Again, we cannot give definitions, only allusions to the historical instances. Gnosticism was a religious movement of antiquity. It can be confirmed as having been approximately contemporary with Christianity—so contemporary, in fact, that it was assumed for a long time that Gnosis involved no more than a Christian heresy.

This notion can no longer be held today. Although there are no gnostic sources that can be dated with certainty before the birth of Christ, gnostic influences and terminology are indeed so clearly recognizable in Saint Paul that they must stem from a powerful movement in existence before his time. On the historical continuity of Gnosticism from antiquity to modern times, let it be said here only that the connections in the development of gnostic sects from those of the eastern Mediterranean in antiquity through the movements of the high Middle Ages up to those of the Western Renaissance and Reformation have been sufficiently clarified to permit us to speak of a continuity.

More important for our purposes than definitions and questions of genesis are the features by which we can recognize gnostic movements as such. Let us list, therefore, the six characteristics that, taken together, reveal the nature of the gnostic attitude.

(1) It must first be pointed out that the Gnostic is dissatisfied with his situation. This, in itself, is not especially surprising. We all have cause to be not completely satisfied with one aspect or another of the situation in which we find ourselves.

(2) Not quite so understandable is the second aspect of the gnostic attitude: the belief that the drawbacks of the situation can be attributed to the fact that the world is intrinsically poorly organized. For it is likewise possible to assume that the order of being as it is given to us men (wherever its origin is to be sought) is good and that it is we human beings who are inadequate. But Gnostics are not inclined to discover that human beings in general and they themselves in particular are inadequate. If in a given situation something is not as it should be, then the fault is to be found in the wickedness of the world.

(3) The third characteristic is the belief that salvation from the evil of the world is possible.

(4) From this follows the belief that the order of being will have to be changed in a historical process. From a wretched world a good one must evolve historically. This assumption is not altogether self-evident, because the Christian solution might also be considered, namely, that the world throughout history will remain as it is and that man's salvational fulfillment is brought about through grace in death.

(5) With this fifth point we come to the gnostic trait in the

narrower sense—the belief that a change in the order of being lies in the realm of human action, that this salvational act is possible through man's own effort.

(6) If it is possible, however, so to work a structural change in the given order of being that we can be satisfied with it as a perfect one, then it becomes the task of the Gnostic to seek out the prescription for such a change. Knowledge—Gnosis—of the method of altering being is the central concern of the Gnostic. As the sixth feature of the Gnostic attitude, therefore, we recognize the construction of a formula for self and world salvation, as well as the Gnostic's readiness to come forward as a prophet who will proclaim his knowledge about the salvation of mankind.

These six characteristics, then, describe the essence of the gnostic attitude. In one variation or another they are to be found in each of the movements cited.

III

For its appropriate expression, the gnostic attitude has produced a rich and multiform symbolism in the modern mass movements. It is so extensive that it cannot be completely described in this essay. We shall deal with only a few of the most important complexes of symbols. Let us begin with that complex of symbols that can be recognized as modifications of the Christian idea of perfection.

This idea represents the insight that human nature does not find its fulfillment in this world, but only in the *visio beatifica*, in super-natural perfection through grace in death. Since, therefore, there is no fulfillment in this world, Christian life on earth takes its special form from the life to come in the next. It is shaped by *sanctificatio*, by the sanctification of life. Two components can be distinguished in the Christian idea of perfection. The first component is that of the movement toward the goal of perfection, which is described by the expression "sanctification of life"—in English Puritanism, by the notion of the *pilgrim's progress*. As movement toward a goal, it is referred to as the *teleological* component. Further, the goal, the *telos*, toward which the movement is directed, is understood as ultimate perfection; and since the goal is a state of highest value, this second component is called the *axiological*. The two components, the teleological and the axiological, were identified by Ernst Troeltsch.

The gnostic mass movements derive their ideas of perfection from the Christian. In accordance with the components just described, there are on principle three possibilities of derivation. In gnostic perfection, which is supposed to come to pass within the historical world, the teleological and axiological components can be immanentized either separately or together. There follow a few examples of the three types of immanentization.

To the first type of derivation, the teleological, belongs progressivism in all variants. When the teleological component is immanentized, the chief emphasis of the gnostic-political idea lies on the forward movement, on the movement toward a goal of perfection in this world. The goal itself need not be understood very precisely; it may consist of no more than the idealization of this or that aspect of the situation, considered valuable by the thinker in question. Eighteenth-century ideas of progress—for example, Kant's or Condorcet's—belong to this teleological variant of Gnosis. According to the Kantian idea of progress, humanity is moving in an unending approach toward the goal of a perfect, rational existence in a cosmopolitan society—though, to Kant's credit, it must be said that he was able to find in the unending progress of mankind no salvation for the individual man, and the relevance of progress for the fulfillment of the person therefore seemed doubtful to him. Condorcet was somewhat less patient than Kant. He chose not to leave the perfection of man to the unending progress of history, but to accelerate it through a directorate of intellectuals. However, his progressivist idea thereby approaches the third type, the activist effort toward perfection; for the three types of derivation are rarely found in pure form in the individual gnostic thinkers, but usually in multifarious combinations.

In the second type of derivation, the axiological, the emphasis of the idea falls on the state of perfection in the world. Conditions for a perfect social order are described and worked out in detail and assume the form of an ideal image. Such an image was first sketched by Thomas More in his *Utopia*. But the design for perfection need not always be as carefully worked out as it is in More. Much more common are those depictions of a desirable final state that are designed as negatives of some specific evil in the world. The list of these evils has been familiar since antiquity; it was drawn up by Hesiod. Chiefly, it includes poverty, sickness, death, the necessity for work, and sexual problems. These are the principal categories of the burden of existence, to which correspond the models of society offering specific deliverance from one ill or another. Incomplete notions of perfections of this sort may be called *ideals,* in order to distinguish them from the complete models of the utopian kind. Under ideals, therefore, should be included fragments of utopias, such as the notion of a society without private property or of one free from the burdens of labor, sickness, or anxiety. It is characteristic of the whole class of these axiological derivatives that they draw up a comparatively lucid picture of the desirable condition, but are concerned only vaguely with the means of bringing it about.

In the third type of derivation the two components are immanentized together, and there is present both a conception of the end goal and knowledge of the methods by which it is to be brought about. We shall speak of cases of this third type as *activist mysticism.* Under activist mysticism belong primarily movements that descend from Auguste Comte and Karl Marx. In both cases one finds a relatively clear formulation of the state of perfection: in Comte, a final state of industrial society under the temporal rule of the managers and the spiritual rule of positivist intellectuals; in Marx, a final state of a classless realm of freedom. And in both cases, there is clarity about the way to perfection: for Comte, through the transformation of man into his highest form, positivist man; for Marx, through the revolution of the proletariat and the transformation of man into the communist superman.

IV

A second complex of symbols that runs through modern gnostic mass movements was created in the speculation on history of Joachim of Fiore at the end of the twelfth century.

Joachim's historical speculation was directed against the then reigning philosophy of history of Saint Augustine. According to the Augustinian construction, the phase of history since Christ was the sixth, the last earthly age—the *saeculum senescens,* the time of the senility of mankind. The present had no earthly future; its meaning was exhausted in a waiting for the end of history through eschatological events. The motives of this view of history are to be sought in the experiences of the fifth century in which it was formed. In the time of Augustine it seemed indeed that, if not *the* world, at least *a* world was approaching its end. But twelfth-century western European man could not be satisfied with the view of a senile world waiting for its end; for his world was quite obviously not in its decline, but, on the contrary, on the upsurge. Population was increasing, areas of settlement were expanding, wealth was growing, cities were being founded, and intellectual life was intensifying, especially through the emergence of the great religious orders since Cluny. The idea of senility must have seemed preposterous to this vital, expanding age, relishing the exercise of its civilizing powers.

Like Joachim himself his speculation arose out of the thriving religious orders. He projected his view of history on a trinitarian scheme. World history was a consequence of three great ages those of the Father, the Son, and the Holy Spirit. The first age lasted from the Creation to the birth of Christ; the second, that of the Son, began with Christ. But the age of the Son was not, as Augustine had it, mankind's last; rather, it was to be followed by an additional one, that of the Holy Spirit. We can recognize, even in this thoroughly Christian context, the first symptoms of the idea of a post-Christian era. Joachim went further and indulged in concrete speculations about the beginning of the age of the Holy Spirit, fixing its inauguration at 1260. And the new age, like the preceding ones, was to be ushered in by the appearance of a leader. As the first age began with Abraham and the second with Christ, so the third was to begin in the year 1260 with the appearance of a *dux e Babylone*.

So ran the Joachitic speculation. It comprises a complex of four symbols that have remained characteristic of the political mass movements of modern times.

The first of these symbols is that of the Third Realm—that is, the conception of a third world-historical phase that is at the same time the last, the age of fulfillment. An extensive class of gnostic ideas comes under the symbol of the three phases. First and foremost would be the humanistic periodization of world history into ancient, medieval, and modern. This classification was derived in its original version from Biondo. It established as the Middle Ages the millennium from the conquest of Rome by the West Goths to the year 1410. Then, in the eighteenth century, the three-phase laws made famous by Turgot and Comte make their appearance: World history is divided into a first theological, a second metaphysical, and a third phase of positive science. In Hegel we encounter a tripartite division of world history according to levels of freedom: antiquity with its oriental despotism, when only one was free; then aristocratic times, when a few were free; and now modern times, when all are free. Marx and Engels applied this tripartite scheme to their question of the proletariat and spoke of a first phase of primitive communism, a second phase of bourgeois class society, and a third of classless society when the final communist realm of freedom is realized. Again, Schelling, in his speculation on history, distinguished three great phases of Christianity: first the Petrine, followed by the Pauline, which will be sealed by the Johannine phase of perfect Christianity.

These are only the principal cases. They are cited to show that the projection of a Third Realm of perfection is in fact a ruling symbol in the self-understanding of modern society and that after several centuries of preparation for final Third Realms, the attempt to bring them into existence by revolutionary action should no longer especially surprise us. The enumeration should further serve to suggest that a type of experience and symbolism that has been built up for centuries will hardly lose its dominant position in Western history overnight.

The second symbol Joachim developed is that of the leader, the *dux*, who appears at the beginning of a new era and through his appearance establishes that era. This symbol was avidly snatched up by Joachim's salvation-seeking contemporaries. The first to fall victim to it was Saint Francis of Assisi. He was considered by so many to be the leader to the realm of the Holy Spirit that he felt it necessary to take special measures to guard against this misunderstanding of his entirely orthodox actions. In spite of his pains, belief in Saint Francis as the leader of the Third Realm persisted, and had a very strong influence on Dante's conception of such a leader-figure. Moreover, the idea dominated the sectarian movements of the Renaissance and Reformation: Their leaders were paracletes possessed by the spirit of God, and their followers were the *homines novi* or *spirituales*. Dante's notion of a *dux* of the new realm emerged again in the period of national socialism and fascism. There exists a German and Italian literature in which Hitler and Mussolini are at times glorified as the leaders foretold by Dante.

In the period of secularization leaders could not be presented as God-possessed paracletes. By the end of the eighteenth century a new symbol, that of the "superman," begins to take the place of the old sectarian categories. The expression—coined by Goethe in *Faust*—is used in the nineteenth century by Marx and Nietzsche to characterize the new man of the Third Realm. The process by which the superman is created is closely related to the movement of the spirit in which the older sectarians drew into themselves the substance of God and transformed themselves into the "godded man," the divinized man. God is understood by the secularist sectarians as a projection of the substance of the human soul into the illusionary spaciousness of the "beyond." Through psychological analysis, this illusion can be dispelled and "God" brought back from his beyond into the human soul from which he sprung. By dispelling the illusion, the divine substance is reincorporated in man, and man becomes superman. The act of taking God back into man, just as among the older sectarians, has the result of creating a human type who experiences himself as existing outside of institutional bonds and obligations. As the main types of the superman we can distinguish the progressivist superman of Condorcet (who even has the hope of an eternal earthly life), the positivist superman of Comte, the communist superman of Marx, and the Dionysian superman of Nietzsche.

The third of Joachim's symbols is that of the prophet. Joachim assumed that the leader of each age had a precursor, just as Christ had Saint John the Baptist. Even the leader out of the Babylonian captivity, who was to appear in 1260, had such a precursor—in this case, Joachim himself. With the creation of the symbol of the precursor, a new type emerges in Western history: the intellectual who knows the formula for salvation from the misfortunes of the world and can predict how world history will take its course in the future. In Joachitic speculation, the intellectual is still deeply immersed in the medium of Christianity, in that Joachim understands himself to be the prophet of the coming, God-sent *dux e Babylone*. In the further course of Western history, the Christian tide recedes, and the prophet, the precursor of the leader, becomes the secularist intellectual who thinks he knows the meaning of history (understood as world-immanent) and can predict the future. In political practice, the figure of the intellectual who projects the image of future history and makes predictions cannot always be clearly separated from that of the leader. In the case of Comte, for example, we doubtless have the figure of a leader before us; but, at the same time, Comte is also the intellectual who prognosticates his own role as leader of world history and, moreover, even transforms himself through the magic of meditative practice from the intellectual into the leader. In the case of communism, also, it is difficult to separate leader and intellectual in the person of a Karl Marx. But in the historical form of the movement, Marx and Engels have been distinguished, by the distance of a generation, as "precursors," from Lenin and Stalin as "leaders," of the realization of the Third Realm.

The fourth of the Joachitic symbols is the community of spiritually autonomous persons. In the spirit of the monasticism of the time, Joachim imagined the Third Realm as a community of monks. In our context, the importance of this image lies in the idea of a spiritualized mankind existing in community without the mediation and support of institutions; for, according to Joachim's view, the spiritual community of monks was to exist without the sacramental supports of the Church. In this free community of autonomous persons without institutional organization can be seen the same symbolism found in modern mass movements, which imagine the Final Realm as a free community of men after the extinction of the state and other institutions. The symbolism is most clearly recognizable in communism, but the idea of democracy also thrives not inconsiderably on the symbolism of a community of autonomous men.

This concludes our discussion of Joachitic symbolism. In it, we have one of the great complexes of symbols that became active in modern political mass movements and has remained so to the present day.

V

The two complexes we have briefly outlined here by no means exhaust the symbolic language of the mass movements. In order to achieve approximate completeness, we would have to add those that can be traced back to the Latin Averroism and nominalism of the Middle Ages. But the symbols deriving from the Christian idea of perfection and Joachitic speculation are doubtless the dominant ones, to which the others are adjusted. And in both the immanentization of the Christian idea of perfection holds primacy.

This position is ontologically determined by the central importance of the question of immanentization. All gnostic movements are involved in the project of abolishing the constitution of being, with its origin in divine, transcendent being, and replacing it with a world-immanent order of being, the perfection of which lies in the realm of human action. This is a matter of so altering the structure of the world, which is perceived as inadequate, that a new, satisfying world arises. The variants of immanentization, therefore, are the controlling symbols, to which the other complexes are subordinated as secondary ways of expressing the will to immanentization.

No matter to which of the three variants of immanentization the movements belong, the attempt to create a new world is common to all. This endeavor can be meaningfully undertaken only if the constitution of being can in fact be altered by man. The world, however, remains as it is given to us, and it is not within man's power to change its structure. In order—*not*, to be sure, to make the undertaking possible—but to make it *appear* possible, every gnostic intellectual who drafts a program to change the world must first construct a world picture from which those essential features of the constitution of being that would make the program appear hopeless and foolish have been eliminated. Let us turn, then, to this specific trait of gnostic models of the world. In three representative cases we shall show which factor of reality has been omitted in order to make the possibility of an alteration in the unsatisfactory state of things seem plausible. For our three examples we have chosen Thomas More's *Utopia*, Hobbes's *Leviathan*, and Hegel's construct of history.

In his *Utopia* More traces the image of man and of society that he considers perfect. To this perfection belongs the abolition of private property. Because he had the benefit of an excellent theological education, however, More is well aware that this perfect state cannot be achieved in the world. Man's lust for possessions is deeply rooted in original sin, in *superbia* in the Augustinian sense. In the final part of his work when More looks over his finished picture, he has to admit that it would all be possible if only there were not the "serpent of superbia." But there *is* the serpent of superbia—and More would not think of denying it. This raises the question of the peculiar psychopathological condition in which a man like

More must have found himself when he drew up a model of the perfect society in history, in full consciousness that it could never be realized because of original sin.

And this opens up the problem of the strange, abnormal spiritual condition of gnostic thinkers, for which we have not as yet developed an adequate terminology in our time. In order, therefore, to be able to speak of this phenomenon, it will be advisable to use the term "pneumopathology," which Schelling coined for this purpose. In a case like More's, we may speak, then, of the pneumopathological condition of a thinker who, in his revolt against the world as it has been created by God, arbitrarily omits an element of reality in order to create the fantasy of a new world.

As More leaves superbia out of his image of man in order to create a utopian order from this new man freed by the intellectual from original sin, so Hobbes leaves out another essential factor in order to be able to construct his *Leviathan*. The factor Hobbes omits is the *summum bonum*, the highest good. Now, Hobbes knows that human action can be considered rational only if it is oriented beyond all intermediate stages of ends and means to a last end, this same *summum bonum*. Hobbes further knows that the *summum bonum* was the primary condition of rational ethics in the classical as well as the scholastic thinkers. Therefore, in the introduction to the *Leviathan* he states explicitly that he proposes to leave the *summum bonum* of the "old thinkers" out of his construct of society. If there is no *summum bonum*, however, there is no point of orientation that can endow human action with rationality. Action, then, can only be represented as motivated by passions, above all, by the passion of aggression, the overcoming of one's fellow man. The "natural" state of society must be understood as the war of all against all, if men do not in free love orient their actions to the highest good. The only way out of the warfare of this passion-conditioned state of nature is to submit to a passion stronger than all others, which will subdue their aggressiveness and drive to dominate and induce them to live in peaceful order. For Hobbes, this passion is the fear of the *summum malum*, the fear of death at the hands of another, to which each man is exposed in his natural state. If men are not moved to live with one another in peace through common love of the divine, highest good, then the fear of the *summum malum* of death must force them to live in an orderly society.

The motives of this strange construct are more clearly discernible in Hobbes than in More. The author of the *Leviathan* formed his image of man and society under the pressure of the Puritan Revolution. He diagnosed the efforts of the Puritan sectarians to set up the Kingdom of God as an expression of the *libido dominandi* of the revolutionary who wants to bend men to his will. The "spirit" that he saw as inspiring these armed prophets of the new world was not the spirit of God, but human lust for power. He then generalized this observation—which was quite accurate in the case of the Puritans—and made the *libido dominandi,* which is the revolt of man against his nature and God, the essential characteristic of human beings. *Every* movement of the spirit became for him a pretext for a movement of the passions. There was absolutely no orientation of human action through love of God, but only motivation through the world-immanent power drive. And these "proud ones," who wanted to rule and pass off their will to power as the will of God, had to be broken by the Leviathan, the "Lord of the Proud," who held them in check with his threat of death and compelled them to accept the peaceful order of society. The result of these assumptions was the same for Hobbes as for More. If men are incapable of ordering their dealings with each other in freedom through love of the *summum bonum,* if society disintegrates into civil war—in fact, into the state of a war of all against all—and if this condition is considered man's "state of nature" from which there is no escape, then the hour has come of the thinker who possesses the formula for the restoration of order and the guarantee of eternal peace. The society that is governed neither by God's will nor its own shall be placed under that of the gnostic thinker. The *libido dominandi* that Hobbes diagnosed in the Puritans celebrates its highest triumph in the construction of a system that denies man the freedom and ability to order his life in society. Through the construction of the system the thinker becomes the only free person—a god, who will deliver man from the evils of the "state of nature." This function of the system is clearer in Hobbes than it was in More because Hobbes recommends his work to a "sovereign" who may read it, ponder it, and act accordingly. More did indeed construct his Utopia; but this humanist's game, dangerous as it was, was still only a game, for More remained aware that the perfect society was, and would always be, "nowhere." But Hobbes takes his construct in dead earnest. He recommends it to a person in power who is to suppress the apparent freedom of the spirit and its order, because in Hobbes's opinion man does not have the real thing.

The third case we shall consider is Hegel's philosophy of history. Let us first state that the term "philosophy of history" may be applied to Hegel's speculation only with reservations. For Hegel's history is not to be found in reality, and the reality of history is not in Hegel. The harmony between construct and history could be achieved in this case, too, only through the omission of an essential factor of reality.

The factor Hegel excludes is the mystery of a history that wends its way into the future without our knowing its end. History as a whole is essentially not an object of cognition; the meaning of the whole is not discernible. Hegel can construct, then, a meaningfully self-contained process of history only by assuming that the revelation of God in history is fully comprehensible. The appearance of Christ was for him the crux of world history; in this decisive epoch God had revealed the Logos—reason—in history. But the revelation was incomplete, and Hegel considered it man's duty to complete the incomplete revelation by raising the Logos to complete clarity in consciousness. This elevation to consciousness is in fact possible through the mind of the philosopher—concretely, through the mind of Hegel: In the medium of the Hegelian dialectic the revelation of God in history reaches its fulfillment. The validity of the construct depends on the assumption that the mystery of revelation and of the course of history can be solved and made fully transparent through the dialectical unfolding of the Logos. We have here a construct closely related to that of Joachim of Fiore. Joachim, too, was dissatisfied with the Augustinian waiting for the end; he, too, wanted to have an intelligible meaning in history here and now; and in order to make the meaning intelligible, he had to set himself up as the prophet to whom this meaning was clear. In the same manner, Hegel identifies his human logos with the Logos that is Christ, in order to make the meaningful process of history fully comprehensible.

VI

In the three cases of More, Hobbes, and Hegel, we can establish that the thinker suppresses an essential element of reality in order to be able to construct an image of man, or society, or history to suit his desires. If we now consider the question of why the thinker would thus contradict reality, we shall not find the answer on the level of theoretic argument; for we have obviously gone beyond reason, if the relation to reality is so greatly disturbed that essential elements are on principle excluded from consideration. We must move our inquiry to the psychological level, and a first answer has already yielded itself in the course of our presentation: The will to power of the gnostic who wants to rule the world has triumphed over the humility of subordination to the constitution of being. This answer cannot completely satisfy us, however, for while the will to power has indeed conquered humility, the result of victory is not really the acquisition of power. The constitution of being remains what it is—beyond the reach of the thinker's lust for power. It is not changed by the fact that a thinker drafts a program to change it and fancies that he can implement that program. The result, therefore, is not dominion over being, but a fantasy satisfaction.

Therefore, we must go further and inquire into the psychic gain the thinker receives from the construction of his image and the psychic needs the masses of his followers satisfy through it. From the materials we have presented, it would appear that this gain consists in a stronger certainty about the meaning of human existence, in a new knowledge of the future that lies before us, and in the creation of a more secure basis for action in the future. Assurances of this sort, however, are sought only if man feels uncertain on these points. If we then inquire further about the reasons for the uncertainty, we come upon aspects of the order of being and man's place in it that do indeed give cause for uncertainty—an uncertainty perhaps so hard to bear that it may be acknowledged sufficient motive for the creation of fantasy assurances. Let us consider some of these aspects.

A complex of derivatives of the Christian idea of perfection proved to be the controlling symbolism in gnostic speculation. Clearly, an element of insecurity must be involved in this idea, which moves men to search for a firmer foundation for their existence in this world. It will therefore be necessary first to discuss faith in the Christian sense as the source of this insecurity.

In the Epistle to the Hebrews, faith is defined as the substance of things hoped for and the proof of things unseen. This is the definition that forms the basis for Thomas Aquinas's theological exposition of faith. The definition consists of two parts—an ontological and an epistemological proposition. The ontological proposition asserts that faith is the substance of things hoped for. The substance of these things subsists in nothing but this very faith, and not perhaps in its theological symbolism. The second proposition asserts that faith is the proof of things unseen. Again, proof lies in nothing but faith itself. This thread of faith, on which hangs all certainty regarding divine, transcendent being, is indeed very thin. Man is given nothing tangible. The substance and proof of the unseen are ascertained through nothing but faith, which man must obtain by the strength of his soul—in this psychological study we disregard the problem of grace. Not all men are capable of such spiritual stamina; most need institutional help, and even this is not always sufficient. We are confronted with the singular situation that Christian faith is so much the more threatened, the further it expands socially, the more it brings men under institutional control, and the more clearly its essence is articulated. This threat had reached the critical point in the high Middle Ages because of widespread social success. Christianity had in fact institutionally encompassed the men of Western society; and in the new urban culture, under the influence of the great religious orders, its essence had attained a high degree of clarity. Coincidentally with its greatness, its weakness became apparent: Great masses of Christianized men who were not strong enough for the heroic adventure of faith became susceptible to ideas that could give them a greater degree of certainty about the meaning of their existence than faith. The reality of being as it is known in its truth by Christianity is difficult to bear, and the flight from clearly seen reality to gnostic constructs will probably always be a phenomenon of wide extent in civilizations that Christianity has permeated.

The temptation to fall from uncertain truth into certain untruth is stronger in the clarity of Christian faith than in other spiritual structures. But the absence of a secure hold on reality and the demanding spiritual strain are generally characteristic of border experiences in which man's knowledge of transcendent Being, and thereby of the origin and meaning of mundane being, is constituted. This may be illustrated briefly in three examples taken from different cultural contexts—the Jewish, the Hellenic, and the Islamic.

In the Jewish sphere, faith responds to the revelation of God. The central experience of revelation is transmitted in Exodus 3, in the thornbush episode. God reveals himself in his nature to

Moses with the expression, "I am who I am." As the formulation in the Epistle to the Hebrews is the basis of Thomas's theology of faith, so that in Exodus is the basis of his teaching on God. Again, one can say of the latter formulation only: That is all. In the contact the human soul in the world has with the beyond, nothing is discovered but the existence of God. Everything beyond this belongs to the realm of analogical-speculative deduction and mythic symbolization. Even in Moses' experience of revelation, we must observe that the thread on which hangs our knowledge of the order of being, its origin and meaning, is very thin. It was in fact so thin that it snapped, and the bulk of the people reverted to the old gods of polytheistic civilization. Furthermore, the prophet Jeremiah made the penetrating observation that nations in general do not desert their gods, although they are "false"; while Israel, who has the "true God," deserts Him. This unique case in the history of the peoples of the time attests perhaps most clearly to the phenomenon we just observed in connection with the experience of faith: With the refinement and clarification of the relationship between God and man, the moment of uncertainty, and with it the need for more solid certainty, is intensified. The example of Israel further shows that the lapse from faith by no means must result in this or that form of Gnosis. If, experientially, the cultural conditions permit it, the need for certainty can also be satisfied by a reversion to a still vital polytheism.

The great demand on man's spiritual strength is clarified in the symbolism of the Last Judgment as Plato develops it in his *Gorgias.* To his sophist opponents, who operate with the ethic of worldly success of the man of power, Plato counters with the argument that "success" in life consists in standing before the judges of the dead. Before these judges the soul stands stripped of the husk of the body and the cloak of earthly status, in complete transparency. And life should be led in anticipation of this final transparency, *sub specie mortis,* rather than under the compulsions of the will to power and social status. What is being expressed symbolically in the Platonic myth, as in all myths of judgment, is the border experience of the examination of conscience. Over and above the normal testing of our actions against the standards of rational ethics, which is called conscience and which we as men perform, the experience of examination can be elaborated meditatively and expanded to the experience of standing in judgment. Man knows that even the most conscientious self-examination is limited by the bounds of his humanity: breakdowns in judgment; on principle, incomplete knowledge of all the factors of the situation and of all the ramifications of action; and, above all, inadequate knowledge of his own ultimate motives, which reach into the unconscious. Proceeding by way of meditative experiment from this knowledge of the limitations of self-appraisal, one can imagine the situation in which a man is to be judged, not at a particular moment in a particular situation of his life and before himself alone, but on the basis of his entire life (which is completed only in death) and before an omniscient judge, before whom there is no longer any pleading of special points and no argument or defense is possible because everything, even the least and most remote, is already known. In this meditation at the border, all pro and con fall silent, and nothing remains but the silence of the judgment that the human being has spoken upon himself with his life.

Plato carried out this meditation—otherwise he could not have composed his myth of the judgment. But if we put ourselves in the situation in which he has his Socrates relate the myth to his sophist opponents and if we ask about the possibility of its having affected these hardboiled *Realpolitiker,* standing firmly in "life," then we must again doubt that many took it to heart and let their existence be formed by it—even though, while listening, they may have been profoundly touched for a moment. The meditation itself and, still more, existence in its tension would be unbearable for most men. At any rate, we find right in the gnostic mass movements a development of the idea of conscience that leads off in the opposite direction from the meditation at the border, toward worldliness. Conscience is readily invoked, even today, especially when a politician's immoral or criminal conduct is to be justified by having "followed his conscience" or by "being aware of his responsibilities." But in this case conscience no longer means the testing of one's actions against the rational principles of ethics, but, on the contrary, the cutting off of rational debates and the stubborn, demonic persistence in actions that passion incites.

The Islamic prayer exercises that have developed since the ninth century will serve as the final example of a high demand in spiritual tension. Structurally, this meditation, which preceded prayer, is most closely related to the meditative experiment on which the Platonic myth of the Last judgment is based. When I want to pray, says the rule, I go to the place where I wish to say my prayer. I sit still until I am composed. Then I stand up: The Kaaba is in front of me, paradise to my right, hell to my left, and the angel of death stands behind me. Then I say my prayer as if it were my last. And thus I stand, between hope and fear, not knowing whether God has received my prayer favorably or not. Perhaps, for the masses, this high spiritual clarity is made bearable through a connection with the neither high nor especially spiritual extension of God's realm by force of arms over the ecumene.

The gnostic mass movements of our time betray in their symbolism a certain derivation from Christianity and its experience of faith. The temptation to fall from a spiritual height that brings the element of uncertainty into final clarity down into the more solid certainty of world-immanent, sensible fulfillment, nevertheless, seems to be a general human problem. Cases of border experience, where the element of insecurity in the constitution of being becomes evident, were chosen from four different civilizational orbits to show that a typical phenomenon is involved in the modern mass movements, despite their historical uniqueness. Empirically, this insight will perhaps contribute something to the understanding of social processes in different civilizations. At any rate, we have managed theoretically to trace the phenomenon back to its ontic roots and to reduce it to ontological type concepts. And this is the task of science.

Index